Memory, Myth, and Time in Mexico:
From the Aztecs to Independence

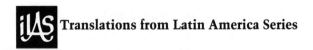 Translations from Latin America Series

Institute of Latin American Studies
University of Texas at Austin

Memory, Myth, and Time in Mexico: From the Aztecs to Independence

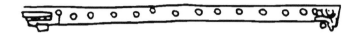

By Enrique Florescano

Translated by Albert G. Bork
with the assistance of Kathryn R. Bork

University of Texas Press, Austin

Second paperback printing, 1997

Requests for permission to reproduce material from this work should be sent to Permissions, University of Texas Press, P.O. Box 7819, Austin, Texas 78713-7819

The paper used in this publication meets the minimum requirements of American National Standard for Information Sciences—Permanence of Paper for Printed Library Materials, ANSI Z39.48–1984.

Library of Congress Cataloging-in-Publication Data

Florescano, Enrique.
    [Memoria mexicana. English]
    Memory, myth, and time in Mexico : from the Aztecs to Independence
/ by Enrique Florescano : translated by Albert G. Bork with the assistance of
Kathryn R. Bork.
        p.   cm. — (Translations from Latin America Series)
    Includes bibliographical references and index.
    ISBN 0-292-72485-3. — ISBN 0-292-72486-1 (pbk.)
    1. Mexico—Historiography. 2. Indians of Mexico—Historiography.
3. Mexico—History—Philosophy. I. Title.
F1224.F5313 1994   94-7482
972'.0072—dc20   CIP

Contents

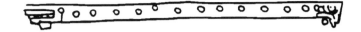

Illustrations

Preface

This book comprises a group of essays that pursue the innumerable memories of the past created by different groups and peoples in Mexico. The groups that peopled the national territory did not produce one, but many, images of the past. They created those images to free themselves of the corrosive passage of time over human creations, to weave solidarity founded on common origins, to delimit the possession of a territory, to affirm identities rooted in remote traditions, to sanction established power, to back contemporary claims with the prestige of the past, to found on a shared past the aspiration of building a nation, or to give sustenance to plans laid toward the uncertainty of the future. In this and other cases, the recovery of the past, or the invention of one's own past, is manifested as an irrepressible compulsion whose final purpose is to affirm the historical existence of a group, a people, a homeland, or a nation.

As these were deep and powerful compulsions, they left traces of their presence everywhere, even among peoples whose main expression was oral discourse. With this testimony, sometimes perfectly elaborated, sometimes fragmented and obscure, I tried to reconstruct the mythic and ideological images that the pre-Hispanic peoples formed of their past; the providentialistic, mystical, and profane images that the conquistadors and friars produced on examining their transformative action on the American world; the patriotic and religious images that the Creoles created to give cohesion to a population split by the inequalities; the surprising recoveries of the past that the indigenous peoples invented and the new ideas of modern human beings who contemplated the past and the future under the influence of the Enlightenment.

The recovery and re-creation of the past is an uninterrupted social process, a collective creation necessary for the survival of a group or a nation, and a process that produces successive and renewed images of the past. From there the explanation that any representation of the past should be sought in the urgencies and aspirations of the collective memory more than in the individuals who appear to produce it and follow through on it, where the vision of the past and the images that represent it are continually renewed.

Each new representation of the past puts into play several procedures to recover it and provides answers to new uses of the past in the present. That is, every recovery of the past forces us to find out how that past was recovered and to what end that reconstruction was carried out. This book intends to answer these questions. But instead of taking as the only expression of the past those works produced by chroniclers and historians, it uses the multiple folk forms and traditions to gather the past. Those forms include myth, legend, ritual, religious symbols, the messianic message that announces the institution of a new kingdom or the return to a golden age, the discourse of charismatic figures who in the name of the past call together the masses to change the course of history, collective movements guided by a mythic image of the past, and, of course, the chronicles, the stories, and historical works that reconstruct and interpret the past.

At the end of the nineteenth century, Ernest Renan wrote, "To forget and I dare say to misinterpret history itself are essential factors in the formation of a nation."[1] This work shows that the formation of Mexican historical conscience is the result of a historical confrontation of some groups with others, of the statements and denials that each group made about itself and its opponents, of the decision made by some segments of society to impose their own image of the past on others, of the decision of many indigenous communities to preserve their own identity, and, finally, of many things forgotten, statements and deformations of the past motivated by conflicting social situations and by the confrontation of different conceptions of historical development. Thus, along with the identification of the different memories of the past, this book also attempts an explanation of the conceptions of time and historical happening that are behind these interpretations of the past.

Giovanni Battista Vico opened a new perspective on the development of historical and anthropological knowledge when he again took up the old thesis that *one can fully know only what one has made* and created, as Isaiah Berlin says, a new type of knowledge based on reconstructive imagination. According to Berlin, the greatness of Vico lies in his having discovered "the principle of agreement by which man can understand himself because he understands in the process, his past; because he is capable of reconstructing imaginatively what he did and suffered, his hopes, desires, efforts, his acts and his works, both his own and those of others. His experience is interwoven with that of others and that of his ancestors . . . whose monuments, customs, laws, and above all words, still speak to him."[2] Following Vico's idea, I attempted to reconstruct the conceptions of time and historical happening, expressed in the cosmogonic myths, in the creation myths, and in the ritual ceremonies of the pre-Hispanic peoples. In addition, there is here an effort to understand how the Hebrew ideas of historical development, the conception of a theological time, and of the eschatological and apocalyptic ideas of Christianity were introduced into the educated and folk mentalities of New Spain and how they dominated the interpretations of time, the past, and historical happening. In the three centuries of the viceroyalty, these conceptions of time and history were expressed in myths, religious movements, populist and revolutionary movements, and in the works and lives of most of the people of that time.

If these reconstructions are correct, one of the conclusions that can be drawn from this book is the following: during most of the viceroyalty, mythic and religious ideas, of both indigenous and European origin, were dominant in the interpretation of time, human happening, and historical development. Only at the end of the eighteenth century, with the Enlightenment, and later, with the revolution of independence, did there appear secular thought and a modern political conception that interprets historical facts as a succession of irreversible, profane happenings that in and of themselves—without the interference of the supernatural or the sacred—make and transform historical happening.

I would like to express my appreciation to Johanna Broda and Alfredo López Austin for their advice and criticism, which helped open my path to the world of myths and conceptions of time in ancient Mexico. Parts of this book dedicated to the recovery of the past during the viceroyalty follow ideas and suggestions developed in the works of David A. Brading, Victoria Reifler Bricker, Serge Gruzinski, Edmundo O'Gorman, and Francisco de la Maza. I would also like to thank Patricia Sámano and Rocío Álvarez for their patience and expertise in typing my drafts. During the preparation of this book, I kept close to me the idea that Vico had with him: a conviction that the products of human thought and creativity are decipherable and comprehensible because they belong to us, and because their transformation in time can be explained if we pursue that transformation with the understanding, rigor, and imagination transmitted to us by the masters of historical recovery.

Memory, Myth, and Time in Mexico:
From the Aztecs to Independence

1.

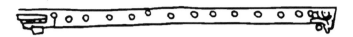

The Nahua Concept of Time and Space

Nahua ideas about time were joined with their concepts of the creation of the world (cosmogonies), the composition of the universe (cosmology), and the sense of what the gods had given humankind as a mission on earth. For that reason, to understand this people's concept of history, we must first define the general concepts of time and space that are expressed in their cosmogonies and religion in order later to relate these concepts to the particular forms of recording and representing historical facts.

The Nahua Creation Myth

The First Creation of the World

Nahua cosmogony accounts mention a divine couple who originated the world and life: Tonacatecuhtli and Tonacíhuatl, a development of the dual god, Ometéotl. As Ometéotl, this couple is self-created, eternal, and the source of all life; they lived in the highest place in the heavens, on the thirteenth level, which gave origin to four deities, each one identified by a color: Tezcatlipoca (red), Tezcatlipoca (black), Quetzalcóatl (white?), and Huitzilopochtli (blue).

After six hundred years of inactivity, Quetzalcóatl and Huitzilopochtli began the creation of the world. They created fire and the sun, but not a whole sun, just a half sun that illuminated very little. They also created a man and a woman and entrusted him to cultivate the land and her to spin and weave. From Oxomuco and Cipactonal (fig. 1), the first human couple, was born the generation of the *macehuales*, who had to be watched by the gods so that they did not stop working. Simultaneously, they created the underworld, with its gods Mictlantecuhtli and Mictecacíhuatl, and also the skies and the water, in which there was "a lizardlike" Cipactli, from which the earth came forth. The gods also created the god of water, Tláloc, and his mate, Chalchiuhtlicue, along

Figure 1. Oxomuco and Cipactonal, the first human couple (Codex Borbónico, pl. 21).

with numerous *tlaloques*, demigods that helped them spill the waters over the land.

This first creation of the universe was done "together and without any time difference," when time was not yet counted, nor were the days, years, or ages.[1] At this moment begins the age of the suns, the age governed by the divine power that created movement and ascribed an origin and an end to the successive eras that the gods established.

Creation and Destruction of the First Four Suns

Nahui Océlotl (Earth Sun). On finishing the creation of the universe, the four creator gods saw that it was somewhat inert and that it only illuminated with twilight.[2] They talked about it, resolving then that one of them should be transformed into a sun and put into motion. Tezcatlipoca, who disguises himself as a jaguar, was the first god to become a sun and thus give a beginning to the eras of the world. Starting with this first sun, years began to be counted.[3] The men of this age were giants who uprooted enormous trees with their bare hands, but did not know how to cultivate the earth. They sustained themselves with acorns and wild fruits and roots. This sun ended abruptly when the giants were devoured by ferocious jaguars and the sun disappeared. This happened on the day called 4-Jaguar. This first sun lasted 676 years.

Nahui Echécatl (Wind Sun). Then the gods created the second sun and restored life to the world. This time the creator god was Quetzalcóatl, who became the sun and shone on the earth. The people of that age ate only pine nuts (*ococentli*). But it happened that Tezcatlipoca, converted into a jaguar, knocked down the sun with one swipe and raised a windstorm that uprooted trees and blew the humans through the air. Those who did not perish from the wind turned into apes. This happened on the day called 4-Wind. This second sun lasted 676 years according to some accounts and 364 according to others (fig. 2).

Nahui Quiáhuitl (Fire Sun). The creator gods made a third sun appear, incarnated in Tláloc, the god of rain and heavenly fire. Under this sun humans ate a seed called *acecentli*, which was like a "water maize." But like previous suns, this third one disappeared in great catastrophes. The sun burned up, fire rained from the heavens, and humans and their houses were destroyed. Those who did not die became turkeys (*pipiltin*). This happened on the day 4-Rain. This third sun lasted 312 years according to some sources and 364 according to others (fig. 3).

Nahui Atl (Water Sun). The gods then created the fourth sun. The goddess Chalchiuhtlicue, "she of the skirts of jade," goddess of water, became the sun at the command of Quetzalcóatl. During this age humans ate a seed similar to corn, called *cincocopi*. This sun ended with a great deluge that flooded the earth, converting humans into fish and making the heavens collapse onto the earth's surface. This occurred on the day 4-Water. This fourth sun lasted 676 years according to some sources and 312 according to others (fig. 4).

Thus, "from the birth of the gods, until this sun's expiration, there were, as counted, 2628 years."[4]

Creation of the Fifth Sun: Nahui Ollin (Movement Sun). Tezcatlipoca and Quetzalcóatl were given the task of beginning the restoration of the

Figure 2. Wind Sun, Nahui Echécatl (Codex Vaticano-Ríos, pl. 6).

universe destroyed by the deluge and by the disappearance of the Fourth Sun. First they cleared away the waters that had invaded the earth; then they tried to raise the heavens that had stuck to the earth, but as they could not do it, they called to their aid the other creator gods. Together they made four roads toward the center of the earth, by which they entered to raise the heavens. Nevertheless, as the sky was big and heavy, they had to create four men to help them. Even then, Tezcatlipoca and Quetzalcóatl had to turn into big trees to raise and hold up the heavens; thus, the former was transformed into "tree of mirrors," and Quetzalcóatl into the "precious willow." And so, "with the men and the trees and gods, they raised the heavens with its stars the way it is now."[5] As a reward for this great effort, Tonacatecuhtli made Tezcatlipoca and Quetzalcóatl into lords of the heavens and the stars and gave them a seat in the Milky Way (fig. 5).

Their task completed, "The gods consulted and said: Who will inhabit [this land], for the heavens stopped and the lord of the land stopped? Who

Figure 3. Fire Sun, Nahui Quiáhuitl (Codex Vaticano-Ríos, pl. 7).

will inhabit it, Oh gods?" After deliberating, the gods decided to entrust Quetzalcóatl with the mission of creating humans anew. Thus, he descended to the underworld, to the kingdom of Mictlantecuhtli, in order to obtain from the latter the bones and ashes of the prior generations of humanity and from them to create humans again. Quetzalcóatl overcame Mictlantecuhtli's resistance with trickery, but when he had the precious bones and was returning with them, he fell in a hole that Mictlantecuhtli had dug and the bones broke there. This is why the new humans were different heights and did not reach the size of the former giants. Finally, Quetzalcóatl reached Tamoanchan, where the gods had gathered, and delivered his burden to them. Immediately, a goddess, Cihuacóatl-Quilaztli, ground up the bones and formed a mass with them, which she deposited in a precious container. Then Quetzalcóatl bled his sex and spilled his divine blood in the container and the other remaining gods made sacrifices, too. Thus, "Two years later, which was the year of the deluge, the gods created the *macehuales* as they had

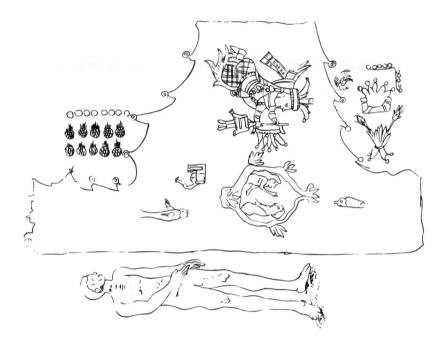

Figure 4. Water Sun, Nahui Atl (Codex Vaticano-Ríos, pl. 5).

existed before, and for thirteen years, nothing else that happened is painted (in their codices)."[6]

Then the gods asked: "What will the *macehuales* eat?" So Quetzalcóatl, who was aware that the red ant knew where the maize, the precious food, was kept, asked about it insistently. Finally, the ant acceded to his requests and indicated the place where the maize was located. Quetzalcóatl turned into a black ant and, together with the red ant, arrived at the mountain called Tonacatépetl, where the maize was hidden. He got it and took it to Tamoanchan. There the gods chewed it and then put it in the mouths of humans, who thus became strong.[7]

Also, so that humans would be happy, the gods made the maguey plant grow. From it they drew pulque. And even before the gods had created humans, Tezcatlipoca had brought fire to the earth. To do that he had gotten flame from some sticks, and that is how fire was made with flints, "sticks that have hearts." So with fire there were feasts with many large bonfires.

And all this occurred while darkness reigned and there was not yet a sun. But twenty-six years after the creation of the earth, the gods decided to create a new sun. In the year 13-Ácatl, in Teotihuacan, the sacred

Figure 5. The Fifth Sun, Nahui Ollin.

place, all of the gods gathered and ordered fasts and sacrifices to propitiate the birth of the sun. Then the gods asked, "Who will be responsible for illuminating the world?" The god called Tecucíztécatl responded to these words, saying, "I'll take charge of illuminating the world." Again the gods spoke and said, "Who will be the other one?" But this time the gods looked around among themselves and asked who else would be the one who would illuminate the world, but none offered. Finally, they looked at a god nobody noticed, who did not speak but only listened. His body was covered with tumors and sores. They said to him, "You be the one who gives light, buboed one." And the god, called Nanahuatzin, ulcerated and humble, willingly obeyed.

And then the two of them began doing penance and sacrifices for four days. Everything that Tecucíztécatl offered was precious. Instead of branches he offered rich quetzal feathers and balls of gold instead of balls of hay; he did not offer maguey thorns, but ones made of precious stones; and instead of blood-covered thorns, he gave red coral spines, and very good-quality copal. On the other hand, Nanahuatzin offered green reeds and balls of hay and maguey thorns covered with his own blood; and in the place of copal he presented the scabs from his sores.

At midnight of the day scheduled for the creation of the new sun, the gods gathered around a great fire they had kept burning for four days and into which Tecuciztécatl and Nanahuatzin were to throw themselves in order to be transformed into bright stars. In place before the fire, all of them said to Tecuciztécatl, "You go into the fire first!" and he tried to do so, but since the fire was very large and active, he grew fearful and stepped back. Four times Tecuciztécatl attempted to hurl himself into the fire and four times he desisted.

Then the gods said to Nanahuatzin, "You try it." And he immediately shut his eyes and threw himself into the fire and began to burn. On seeing this, Tecuciztécatl gained courage and threw himself into the fire, too.

After both of them had fallen into the fire and burned, the gods sat down and waited to see where the sun would rise. After a while, they saw that the sky was turning red and getting light everywhere, but they did not know in which direction the sun was going to rise, so they looked in all directions. Only Quetzalcóatl and Tezcatlipoca, Xipe Tótec, and a few others predicted that Nanahuatzin, converted into a sun, would appear in the east. And indeed, from that bearing appeared the sun, red and radiant. It was so resplendent that nobody could look at it without hurting his or her eyes. Behind it came the moon, also luminous and brilliant, so much so that the gods asked themselves, "Is it good for both of them to go at the same time? Is it good for them to illuminate equally?" They agreed that it could not be thus, so one of them threw a rabbit at Tecuciztécatl and dimmed his splendor, darkening his face and leaving the moon the way it is today, with diminished light.

With this accomplished, the gods discovered to their consternation that the new sun and the new moon remained immobile on the edge of the sky toward the east. For four days the sun did not move, nor did the moon. Frightened, the gods asked, "How will we be able to live? The sun does not stir? Then they decided to carry out a supreme sacrifice to set the sun into motion. They resolved to offer their lives so that with the divine blood of the gods the sun would have the strength to begin its journey through the universe. "Let us all die and make it resuscitate through our deaths," they said. And this is what was done, so that each of them gave his blood to give motion to the sun. Afterward, from the clothing that the dead gods left, and with their jade jewels and snake and jaguar skins, their worshipers made bundles that were given the names of the late gods. And henceforth, these objects were revered as if they were the gods themselves who had sacrificed themselves at Teotihuacan.

But the sacrifice of the gods was not enough to satisfy the new sun's thirst for blood. That is why humans, following the example of the gods, had to sacrifice themselves. This divine need gave rise to war, which has as its purpose obtaining victims for the sun sacrifice. One chronicle says that even before the Fifth Sun was born, the gods had instituted war so that the sun that was to reign in that age would have many hearts. According to this chronicle, when the world was still in darkness, the gods resolved to make "a sun that illuminated the earth and . . . this sun ate hearts and drank blood, and for this [it was necessary] for them to create war where hearts and blood could be had."[8]

The Myth's Cosmogonic Creations

As has been observed, there are three divisions established in the cosmogonic story: (1) first creation of the universe; (2) the cyclical creation of the suns; and (3) creation of the Fifth, or Movement, Sun, which gives rise to human sacrifice as necessary nourishment of the sun and the gods.

The First Creation of the Universe

In contrast to the last two creations, the primitive creation of the universe occurs in a moment without time. The creation of the sun, of the first human couple, and of the primordial earth, heavens, and waters occurs simultaneously, or, as the myth states, "together and with no time difference." Clearly, the absence here of temporality, chronological references, and movement is associated with the sun, because in contrast to the other ages, only in this one was there a diminished sun, without sufficient energy to give the universe full life.

The Cyclical Creation of the Suns

In contrast, the second part of the myth is dominated by an incessant, cyclical, and fatal movement that is governed by the appearance and destruction of the suns, for each sun creates a new cosmic order, supposes a new re-creation of the universe and of human life, in the same manner as its disappearance implies the sudden destruction of what was created before.

In spite of this to-and-fro cycle, some authors have seen progression in the temporal sequence of the four suns, not only because the majority of the sources record the duration of each sun in a progressive fashion, measuring time backward to forward, but also because, as Alfonso Caso says, the very plants that are described as the food of humans (acorns, pine nuts, "water maize," *cincocopi*) draw progressively closer to the primary food of the peoples of Mesoamerica, maize. Following an order that is different from the one we have adopted here for the sequence of the four suns, Caso concludes that, in the creation of humans, there is an evolutionary sense, for in his arrangement of the suns, humans first became fish, then birds, later on apes, and finally giants.[9]

But this progressive interpretation of the cosmogonies is denied by the cyclical character of these creations and by the absence of continuity between the event that occurred between one sun and another. Setting aside the serious problem that there is no agreement among authors on even the sequence of the suns, what is certain is that, while the chronological time that records the succession of suns is linear and progressive, the temporality of the events that occur in each sun is cyclical. There is a separation between chronological time and the temporality of the mythical happenings, for while the former flows incessantly forward from the past, human time has a precise beginning and ending, a duration that is inevitably and violently complied with.

What is characteristic in the succession of the four suns is their fated destruction and the certainty that, once that world is ended, another one will begin, with other humans and under other guardian gods. Also characteristic is the antagonism of the gods and the forces of nature, put into motion by the combating gods themselves. Each sun is born under the auspices of one god, who dominates or embodies certain natural forces, which in turn are in conflict with other gods and other forces. Thus, the struggle between these forces and gods is what breaks the equilibrium in the universe and brings with it destruction and chaos. That is why every new sun begins by conjuring the chaos and imposing order in its place. In that sense, the cyclical repetition of the cosmogony is a celebration of the powers that regenerate the world and introduce order.

The Creation of the Fifth Sun

As in prior cosmogonies, the creation of the Fifth Sun signifies a total re-creation of the universe, which, in this case, the sources detail with greater breadth. From the chaos and darkness appears again the new order: the collapsed sky is lifted and returned to its place; the earth and water, furnished with their generative powers, surge forth again from the chaos; the gods create humans anew, along with the necessary gifts (fire, foods) so that they can reproduce and people the earth.

What is distinctive in the cosmogony of the Fifth Sun is the insistence on order, just as the creation of humans and the sun is a gift from the gods and the maintenance of life in the world implies sacrifice. Time and again, the cosmogony account points out the creative effort by the gods to impose order and bring life into the world. The culminating moment in this series of efforts is the self-sacrifice of the gods to impart motion to the new sun. And precisely what makes the myth stand out is that if the purpose of divine creation was to create life in the world, the final purpose of earthly creatures is to maintain by their own blood that created order, the permanent vitality of the universe.

The synthesis of this Mexican vision of the cosmos is the monument known as the Sun Stone (fig. 5). In the small squares that surround the central facet of this monument are represented the four suns, or prior eras of the world, with their dates of creation. Earth Sun, Wind Sun, Fire Sun, and Water Sun are set out in a counterclockwise fashion. From the central disk emerge solar rays that point to the four bearings of the cosmos and to the intercardinal directions. On the upper part of the monument is inscribed the date 13-Reed, which corresponds to the year 1011, the year of the birth of the Fifth Sun. The royal diadem and the glyph 1-Tecpatl, placed on either side of the sun's ray that points to the east, the direction in which the sun rises, refer, respectively, to the royal power with its seat in Mexico-Tenochtitlan and the calendar date of the birth of Huitzilopochtli, the protector god of the Mexica. In the center of the disk, in the place where the four prior suns articulate with the four bearings of the cosmos, emerges the terrible effigy of the Fifth Sun, the Movement Sun, whose motion is at once continuous and life-renewing and must be fed by the sacrifice of human hearts.[10]

The Founding Order of Cosmogonic Creation and the Integration of Space into the Cosmic Order

Paul Kirchhoff wrote, "Ancient Mexico is a world of order, in which everything and everybody has his proper place . . . it is also a world that terrifies us because of its universality . . . These cultures did not know chaos."[11]

The cosmogonic myth that we have been considering is the model of that order, an order that, for the purpose of creating harmony and unity between space, time, nature, and the social world, integrated all of these parts into a system or universal model governed by sacred principles. As has been seen, the significance of the cosmogonic creation is to avert chaos and establish order. Creation is an ordering of the universe, a placing and a definition of its components, in such fashion that beginning then each of its parts occupies a precise place in the universal order, with defined attributes and functions. The separation of the heavens and earth places: in the lower, feminine, world those generative forces of nature and in the upper, heavenly, masculine world those fecundating forces, although in both sectors, as in the essential duality, malefic powers also dwell. Thus, beginning with the act of creation until the disappearance of the Fifth Sun, the world will be conceived as an essential duality—heaven and earth, above and below, light and darkness, masculine and feminine, life and death—that repeats the duality that originated it: Tonacatecuhtli-Tonacíhuatl.

The creator gods, Tezcatlipoca and Quetzalcóatl, are likewise a development of the essential duality. In turn, the successive divinities that create the primordial gods to govern the various parts of the universe—the heavens, the earth, the waters, the underworld—are also dual deities, which are represented as divine couples.

Together with this dual and symmetrical division of the universe, the cosmogony establishes a geometric division of the space of the earth, which is conceived as a horizontal surface in the shape of a rectangle surrounded by water. On this horizontal plane that makes up the earth, the sacred center that unifies the various parts of the universe is founded. This is the point that establishes vertical communication among the heavens, the earth, and the underworld and that horizontally ties together the four cardinal points: east (the guide direction, because it is the one in which the sun rises), north, west, and south. Thus, according to the story of cosmogony contained in *Historia de los mexicanos por sus pinturas*, the paths made by the gods on the four points of the universe converged at the center of the earth, there where all the parts of the created world were fused. This division of the universe into four parts oriented to the cardinal points is the one found in all the codices and texts that represent the distribution of the universe (fig. 6).[12]

One of the versions of the cosmogonic myth states that Quetzalcóatl and Tezcatlipoca were transformed into trees in order to lift the heavens and hold them up. In the codices that refer to the cosmogonic creation, these trees appear distributed in the four parts of the earth's surface (Codex Borgia, pl. 49–52; Codex Fejérvary-Mayer, pl. 1), establishing permanent communication between the heavens and the earth (fig. 7). These cosmic trees, along with the four axes that led to the center of the earth, "ran the paths traveled by the gods and their forces in order to reach the surface of the earth. From the four trees, the influences of the gods of the upper and lower worlds radiated toward the central point."[13]

Thus, from the cosmogonic creation, the earth's surface is converted into a sacred space, divided into parts governed by divine powers, with spatial orientations, colors, and symbols that infuse each space and place with a transcendent sense, a significance that goes beyond its material reality. Space on the earth is converted into a replica of the sacred order that governs the universe, into a reproduction of the cosmogonic arche-

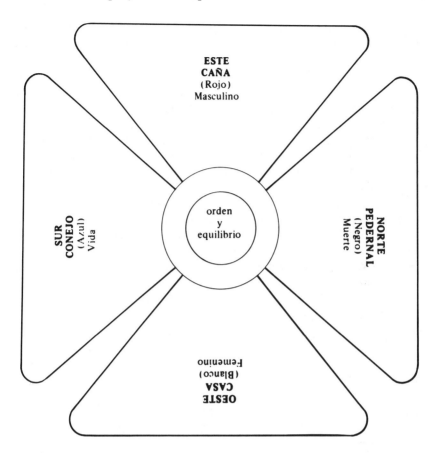

Figure 6. Map of the world.

type. An example of this transformation of the earth's space into cosmic space is the hills and mountains, which all the peoples of Mesoamerica considered sacred places, points where the heavens and the earth were joined, equivalent to the center of the world.

The Mexicas took this conception to the extreme, as they made the space on earth and the social order an exact replica of the cosmic order. In the same fashion as Mexica vertical space (heavens, earth, underworld) reproduced the vertical division of cosmic space, thus also did horizontal space reflect, like a mirror, the four directions of cosmic space, integrated to a center that articulated all the directions, gods, and forces. The greater space, that which constituted the terrestrial extension of the so-called Mexica empire, was divided into four great regions divided up along the four cardinal points and united by a center, or fifth, region: Mexico-Tenochtitlan.[14] In this manner, the conquered territories were assimilated into the archetypal cosmic order and integrated into a new spatial and religious distribution.

The founding and later spatial division of Tenochtitlan also repeat with great accuracy the organizational principles of cosmic space: "in the center of what was to be the city was erected the temple to Huitzilopochtli, and in it were joined the vertices of the four major divisions (*nauh*) *campan* (or wards) called Moyotlan, Teopan, Atzacualco, and Cuepopan,"[15] distributed along the four cosmic points (see pl. 1 of the Codex Mendocino, fig. 8). The central part of this quadripartite division of urban space was the sacred area of Mexico-Tenochtitlan, in the center of which the Templo Mayor was raised. Counting this center, urban space adopted the same form and division as the cosmic surface: a square cut into a cross, in whose center was the navel of the universe. The *calpullis*, or smallest territorial units, were distributed in the four large segments into which the city was divided. According to one author, these totaled twenty, as twenty was the number of tributary provinces of the empire. Recent studies have demonstrated that the *calpullis* were organized around temples, gods, and social groups distributed in the four principal segments that divided the city.[16]

Finally, the center of the city was taken up by the great sacred precinct surrounded by a wall of serpents, a square measuring two hundred rods [eleven hundred yards] per side. Here each of the twenty *calpullis* had its particular temple, sharing the space with the temples of the principal gods of the Aztec pantheon and the gods of the conquered provinces. On each side of the sacred area four doors opened, from which the four roads exited that communicated with the four cosmic points. In the center of this area of the gods was erected the preeminent sacred space, the great *teocalli*, or Templo Mayor. It, like the position the center of the earth has in the cosmogonic myth, was the navel of the earth and the divine mountain where the heavens, the earth, and the underworld united, the place where the heights and the depths were articulated with the four bearings of cosmic space. In this essential point, the confluence of sacred forces that infused order into the cosmos, the Mexicas ratified the pact established in the cosmogonic myth and presented the gods with human sacrifices.

Fray Diego Durán furnishes further evidence that the Mexicas had arranged their city's space in accordance with the cosmogonic myth's model. Based on ancient documents and eyewitness reports from the time of the Conquest, such as that of Francisco de Aguilar, who was one of Cortés's soldiers and Motecuhzoma's guards during the latter's captivity. Durán explains the orientation of Tenochtitlan's sacred area:

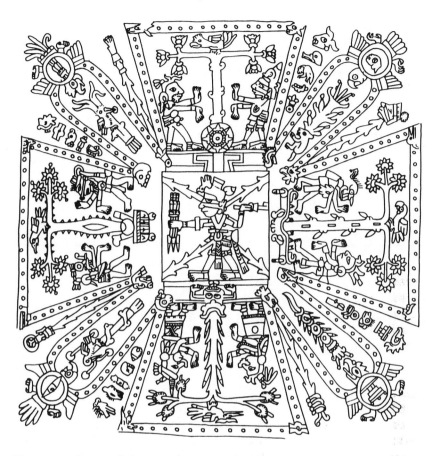

Figure 7. The quadripartite division of space (the rays that form a Latin cross and that meet in the fifth central region) and the four directions of the universe (the four petals that form a Saint Andrew's cross) (Codex Fejérvary-Mayer, pl. 1).

This patio had four doors or entrances: one toward the east, one toward the west, and another at midday and the other toward the northern part . . . The four main temples also had their portals facing said parts and the four gods that were in them were turned facing those same parts. I will not let pass without saying . . . the cause of that, so that we will understand the mystery. The ancients pretended that before the sun rose or was even created, the gods had a great struggle among themselves, stubbornly arguing among themselves in which direction it would be good for the sun to rise

... Each trying to get it to rise by their will, one said it was very important for it to rise in the northern parts, another ... that it rise in the southern parts; another ... to the west; another ... to the east ... Which did rise according to his opinion, and thus, his face (the god's) was placed where he said it would rise, and the other (gods) were placed facing the directions where they wished it to rise, and *that's why there are four doors,* and, *thus they say such and such a god's door, and the others the same, giving each door its god's name.*[17]

Figure 8. The quadripartite division of Mexico-Tenochtitlan, with the eagle in the center (Codex Mendocino, pl. 1).

This obsession in repeating in all earthly creations the archetype of the cosmogonic creation reveals that, in Nahua mythic thought, the essential was not the becoming, but rather, the founding act that by eradicating chaos and creating an order in the universe established a harmony in the world and averted the dangers of its disruption. That is, to have order, foundation, and duration, all human creations had to re-create the preeminent creative act, because it is an exact replica of the original act that gave birth to the universe. Every creation is thus a repetition of the creation of the world, and everything's foundation is based on the center of the world,[18] just as everything that is thus created is converted into a sacred space, governed by the primordial forces. The repetition of cosmogonic creation in human foundations is, then, an entreaty against the change and instability of historical happening, a calling to the permanence of primordial order.

Time and Its Integration into the Cosmic Order

The cosmogonic myth tells that, every time one of the suns disappeared, the order of the universe was crushed and chaos overcame it. In the myth, chaos is the result of a violent eruption of natural phenomena that provoke universal cataclysms and undo the created order. Another expression of chaos, indicated in the first part of the myth, is the absence of light and movement, when the gods initiated creation but did not create a complete sun. This is why in the four solar cosmogonies that follow this twilight period, the sun's creation appears, without being stated, as the direct cause of life, light, and movement. In the case of the creation of the Fifth Sun, this is stated expressly: once the heavens were raised and the earth, the underworld, and humans created, the gods made their greatest efforts to give life to the Fifth Sun, which was born precisely from the individual sacrifice of one of the gods and from the penance of all the gods gathered in Teotihuacan.

It is clear that what matters about the sun is not just that it illuminates, but also that it is put in motion, because the birth of day, the sequence of the seasons, and the incessant flow of time depend on its journey through the cosmos. Therefore, the gods, in consternation at the sight offered by the sun suspended at the eastern edge of the heavens, decide to sacrifice themselves and offer their blood to put the sun into motion. Also, the association of the sun with the birth of time and the calendar record of the occurrence of time are clearly indicated in the same text that narrates cosmogonic creation: "And because the counting begins with this first sun and the counting figures go forward continuously, leaving behind six hundred years, at the beginning of which the gods were born."[19]

The creation of the Fifth Sun signifies, then, the putting into action of life, as is expressed in its very name: Ollintonatiuh, Movement Sun. This movement also creates an order, for cosmogonic creation clearly indicates that from the birth of the sun the cosmos begins to function in a regular fashion: day succeeds night; the stations follow one after the other; time flows eternally; the earth, the heavens, and the underworld take their places; the gods govern the world and humans fulfill their mission on earth. Everything created has a precise place and function, a beginning, a duration, and an end. The essential idea the myth transmits is that the sun not only created life and movement, but also imposed a fundamental order on cosmic and human becoming.

By putting into motion the other heavenly bodies (the moon, the stars) and regulating the action of celestial forces, the sun establishes the necessary link between these and earthly forces. No other heavenly body established with such certainty the fundamental unity between the fecundating power of heavenly forces and the appearance of life on the earth's surface, or exercised such determining power on the cyclical regulation of nature, given that the sun's motion divided the year into four seasons and the sun's first passage through the zenith announced the imminent arrival of the rains.[20] By imposing this cyclical movement on the forces of nature, the sun's motion also determined the distribution of agricultural tasks over the stations and the year and ultimately subjected the lives of humans to the empire of its movements.

The sun's trajectory from east to west and the astronomical position that the equinoxes and the vernal and winter solstices occupied during its annual movement defined the east-west and north-south axes in Nahua thought and established the quadripartite division of cosmic and earth space. In this way, the movement of the sun organized the space also, defining its four bearings, or principal directions. In turn, this definition of the bearings of the universe by the annual movement of the sun established an association between space and time, between the four directions of the universe and the four seasons that divided the year. "In the Mexican system each season is associated with the cardinal point where it ends with a solstice or an equinox, ordering the cardinal points in a counterclockwise fashion (east, north, west, south)" (see fig. 9).[21]

Another example of the organizing function that was attributed to the sun is the relationship between the astronomical observation of the positions of the sun in its annual course and the orientation of the principal temples and axes of the ceremonial centers. Just as the spatial division of Tenochtitlan corresponded to the quadripartite division of cosmic space, so also was the orientation of the religious temples and monuments made to correspond to the movement of the sun. The

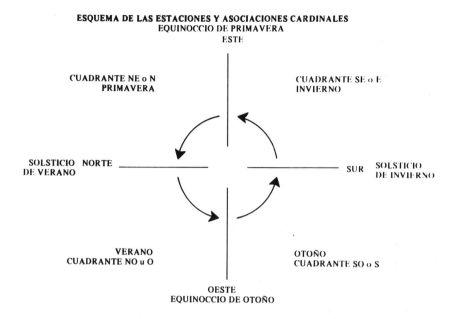

ESQUEMA DE LAS ESTACIONES Y ASOCIACIONES CARDINALES
EQUINOCCIO DE PRIMAVERA
ESTE

CUADRANTE NE o N
PRIMAVERA

CUADRANTE SE o E
INVIERNO

SOLSTICIO NORTE
DE VERANO

SUR

SOLSTICIO
DE INVIERNO

VERANO
CUADRANTE NO u O

OTOÑO
CUADRANTE SO o S

OESTE
EQUINOCCIO DE OTOÑO

Figure 9. Diagram of the seasons and their cardinal associations, according to Pedro Carrasco.

Templo Mayor in the Mexica capital was oriented in such a fashion that at the equinox the sun would pass through its center. The other temples were also oriented "toward the east, that is, facing in the same direction in which the sun moves. The Tenayuca [pyramid] has a deviation in regard to the cardinal points, so that it faces the point where the sun sets on the day it passes through the zenith."[22] In recent years, astronomical and archaeological studies seem to prove that the temples and buildings of the cities were oriented to the principal points of the annual solar cycle, that is, toward sunrise and sunset on the days when the solstices, equinoxes, and passes of the heavenly body through the zenith occurred.[23]

Full incorporation of the suns' movements into human happenings was accomplished by the priests, who watched the sky, and by means of the calendar. As the cosmogonic myth points out and as contemporary studies prove, the calendar was drawn up based on the record of the sun's movements that marked the duration of the days, the succession of the stations, and the annual cycle of solar movements. In this way, the calendar not only reproduced accurately the cyclical changes of the solar year, but also imposed on the population a ceremony founded on the religious and ideological conceptions that the ruling groups had made around the cult of the sun.

Pedro Carrasco has demonstrated that the eighteen "months" or twenty-day periods that made up the Mexican year (Xihuitl) were closely associated with the solstices, equinoxes, and the sun's passes through the zenith and with the spatial division of the four directions of the world. During the eighteen twenty-day periods of the year, different ceremonies were celebrated. As these were feasts organized by the high religious and military officials, they came to be a public ritual directed by the "state." Among the multiple ceremonies that populated the year, three cycles of principal feasts stood out: (1) those dedicated to the four gods that intervened in the creation of the world; (2) the feasts of the gods of water, rain, and cultivated plants; and (3) the feasts that celebrated the gods of the underworld, fire, and earth. Each of these feasts took place during the period associated with the cardinal direction that corresponded to the god being feasted and was connected to the stations. That is, the ceremonies distributed in the calendar reproduced the principal ordering divisions of the cosmos: the vertical division of the world into three levels (heavens, earth, underworld) and the quadripartite spatial division of the universe, divisions that in the religious ritual appeared associated with the cyclical movements of the sun throughout the year.[24]

In this way, the rites for each of the feasts served as historical memory that reactualized the great happenings of the foundation and organization of the cosmos at the same time that they inculcated the population with the ideology formulated by the governing groups. Thus, through a system of political and ideological domination, the observation of the heavenly bodies, astronomical calculations, and the complex calendars became a sacred order, a transcendental record of temporal happening. Like the transformation of the earth's surface in sacred space, the time and its chronological expression in days, weeks, months, and eras was transformed into a succession of temporal units governed by gods and cosmic forces. Each temporal unit that measured the passage of time was transformed into a deity or a manifestation of the divine powers, so that the future became a process that could be explained only through the deciphering of symbolic and religious burdens that the gods imposed on each temporal unit. This conversion of temporal happening into sacred happening occurred in very remote times, probably dating from the very invention of the calendar.

According to Eric S. Thompson, "Among the Maya the days themselves were divine in and of themselves . . . each day is not simply under the influence of some god: it *is* in and of itself a god, rather, a pair of gods, as each day is made up of the combination of a number and a name—1-Ik, 5-Imix, 13-Ahau, etc., and both components are divinities."

From this conversion of temporal happenings into sacred ambit, the Maya conceived of the divisions of time into burdens that were transported by divine bearers through eternity: "Using a similarity in terms of our calendar, it is as if for December 31, 1952, for example, there were six bearers: the god of the number 31 bearing December on its back; the special god of the one the millennia; the god of the number nine the hundreds; the god of the number five, the decades; and the god of the number two carrying the years."[25]

The Nahuatl-speaking peoples, particularly the Mexicas, also practiced this identification of time with the sacred. For them "each sign, each numeral, each day [and each of the temporal units] is associated with a deity that governs the happenings that occur in its time. It's as if the gods spelled each other to govern the world."[26] And, truly, in the Mexica society the gods governed each act of people's lives, from their births to their deaths, through the *tonalpohualli*, or divining calendar. In this calendar, each day and each temporal unit were governed by a combination of sacred forces, auspicious and ominous, that determined the destiny of humans by the date of their births and also predicted the benevolent or adverse character of the activities of each of the days of the year. The significance of this transformation of temporal happening into sacred calendar is summed up very well by Soustelle: "[Man is] governed by predestination; neither his life nor his after-life were in his own hands, and determinism ruled his short stay on earth. He was crushed under the weight of the gods and the stars: he was the prisoner of the omnipotent signs."[27]

This subjection of humans to a superhuman order was a consequence of the perfect integration of time and space into religious ideology. The conversion of the earth's surface into a sacred space where each province, each ethnic group, each neighborhood, each social sector, and each individual were assigned a precise space governed by cosmic forces, gods, and sacred symbols, was completed with the transformation of temporal happening in time governed by the gods, in such a fashion that every human action carried out in space and time lost its earthly and profane sense and was converted into an action dominated by the sacred.

This fusion of sacred space and time was accomplished in ritual, in multiple ceremonies that populated the calendar. In each of these ceremonies, the spatial division of the territory served as the principal organizer of the participating population, as each social group and sector participated in them as a function of the gods, temples, and symbols that corresponded to their territorial space. In turn, each of those spaces was associated with a station, a month, or a day of the year defined by the religious calendar. The geographical-political order of social organization thus corresponded to the cyclic order of the feasts and ceremonies of the religious calendar.

The feast itself was, then, a celebration of the unity between time and space, a reactualization of the sacred principles that governed the universe and a communion of humans with the sacred order. As these ceremonies took place in the sacred centers par excellence, in the temples and palaces that were the territorial symbol of political power, the rite and feast came to be a legitimization of the ruling group, a cosmic celebration of established power.[28]

Rejection of the Temporal Passage and Affirmation of Primordial Creation

This obsession with averting the passage of time by returning to the founding origins of the cosmogonic creation was also expressed in the "tying of the years" ceremony, or feast of the "New Fire." It took place every fifty-two years, when a "century" was completed by Nahuatl time computations. It was celebrated "in all the provinces, towns and houses," but its principal stages were Cerro de la Estrella (two leagues to the east of Tenochtitlan), particularly the great *teocalli* of the Mexica capital, the center of political and religious power, and the navel of the world. This ceremony was preceded by a three-day general fast. The population then broke all the pitchers, pots, grills, and vessels for domestic use. In Tenochtitlan inhabitants threw the household gods and home utensils in the lake and everyone proceeded to clean their houses. The evening before, or four days earlier, all the fires were put out, the home fires and the fire that always burned in the temples. Thus, as in the era that preceded the cosmogonic creation, the world was enveloped in darkness, so that from the time the sun disappeared in the sunset, the population was in a state of anxiety, waiting for the priests to announce that the sun had not died, that it was being reborn, and that once again life had returned to the world.

At sunset, the priests of the temples of Tenochtitlan "dressed and made themselves up with the ornaments of their gods, so that they appeared to be the gods themselves; and at the fall of night they began to walk [in the direction of the Cerro de la Estrella], bit by bit and very slowly, and very seriously and silently—that is why they called it *teonenemi*, which means, they walked like the gods . . . and arrived at the aforesaid hill around midnight. The priest of the Copolco neighborhood, whose job it was to start [the] new fire, carried in his hands the instruments for starting a fire."

Shortly before reaching the Cerro de la Estrella, the priests observed the nocturnal sky for the movement of the Cabrillas, or Pleiades: "They looked . . . to see if they were in the center, and if they were not, they waited until they were; . . . and when they saw that they were passing through the center, they understood that the sky's movement had not stopped and that was not the end of the world; rather they would have another fifty-two years, certain that the world would not end."

At the moment that the Pleiades passed the zenith, the priest from Copolco section proceeded to start the new fire with the fire stick, which was "placed on the chest of a captive . . . taken in war." Once the new fire was started, the priests opened the warrior's chest, took out his heart, and threw it and his whole body into a large bonfire that they all tended so that it would be visible from afar

> At that time, on the hills . . . that surrounded this entire prov-
> ince of Mexico, Tetzcoco, Xochimilco, and Quauhtitlan a great
> number of people waited to see the new fire, which was a signal
> that the world was going ahead; and [as soon as the new fire was
> lighted again, those who were there . . .] raised up a cry . . . of joy
> [because] the world was not ending and [because] they were certain
> of another fifty-two years. . . . And everyone, having seen that
> light, then cut their ears with knives and took the blood that ran
> out and spread it toward that direction where the flame appeared
> . . . and everyone was required to do it, even the children . . . be-
> cause they said that in that manner, everyone was doing penance.[29]

Having built a large bonfire of the new fire, they lighted a torch in it. Before anyone else lighted another one,

> with great haste and brevity, they took it to the principal Mexica
> temple; and having set the new fire before the idols, they brought a
> prisoner taken in war, and before the fire . . . they took out his
> heart, and with the blood, the highest minister sprinkled the fire,
> as a form of blessing. Having completed this, they were waiting
> there from many towns to take the new flame to their temples,
> which they did with permission from the high priest; and this was
> done with much fervor and brevity, although the place was fifteen
> or twenty leagues from there. In the provinces and towns far from
> Mexico, they performed the same ceremony, and this was done
> with great rejoicing and happiness. And beginning the day, thus on
> earth, as mainly in Mexico, they held a great feast and sacrificed in
> Mexico four hundred men [fig. 10].[30]

On New Fire Day, the population renewed the home fire and replaced all the household utensils, "so that all the things that were needed at home were new, as a signal of the new year beginning; therefore, everyone was happy and they held great feasts."[31]

As can be seen, the same calendar and astronomical, religious, and ideological elements that are present in the creation myth are present in the New Fire celebration. The celebration of the end of one era and the beginning of another, which the calendar system dated on a precise year and day, is associated with the movement of the sun to express, as does the cosmogonic myth, the return of the founding moment of the creation of the universe. The New Fire ceremony repeats the archetypal act of the creation of fire related by the cosmogonic myth (when Tezcatlipoca for the first time made fire with the sticks) and associates this fact with the solar cult and the human sacrifices dedicated to the maintenance of the Fifth Sun's life. It is evident that the ritual that organizes the New Fire ceremony is oriented to reactualizing the vitalizing and organizing moment of the universe, when the sunrise exiled darkness and gave heat and movement to the world. The ritual is also charged with the political and ideological message that is typical of the Mexica system of domination: the culminating act of the New Fire ceremony, the sacrifice of the captives of war, was the ratification and a justification of the providential mission that had been assigned to the Mexica people as provider of the divine food of the sun and sustainer of the cosmic order.

As Johanna Broda has shown,[32] the New Fire ceremony was a symbolic staging of Mexica power; it was organized and presided over by Mexica priests, who dressed in the garments of the gods and appeared before the populace as if they were the gods themselves. The original site of the ceremony, the Cerro de la Estrella, had been displaced by the Mexica Templo Mayor, center and axis of the world. From here the new fire was transported by torches to the temples of the wards into which the city was divided, then to the people of the Valley of Mexico, and finally to the most remote provinces under Mexica rule. In this fashion, the symbolism of the ceremony sanctioned the relationships of power between the Mexica capital and its subjugated provinces.

The New Fire feast is also one of the most representative examples of the rejection of the passage of time that the Mexicas share with other ancient peoples studied by Mircea Eliade. The New Fire ceremony was one ritual form of killing the time past, of canceling history constructed by the successive accumulation of happenings, and a means of reactualizing the original moment of creation, the time without wear in which the organizing principles of the universe were established. The ritual of the feast abolishes past time, destroys things worn by the march of time, and returns the population to the inaugural beginning of the

Figure 10. The New Fire ceremony (Codex Borbónico, pl. 34).

world, making it represent live the moment when everything was created anew. Here, again, the return to the founding origins acts as an exorcism of the march of time, against wearing down, instability, and the change that threatened the permanence of the primordial order.[33]

Primitive Time and Cyclical Time

In the cosmogonic creation myth and in the rite that celebrates the feast of the New Fire, several conceptions of time are intermingled. Cosmogonic creation stresses the importance of the original moment in which the cosmos was created and attributes to that primitive time the virtues of creating time and ordering the cosmos. It was the time of absolute beginning, the moment when chaos was exorcised. This was the preeminent sacred time, the time when everything existed for the first time. This original time was also perfect time, the age when the cosmos existed charged with all its vital force. But this simultaneously creative, organizing, and vitalizing perfect time of the cosmos is immediately attacked by the passing of time, which brings with it wear and cosmic deterioration. The destruction of the primitive order by the passage of time is represented in the cosmogonic myth by the cosmic catastrophes that periodically put an end to the order created. The conception of perfect original time is thus interwoven, in the Mesoamerican creation myths and in the cosmogonic myths of other peoples,[34] with the idea of a cyclical creation and destruction of the cosmos. That is, in Mesoamerican creation myths, the idea is present that everything that lasts becomes worn, degenerates, and ends up perishing. Also present is the idea that primitive creation is recoverable, that the destruction of the cosmic order is followed by a new creation that establishes again the primordial moment when everything is created anew. In the Nahua cosmogonic myth, each of the suns, or ages, is suddenly destroyed at the end of a certain time, but each of these destructions is followed immediately by a new cosmic creation that restores the annihilated world.

The ritual of the feast of the New Fire takes from the cosmogonic myth both the notion of perfect primitive time and the idea of the cyclical renovation of the cosmos and introduces them into human time. The purpose of this ceremony in which all of the population participated was to revitalize the cosmos through the double procedure of abolishing time past and returning to the origin of creation, to the perfect moment when creation possessed full vitality. The celebration of the New Fire ceremony anticipates the final cataclysm that the cosmogonic myth relates through the procedure of restoring vitality to the cosmos every fifty-two years. It does this by returning the cosmos to the moment of its first creation, when everything was new for the first time and it enjoyed the beatitude of the origin. Every time the calendar marked the end of one era or the end of a cycle of the movements of the sun, the ceremony and rite intervened to abolish the wasting effects of the passage of time and to return to the first moment of creation. The periodic reactualization of the origins is the essential purpose of the rite, the means of combating permanently the corrosive flow of time. The rite assumes the form of a collective restoration of the original act that gave a foundation to creation and serves as an exorcism against the wear caused by the passing of time.

The notion of the perfect time of the origins and the cyclical concept of cosmic time are completely alien to the idea of a profane time constructed by the action of humans. The former, on making of creation the essential moment of cosmic happening, converts past time into a time lacking significance. Furthermore, to the extent that distancing of the original plenitude implies a degeneration of creation, religious and human effort concentrates on recovering original time, which is translated into an eternal return, in a constant turning backward, in search of primordial time. Therefore, it can be said that the recovery of the original plenitude is a form of escaping real time. There is a flight from effective time by the procedure of returning to the moment of absolute time of the creation. Thus, by going back to the origins of the creation of the world, the myth and the ritual do not seek to place events within a temporal framework; rather, they create a religious experience by means of which it will be possible to reach "the very depth of being, discover the original, the primitive reality from which the cosmos came and which permits understanding coming into being as a whole."[35]

The idea of a constant creation and destruction of the cosmos is also alien to the profane temporal happening of humans. The chronology that measures the duration of eras of that cyclical time is not constructed to create a temporal perspective of human events, nor does it intend to establish a framework that explains the sense of human actions. Rather, it is made to signal the cyclical character of the creation and destruction of the cosmos. More than a chronology of temporal happenings, these measures of the duration of eras or cycles appear to certify that, whatever might be the duration in years or centuries of those cycles, the world created will inevitably be destroyed and that destruction will ineluctably be followed by a new creation, and so on successively.

The idea of a perfect primordial time establishes a relationship between past, present, and future that is foreign to the modern, contemporary, western conception of history. According to this conception, there is no difference between past, present, and future, for those temporal categories, so clear and distinct to us, form a single block, an uninterrupted sequence of the act of creation. The past does not have the character of what has happened because it is always present as founding act; on the other hand, it lacks the charge of what has occurred acting on the present because the accumulation of past human events has no weight, no significance in that conception of temporality that makes the moment of mythical creation the act that constitutes human destiny. In turn, the present is not conceived as being forged by the accumulation of the past and the perspectives of the future, for it has sense only as a realization of the founding act. And the same occurs with the future, which is seen as one more compliance with the original designs revealed in the act of creation. More than a temporality or a chronology, mythic thought proposes a genealogy, a continual affiliation of the present with respect to the past.

Eschatological Ideas and Circular Time

The idea of the perfection of the origins and of cyclical time is intermingled with the idea that, "for something genuinely new to begin, the . . . ruins of the old cycle must be completely destroyed." The possibility of restoring the original perfection implies the radical destruction of the world that has degenerated. In the Nahua creation myth and in other creation myths studied by Mircea Eliade, it is clear that the New Creation cannot take place without the complete abolition of the old cycle: "The obsession with the beatitude of the beginnings requires the destruction of everything that has existed . . . and has been degraded."[36] These ideas gave a basis to the eschatological conception of the cosmic coming into being, as they predicted that each sun or world created would have to terminate in total destruction. In this way, the conception of cyclical time gave way to an at once pessimistic and optimistic concept of cosmic and human destiny—pessimistic because it supposed that everything created would have an end, and this end was conceived as being sudden, catastrophic, and total; optimistic because it nourished the conviction that, after that annihilation of the world, there would be a new creation, that to be truly new presumed the radical destruction of the ancient world. The cyclical conception of creation and destruction of the cosmos is, then, the basis of the eschatological ideas so deeply rooted in the Indian mentality, ideas that sooner or later, after the Conquest, would be reborn strongly under messianic and apocalyptic forms, mixing with and enriching themselves with the eschatological ideas of European and Christian thought.[37]

The ideas concerning a perfect primitive time and a time that was cyclically renewed were linked to a conception of circular time, to the idea that, in the infinite sequence of cycles, these would be repeated after a prolonged time. In the Florentine Codex there is a Nahua proverb and following it an explanation of it that express this idea:

> Another time it will be like this, another time things will be the same, some time, some place.
> What happened a long time ago, and which no longer happens, will be again, it will be done again, as it was in far-off times: those who now live will live again, they will be again.[38]

The idea of the repetition of time, that the cycles and events that have occurred once will be repeated, is the basis of the calendrical, astronomical, and divining systems of the Mesoamerican peoples. In the same fashion as the solar calendar and the astronomical calculations revealed the periodicity of the sun's movements, it was thought that the record of natural events that affected human lives would permit forecasting their next appearance and creating means of preventing their effects. These observations had led the Mexicas to discover that *ce tochtli* years coincided with the years when crops were destroyed, with the periods of hunger and death. That is why they believed that the return of each cycle of fifty-two years would present the same danger.[39] The prophecies that the Maya priests inscribed in their sacred books had the same basis: they predict what will happen in the future based on what was known to have occurred on *katunes*, or prior temporal cycles:

> 6-Ahau: trees will be eaten, stones will be eaten; great hunger will be its burden, death will be seated on its mat and its throne . . . It will happen three times that there will not be wild jicama bread and tree fruits; great hunger and depopulation and destruction of peoples.[40]

What unites the perfect time of original creation to cyclic time and to the circular time that returns anew is the fact that all these times refer to preeminent sacred events: the creation and ordering of the cosmos, the rhythm of cosmic temporality, the end of the world, the circular regeneration of the ages. These different times do not seek to explain a happening; rather, they reveal the sacred reality that gave beginning, organization, and movement to the universe. These are essentially founding acts, constituting a reality, that become archetypal acts. By revealing a reality—the passage from chaos to the cosmos, the organization of space, the rhythm of time, the creation of humans, the extinction and renovation of the earth—the myth converts it into an archetypal reality, revealing its sacred character and codifying its manifestations. As Malinowski says, the myth "makes an original reality revive . . . The myth is . . . a living reality to which recourse never ceases to be made."[41]

2.

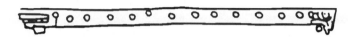

Representation and Uses of the Past

Origin and Functions of the Gatherer of the Past

In Mexico we do not find the cultural sequence that in Greece defines the contours of the folksinger of legendary deeds (Homer), then defines the traits of the first explainers of myths or mythographers (Hesiod), and finally gives an account of the lives and works of those who proposed to gather past events so that "the memory of the public deeds of men will not disappear with time" (Herodotus). Instead of this progression, the first clear image of the historian given to us by the oldest literature is that of the historian-priest, the specialized historian who gathers and explains the past to serve the interests of the *hueytlatoani*, or highest ruler. The texts that describe him sometimes elevate him to the category of a sage, or represent him as an individual who possesses specialized techniques and knowledge. In all cases, the high rank that he occupies comes from his knowledge of pictographic writing, which was a specialized knowledge.

Among the Mayas, the figure of the scribe stands out sharply in the codices and particularly in the painted ceramics of the Classical period. For the Mayas, writing and painting were synonymous, and the practitioner of these arts was considered a superior personage. Among the diverse representations that show us the Maya scribe, some represent him handling the instruments: the brush and the paints, the latter contained in shell receptacles (fig. 11).

Other images show him in the very act of painting his signs in the sacred books, often bound in jaguar skin (figs. 12–14). In others we see him reading and leafing through the painted books (fig. 15). Frequently, these scenes occur before the sovereign or in the royal chambers. In different ways, these images suggest that the tasks of painting the codices and inscribing in them the outstanding events of the cosmos, the events of the earthly world, or matters related to supernatural beings were actions charged with a special sense, almost sacred or divine.[1]

Figure 11. Two Maya scribes handling the paintings and the brush. Drawing based on Robicsek, *The Maya Book of the Dead*, p. 55. (Photo © Justin Kerr 1980.)

We are in debt to the Maya scribes for some of the most beautiful codices preserved, the most refined calligraphy, and the most sensitive, natural, eloquent, and dedicated plastic representation of the human figure that we know from the ancient world. They probably perfected their art in schools or workshops established for that purpose and occupied one of the highest places among the elite who led the kingdom. Recent studies show that the Maya scribes of the Classical period formed lineages that transmitted the profession from father to son.[2] In Copán, one of these scribes came to be so important that he erected a sumptuous palace and inscribed his name on it, next to that of the sovereign of the realm, who apparently presided over the inauguration of the residence.[3] At the end of the Classical period, it appears that each important lineage of the Maya kingdom had its own scribes, who were charged with the memory and exaltation of the family.[4]

Among the Aztecs this tradition was prolonged. The Nahua texts that describe the scribe, or *tlacuilo*, sometimes elevate him to the category of sage, or they represent him as an individual possessing specialized techniques and knowledge. The upper range that he occupies is denoted by his knowledge of pictographic writing, which was a specialized field of knowledge.

When he is equated to the sage, the knower of the past is indicated as a "torch that doesn't smoke," as a bright, clear light, and as the incarnation of wisdom itself: he is the depository of ancient and deep learning, the one who preserves and communicates the secrets con-

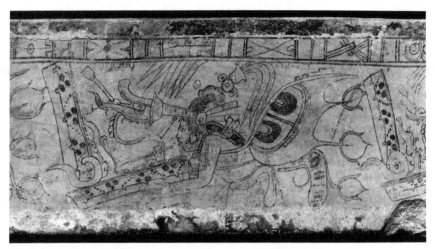

Figure 12. Maya scribe in the act of painting a codex bound in jaguar skin. Drawing based on Robicsek, *The Maya Book of the Dead*, p. 55. (Photo © Justin Kerr 1980.)

tained in the painted books, the one who illuminates what happens on earth. He is a guide, a master, and a light for other human beings. He combines the qualities of the sage, the seer, and the priest. Because of that knowledge and those powers, he is above others. He is an exceptional being.[5]

Other texts stress the technical knowledge and capacity that distinguished the knowers of the past. They are "the ones who are looking (reading), the ones who tell (or report what they read). The ones who noisily turn the leaves of the codices. The ones who have the black and red ink (writing) and drawing, they take us, they guide us, they show us the path."[6]

In this and in other Nahua texts, the scribe appears as a person who, because of his knowledge, has the power to see and make seen that which remains hidden to the common human being. His prestige and his powers to illuminate the occult take root in his knowledge. But unlike the witch doctor or the shaman, who established their relationships with the supernatural through individual practices of ecstasy or trance,[7] the scribe-historian came into contact with the unknown through the discipline and practices of institutionalized priesthood. What distinguished the priest from other individuals was, on the one hand, the rigorous discipline and special knowledge that he acquired in the *calmecac*, or school where priests were trained, and, on the other, the

Figure 13. Maya vessel with the figure of a scribe painting a codex. Drawing based on Robicsek, *The Maya Book of the Dead*, p. 58. (Photo © Justin Kerr 1980.)

austerity, the asceticism, and the intense dedication that the practice of priestly duties implied. Added to these differences in training and functions is the priests' physical segregation in temples and palaces, and a way of life and vestments that made them appear different to common mortals. Secluded in their temples, they were displayed for others to see only on the occasion of the great ceremonies and religious feasts, when they officiated as intermediaries of the gods, led the ritual, and transmitted divine plans to the people. In these ceremonies, the highest priests were identified with the gods themselves, adopting their names and clothing.

Even though the majority of the priests were trained in the writing, reading, and interpretation of the painted books, not all of them occupied the highest religious posts, nor were all of them specialized in the techniques of recollection and transmission of the past. The available testimonials indicate that, parallel to the strengthening of Mexica

Figure 14. Elegant figure of a Maya scribe in the act of painting a codex. Drawing based on Robicsek, *The Maya Book of the Dead*, p. 58. (Photo © Justin Kerr 1980.)

power, the group of priests grew, as did the internal division of labor among them. The demand for specialized knowledge and techniques, limited at the beginning to the requirements of the governing families and to a reduced group of administrators, increased considerably as political dominance extended over numerous peoples. The specialists then trained in gathering the political and military feats of the *tlatoani*. Together with them, the specialists dedicated themselves to composing the texts wherein were recorded the population and the tribute of the dominated provinces, the organization of collective labor, the composition and recruitment of the army, the handling of the waterworks and of public works, the ritual, religious, and agricultural calendars. That is,

Figure 15. Maya scribe reading and leafing through a codex. Drawing based on Robicsek, *The Maya Book of the Dead*, p. 54. (Photo © Justin Kerr 1980.)

the development of writing and of scribes came to be a direct consequence of the growth and complexity acquired by political power and the administrative apparatus that served it.

One idea of the complexity of the written register of the events in the last era of Mexica power is transmitted by the following text by mestizo historiographer Fernando de Alva Ixtlilxóchitl. This historian says of his ancestors:

> They had writers for each genre: some who handled the Annals, putting in order the things that happened each year, by day, month, and hour. Others were in charge of genealogies and ancestors of the kings and persons of lineage . . . Some of them took care of painting the limits, boundaries, and boundary lines of the cities, provinces, towns, and places, and of the lots and distribution of lands . . . Others of the books of laws, rites, and ceremonies that they prac-

ticed as infidels; and the priests of the temples of their idolatry . . .
and of the feast of their false gods and calendars. And finally it was
the responsibility of the philosophers and sages who were among
them to paint all the sciences that they knew and attained and to
teach from memory the songs that [preserved] their sciences and
histories.[8]

In addition to specifying the variety of pictographic records that
occupied the priests, this text allows us to see another important
division of labor among them: there were those who "were in charge of
painting all the sciences that they knew," and those who taught "from
memory the songs that [transmitted the cumulated knowledge of] their
sciences and histories." This distinction between the pictographic
record and the memorization of the songs that transmitted what was
written in the codices refers to a cultural process wherein the written and
the oral discourse were still mixed, without either of them existing
independently of the other. That is, the oral culture was no longer the
preeminent one, nor was it based exclusively on memory,[9] for it was
guided by the pictographic record. In turn, reading the pictographic
record was accessible only to the limited group of priests, so that for its
contents to be communicated to wider sectors of the population, it
necessarily required oral discourse. These characteristics of the development of the oral and pictographic culture exercised a decisive influence
on historical discourse.

The greatest limitation of the Nahua historical discourse was the
absence of a fully developed writing system. Pictographic writing transmitted its message through pictures that represented objects or actions.
These were representations that distinguished the qualities of attributes
associated with the object painted.[10] That is, the pictographs and
ideograms were a technique that permitted, through the association of
drawings and symbols, the recording of a precise idea in the document
and the transmittal to the reader of a "unique message." Because of these
technical limitations, the codices and historical annals also transmitted
their message in unique units that expressed an idea. This made it
necessary to draw a separate message to connect one idea with another
one (see figs. 16–19). That is, the annals in which the events were
inscribed could gather multiple events that happened over the course of
the year, but they were able to transmit only a brief and symbolic
message about each of those events.

Constrained by the technical limitations of his writing system, the
Nahua scribe was not able to create a representation of past events that
was as rich in nuances of time, place, and action as the Indo-European
historical literatures. The text or codex in which the historical happen-

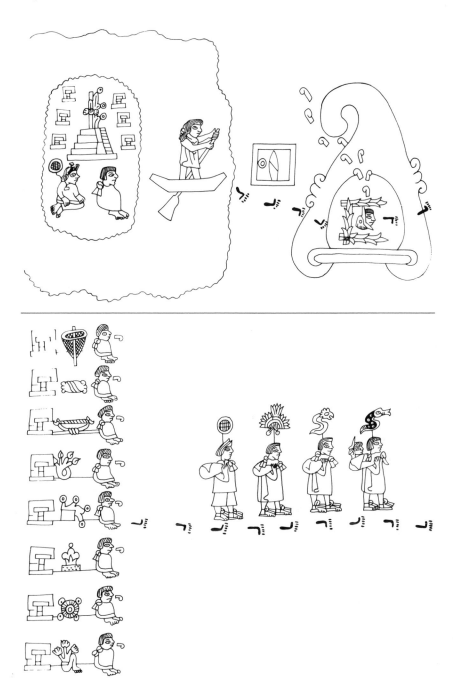

Figures 16 and 17. *Tira de la peregrinación* (depiction of the journey).

Figures 18 and 19. *Tira de la peregrinación* (depiction of the journey).

ings were inscribed was thus a mnemonic device, a memory aid that permitted retention and transmission of essential facts, but without the capacity to describe them with depth, breadth, and richness of detail.[11]

In order to describe with breadth and to shade the facts recorded in the documents, the Nahua-speaking peoples availed themselves of other procedures. Beside the *tlacuilos*, or specialists who painted the books, there were specialists who read them, interpreted them, memorized them, and expounded on them in detail before audiences of nonspecialists.[12] Because of these technical limitations, the Nahua historical discourse was divided into two parts: one recorded the events that occurred through simple, precise ideograms; another transmitted them to a broader public through oral language that gave the account expressive force, nuance, and coloration. Both parts demanded a high degree of specialization; thus, its practice was limited to the select group of priest-scribes.

It would be anachronistic to think that the scribe had autonomy over the historical story that he recorded and spread. At the time of Mexica domination, as before in Monte Albán, in the Mayan cities, in Teotihuacan, or in the Toltecs' Tula, the recovery and explanation of the past was a function of the governing group. The rulers of the state determined what to recover of the past and why. In the reconstruction of the past, the Mexica scribe, like his Chinese or Babylonian counterpart, played the role of a specialized functionary who gathered and organized the events that had been selected previously by the current ruler. Socially, the priest educated in the *calmecac* was a natural reproducer of the message of his class; he was not a person who had an individual criterion or conscience. In Mexica society, the individual was subservient to the collectivity, which in turn was conditioned by the power structure whose strings were centrally controlled by the sovereign. Because of this power structure and since in these societies individual existence had no more meaning than that of preserving the life of the collectivity, it was unthinkable for the scribes who composed the historical texts to express individual ideas or opinions.

Also, like every society ruled by an absolute central power, the Mexica society was severely controlled by censorship. According to indigenous testimony preserved by Bernardino de Sahagún, every new song or text that was composed was submitted to the censorship of priests dedicated to looking out for the maintenance of the current orthodoxy. Thus, Tláloc's priests, in their avocation to Epcohua, or "mother-of-pearl serpent," had the evaluation of new songs as their job, so that "when someone composed songs, he gave his opinion about them."[13] Another priest, called "conservator," was charged with making sure the teaching and transmission of the approved songs was faithful:

The conservator was in charge
of the songs of the gods,
of all divine songs.
So that nobody erred,
he watched with care
to teach the people
the divine songs in the neighborhoods.
He preached
so that the townspeople gathered
and learned the songs well.[14]

Above these censors and conservators was the censorship of the supreme ruler. The *tlatoani* imposed decisive censorship on the contents of the historical texts and their forms of pictographic, ritual, or symbolic expression. Because of his functions, he and his closest advisers agreed on the selection of what was to be gathered from past events, the rank of importance that he should grant to each event, and the forms of representation of those events. The systematic ordering of the historical traditions was attributed to Huémac, king of Tula.[15] There is also proof that the Mexicas' *tlatoani* periodically reconstructed the interpretation of the past made by his predecessors and adjusted it to the present situation. Sufficient testimony is known to say that the image of the past that the Mexicas transmitted to posterity was a retrospective elaboration that began with the consolidation of Aztec power in central Mexico. We know that from the reign of Itzcóatl (1427–1440), when this ruler ordered the burning of ancient codices, a systematic rewriting of the past was undertaken. It is most likely that the texts that tell of the Mexica migration as an edifying pilgrimage to the promised land, the identification of Aztlán (the place of obscure origin) with Tenochtitlan (the place of the splendor of Mexica power), the transformation of the new arrivals into the peoples inheriting Toltec culture, and the image of the Mexica as the peoples predestined to dominate their rivals and initiate a new era correspond to these years.[16]

It is clear that in these societies the preservation and interpretation of the past were a function of the sovereign and that this function developed most strongly in those metropolises that managed to dominate extensive regions and in which a continuous and systematically reelaborated historical discourse flowered. This is why the house of paintings, where the codices were preserved, was in the sovereign's palace, for it was a proper function of the ruler to preserve historical memory. For the same reason, the writer who "paints or puts in writing the memory-words," the specialist in explaining "the contents of the books of years,"[17] and the priests who were experts in preservation of the memory of the past were directly attached to the *tlatoani*.

The scribe who specialized in recording and transmitting the past was, then, separated from the majority of the population by his function and by the very knowledge he managed, which was accessible only to his peers. This separation began at birth, that watershed that divided the nobles from the *macehuales* and decided the former would have a specialized education in the *calmecac* prepare them to occupy the highest administrative and religious positions and to be directors of the *macehuales*. As occurred in ancient China, in Mesoamerica the recording and reading of the past were the exclusive knowledge of the ruling class. The rest of the population was acquainted with this record of the past through oral discourse and, more precisely and in a livelier fashion, through the myths, the ceremonies, and the ritual stagings that transmitted the cryptic message of the sacred texts by multiple means.

While available data are still precarious for illuminating the figure of the ancient gatherer of the past, it is clear that one of the processes that affected his social position and functions most was the passage of the tribal groups into political forms such as kingdoms or "city-states," or to more developed political organizations, such as the Triple Alliance that the Mexicas commanded. This transition to more complex forms of political organization caused an amplification and systematization of the historical records. It favored the ascendancy of written over oral discourse, and it stimulated the replacement of the historical record based on the ruling family with a different one, whose axis would be the ethnic group and the broader political organization that contained it.

As these transformations occurred, the ancient rememberer of the past, who was a charismatic being whose prestige depended on his power to retain and recite the oral tradition, was replaced by the scribe, who from an early age specialized in knowledge of writing, religion, calendrical systems, and sciences and arts. From that time, rigorous domination of these fields of knowledge, not his expressive or charismatic abilities, raised him to the status of superior being, possessor of techniques that gave him access to events that occurred a long time ago and that allowed him to enter into what was secret and unknown to others. Knowledge of the calendar and chronological records, and the handling of techniques to inscribe events systematically depended, then, on the domination of writing. As the ancient texts said, only those who had in their power "the black and red ink and painted with it" were in possession of knowledge. Writing was, then, a synonym for knowledge, and the priest, he who had the black and red ink, a synonym for sage.

The superiority of writing over memory and the oral tradition also converted the scribes into a specialized group that reproduced itself by means of an educational system whose stability and development depended on political power. Unlike the shaman, who hid his knowledge from others and transmitted it only by inheritance from father to son, the knowledge of the priest-scribes was transformed into institutionalized knowledge that was learned and transmitted in the *calmecac*, the place where institutional continuity made specialized knowledge into an accumulative process. Beginning with the institution of the *calmecac*, or its equivalent, the group of scribes acquired permanence. Its development ran parallel to that of political power, which required the services of these specialized schools to produce men to direct and organize society.

The differences between this "state bureaucracy" of specialists occupied with gathering and transmitting the past and their ancestors should be clarified, because these differences illuminate the step that goes from the scribe entirely devoted to recording the deeds of the *tlatoani* and to justifying the legitimacy of the governing family, from the scribe dedicated to creating a historical memory of the ethnic group, the kingdom, or the state. An example of the first type of rememberer of the past is offered by the admirable reconstruction that Alfonso Caso did of the kings who governed the small, dispersed domains of the Oaxaca Mixtecs between the year A.D. 692 and the sixteenth century.[18] This extensive and surprising reconstruction of the genealogy of the Mixtec rulers was possible because in those diminutive kingdoms the history of the realm was confused with the person of the ruler, and because the basic function of the scribe was to record the principal events in the life of the ruler, to exalt his deeds, and to inculcate in the population the idea of the divine and inextinguishable character of the royal office.

The apogee of Mexica power also had scribes dedicated entirely to narrating the *tlatoani*'s victorious campaigns and to composing songs that exalted his virtues and biographies that detailed the principal events of his life. But not all of the history of the expansive Mexica kingdom was centered around its *tlatoque*, nor were all the scribes dedicated to collecting and recording the feats of its rulers. Although the Mexica kingdom was a political and social entity centered around the *hueytlatoani*, or supreme ruler, at the time of its apogee it acted as a state whose purposes went beyond the person of the current ruler. The last decades of the Mexica kingdom reveal a political process that was headed in the direction of state institutionalization of power and show the strengthening of groups and institutions that imposed a limit on the previously all-embracing powers of the *tlatoani*. The progressive stratification of the Mexica kingdom is not expressed only in the political organization of the Triple Alliance, or in the formal participation of warriors, priests, and merchants in the principal foreign and domestic policy decisions, or in the formation of a complex administrative apparatus in charge of religious, economic, military, and judicial matters.[19] It is also manifested in the appearance of a form of historical record that we could classify as "state," in the sense that it gathers and orders events connected with the historical formation of the kingdom as such, independently of the person of the sovereign. Thus, alongside the genealogies of the lords and principal families, alongside the annals that described the lives of the rulers, there appears a form of historical account that collected the events that constituted the kingdom and another that fused the history of the rulers with that of the ethnic group and the political organization that contained all of these parts, both of which gave rise to what we could call the history of a people or of a nation. An example of what has been called a historical state record would be the books in which they painted "the boundaries, limits, and landmarks of the cities, provinces, towns and places," the books in which the agreements entered into with the conquered provinces were recorded, the books in which was registered the amount of the tribute that the enslaved peoples were to pay, and the books that gathered the names and characteristics of the various gods, arts, sciences, and laws. The *Tira de la peregrinación*, the *Historia de los mexicanos por sus pinturas*, or the *Historia Tolteca-Chichimeca* are examples of accounts that proposed to gather the origin of ethnic groups and tribes, joining them with the history of their caudillos and gods, and with the story of the triumphs and failures of the ethnic group. In these accounts, the historical record, instead of focusing on the biography of the ruler, has as its subject the ethnic group and the political entity that had managed to unify and grant social identity to vast human groups.

Ethnic group, tribe, or kingdom were social and political organizations that had absorbed the individual, family, and familial groups into larger units, that endowed individual existence with meaning and proposed a collective future and destiny. At the same time as the accounts centered on the ethnic group strengthened the ties of identity and recognized a common past, they proposed a collective destiny, which in the case of the Mexicas was offered as grandiose and predestined.

The Representation of Historical Reality

The representation of the Mesoamerican peoples' historical events is incomprehensible if we do not refer to their conceptions of space and time,[20] to their idea of how the universe worked, and human groups within it.

The Nahuatl idea of the composition of the cosmos is founded on a precise conception of nature and of nature's relationship to the world of humans. The cosmos was conceived of as being formed by specific elements: water, earth's surface, heaven, fire, air, generally represented as pairs of opposites—heaven-earth, darkness-light, cold-heat, wind-fire. These different elements were thought to be inhabited by forces, fluids, or divine powers that spread throughout the universe and its different spaces, so that the heavens, the earth, and the underworld were at the same time receptors and bearers of these forces.[21]

The dynamics of the cosmos were a result of the interaction of the celestial forces with those of the underworld when assembling on the earth's surface (the human world), where they arrived transported by the four cosmic trees and by the four roads that met at the center of the earth. There, on the surface of the earth, they united and ordered the multiple cosmic forces; they divided spatially and received their temporal dynamic. In the cosmogonic myths, the spatial division of the cosmic forces is simultaneous with their being put into motion: each one of the forces left its place and became present on the earth's surface in accordance with an order "strictly determined by the calendrical cycles." Each hour, day, month, year, or chronological era was governed by one of these forces or divine powers, so that its dominion encompassed simultaneously a precise space and temporal lapse, until with the advent of another temporal moment that force was displaced by the new one, which from that instant ruled its corresponding space and time.[22]

The alternating dominance of these forces in space and time implies, then, the belief in a constant increase and decrease in the energy that gave life to the universe. The dynamics of the universe is conceived in a manner similar to that of nature, as an uninterrupted process of birth, plenitude, degeneration, and death that varied only in the quality of the forces that presided over that process at each moment. The coming into being of the cosmos was seen as a succession similar to that of the seasons, the annual renewal of nature, or the cyclical movements of the stars. And thus, as nature experienced processes of generation, plenitude, and decay, it was thought that the cosmic forces passed through similar processes; thus, it was necessary periodically to revitalize the energy that imposed movement on the cosmos.

In extreme terms, it could be said that the calendar and the chronological computations served especially to record changes in nature, changes that, since they affected the principal human activities (the agricultural cycle, the hunting seasons, and the gathering of wild fruit), were the principal ritual acts of the religious and state calendar. By means of this transformation of the natural calendar into ritual calendar, the priests and rulers were able, on the one hand, periodically to revitalize the forces of nature; on the other, they were able to organize the population's activities in a centralized fashion.

The idea that the cosmos was activated by forces that acted on specific moments and spaces was transferred to the time and space in which humans acted. The warrior, expansionist ideology of the Mexicas was based on the conception that, to maintain the vitality of the Fifth Sun, it was necessary to nourish it with the blood of captive warriors. War and human sacrifice thus became acts that sustained the cosmic balance. At the same time, since cosmic vitality was what infused human events with strength and meaning, it was thought that, to have strength, each act of human life had to be fortified by the presence of these divine powers.

The social and political organization of the Mesoamerican peoples was sustained by the idea that the forces that imparted energy and balance to the cosmos were manifested in the persons of the rulers, who were the representatives of the strength of the gods: "Cosmic duality was a model for political organization. In Mexico-Tenochtitlan, the delegation of divine is clearly seen in the two supreme lords of the *tlatocáyotl*: On the one hand, there was the *tlatoani*, who received his attributes of divinity in their masculine form, and, on the other, the *cichuacóatl*, whose name links him to the feminine aspect of divinity. Whereas the first was the supreme head of the *tlatocáyotl* and functioned as a military leader, the second was the chief administrator, who received, amassed, and distributed wealth."[23]

In the same manner in which the ruler was invested with cosmic forces that nourished the world, the political and social organization rested on the pillars that were the foundation of the cosmos. In order to have strength and vitality constantly renewed by the divine powers, the Triple Alliance, the Mexica state, its capital, and each one of its towns founded a political organization similar to the organization of the cosmos, dividing it into the four parts of the cosmic bearings through which circulated the divine forces. The center, where the four bearings of the universe and the forces that emanated from those regions converged, was occupied by the Mexica capital, the Templo Mayor. And in turn, the *hueytlatoani*, or supreme ruler, was the highest expression of the center of the world and of the concentration of the forces of horizontal and vertical space.[24] In Tenochtitlan, the *tlatoani* was considered the heart of the city (*in iyollo altépetl*).[25]

The social world was, then, a replica of the organization and founding of the cosmos, not a reality in itself. And the same thing occurred with time, which instead of recording the temporality of human events, assimilated these into a sacred temporality. Thus, to cite one example among many, the calendar date Ce-técpatl (1-Flint), dedicated to the god

Huitzilopochtli, as it was his birthday, is the mythical date in the historical accounts that was made to coincide with the day and year of the departure of the Mexicas from Aztlán, with the beginning of the pilgrimage, with the founding of Tenochtitlan, and with the naming of the first *tlatoani*, Acamapitchtli. In this way, the real temporality of the beginning of the pilgrimage, of the founding of the city, and of the creation of the monarchy was subsumed by a sacred temporality, through which these dates were assimilated to the calendar date of the god Huitzilopochtli, a date charged with all of the power of the protector-god of the Mexicas. As Richard F. Townsend summarizes it so well:

> Historical commemorative monuments recorded the decisive events of Mexica national history—as it was officially interpreted according to imperial policy—and celebrated the role of kings, priests, and other major functionaries of the Mexica social hierarchy. But these events and offices could only be meaningful when legitimized by portraying them symbolically in cosmological settings; the state and the social order were only valid and therefore understandable in the measure that they were equated with the sacred world.[26]

In the majority of the Nahua historical texts, these cosmological, religious, mythic, and sacred conceptions that made the world coherent are constant. The Mexica pilgrimage in search of the promised land, the foundation of Tenochtitlan, the successive conquests, the coronation of each *tlatoani*, and every significant event were tied, in order to have reality, to symbolic calendar dates, to numens that assigned it its "true" importance and significance, for, as a profane event, it appeared to be stripped of transcendence. In this conception, the human act in itself did not found a historical reality; rather, that act conformed to a group of religious or mythical symbols and beliefs that framed it. For example, "the history of the Mexicas, prior to settling in the valley that they dominated later, is totally wrapped in the myth that tells of the birth and life of the guardian god Huitzilopochtli, and in turn is the story of the tribe itself."[27]

Nothing expresses this constant immersion of the historical reality in the realm of the mythical and sacred better than the Mexicas' own testimony dedicated to reviving the memory of past events. Let us see how the *Tira de la peregrinación* explains the Mexicas' first steps in search of the promised land. In figure 16, the first of this codex, an island (Aztlán) appears on the left side with a temple surrounded by three houses on one side and a like number on the other, indicating the seat of six families or ethnic groups. The man in the canoe and the footprints signal that the place was abandoned in the year Ce-técpatl, or 1-Flint (according to the little square in the middle) and the voyage toward the twisted mountain that is seen on the right side. In the interior of this mountain, in a cave, there is an altar made up of branches, in whose center is the god Huitzilopochtli. His face comes out of the beak of a hummingbird. From there he speaks to his followers, as the commas that come out of his mouth, representing words, indicate.

At the twisted mountain, the Mexicas find eight tribes, or ethnic groups (fig. 17), represented by a seated individual, with a hieroglyphic name and a house. These groups are the Matlatzinca, the Tepanecas, the Tlahuicas, the Malinalcas, the Colhuas, the Xochimilcas, the Chalcas, and the Huexotzincas. With them, the Mexicas take up their path again, guided by three priests and one priestess. The priest who heads the group carries the guide god, Huitzilopochtli. In the following plates (figs. 18, 19), Huitzilopochtli maintains the role of oracle and guides the actions of his followers. That is, in this and in the majority of the Mexica historical texts, the events that are told are commanded by the gods and are not explained by themselves; rather, their significance is revealed when the mythical or religious symbolism they are wrapped in is explained.

Thus, if for western thought an event is historical only if it is produced in a profane time and space, stripped of transcendental meaning,[28] for the Mexica mentality, the historical is exactly the opposite: the event that has weight is the one that is endowed with significance that transcends the time and place in which it is located. While western historical thought has worked for centuries on disconnecting human events from their supernatural, sacred, or suprahistorical implications, Mexica conception inextricably fuses human action with the sacred, to such an extent that, for the Mexica conception, the only reality is that which is imbued with the sacred. In fact, by making space and time sacred realms, all reality in the Nahuatl world becomes a sacred "reality."

Therefore, the chronological record of events, even though it is kept with notable precision, does not produce the sensation of a profane happening, of a succession of human events, of a time that creates history. Apparently, the calendar and the chronology record and date human events that succeed each other in time. What is significant, however, is that these actions are devoid of effects on temporality and on human actions—first, because human beings themselves are not considered autonomous beings in the historical stage, but mediators, agents of the gods; second, because in the Mexica conception of coming into being, the individual, unrepeatable, and irreversible happening, more than an act that forms history, appears as a disrupter of the established order when it is not subject to the principles that give harmony to the universe.

Therefore, instead of being accepted, it is fought. Cosmology, myth, religion, rite, and social and political organization are constructed as a defense to prevent the disruption that the uncontrolled event causes; their function is to maintain the order that was established once and for all in the original moment of creation.

Mexica interest in becoming is not, then, centered on the succession of irreversible events, but on the acts that are repeated and that manifest the fulfillment of what was ordained at the moment of creation or of mythic time. It can be said, therefore, that the Mexica conception of time is opposed to the western idea that becoming is in and of itself the creator of history, that it is the succession and relation of human events in time that creates history. For the Mexicas, on the contrary, what constructs history is the inaugural act that gave the cosmos its basis. Stated briefly: in the Mexica conception of temporality there is no history, but destiny. Human action and the succession of human events in time lack creative power on becoming because, from the moment of cosmic creation, everything was ordered and determined.

Together with this mythic, sacred conception of temporal happening, a more earthly, profane conception of historical development was formed. The *Historia de los mexicanos por sus pinturas*, the *Anales de Tlatelolco*, the *Anales de Cuauhtitlan*, and the *Historia Tolteca-Chichimeca* are examples of historical narrations in which real human events are mixed in with mythic and legendary stories. Thus, the farther back in time the stories go, the less visible are human actions and the more overwhelming is the presence of myth: Teotihuacan is a sacred city; Tula, a mythic kingdom; Topiltzin-Quetzalcóatl, a legendary being with archetypal qualities—he is the model of the priest, cultural hero, and wise ruler.

But as the events recounted approach the present, a gradual separation can be observed between the sacred and the profane. This distinction became more marked as the concrete human events, particularly the political ones, became more significant in the historical formation of those peoples. Just as at their beginnings the cosmogonic myth offered the Mesoamerican peoples a foundation for the world and an explanation of its dynamics and of the sense of human destiny, later, the constitutive force of political events made political events part of the explanation of human becoming, although the constitutive events of political reality never ceased to intermingle with the events of mythic reality. This process is seen clearly in the accounts that explain the origin and the pilgrimages of the different ethnic groups.

Almost all of the accounts that narrate the origin and migrations of a group follow an archetype that refers to the mythic tradition of the seven caves or original areas, to the departure from that mythic place in search of a promised land, and to the happy arrival at the latter, after several tests, under the guidance of the group's guardian god. But there is also in these accounts an abundance of data concerning the historical reality: the actual founding of the city, the remembrance of the first ruler who politically unified the group, the names and principal feats of the caudillos, the dates that record the conquest of other peoples, the earthly causes of the struggles in which they oppose ethnic groups and tribes, until alongside the mythic account a patently historical account appears and concentrates on profane and earthly events: dynastic lists of rulers, accounts that narrate military triumphs, monuments that record in imperishable fashion the great happenings that occurred during the rule of a *tlatoani*.

And in the same way that the history of political events replaces the history of mythic events, so also do human action and figures become more clear, real, and precise, until a point is reached at which the god-kings, god-heroes, and legendary beings acquire an almost entirely human personality: they are born and die on precise dates, they are remembered for daring or pusillanimous actions, and the judgment that qualifies their actions rests more and more on earthly values, not on sacred or religious ones.

From Sacred Time to the Time of Human Beings

Together with the sacred times of the mythical account, continuous time is also found, expressed in chronological units that measured the temporal development of the earthly actions of humans in a linear and continuous form. As we have seen, the myth of the cosmogonic creation of the Four Suns contains a successive record of time beginning with the first creation of the world. In this record are chronologically inscribed the destruction and re-creation of suns. Nevertheless, this chronology is interested only in specifying the various moments of cosmogonic creation; it does not record the time of humans, nor does it gather human life except when the latter reflects the intention of the gods.

The appearance of a linear and continuous chronological record of human events worthy of being recorded appears tied to two facts: the perfection of hieroglyphic writing and astronomical and calendrical computations and the appearance of stable and long-lived political organizations. Or rather, once the calendrical system was invented, the capacity of this system to record historical events continuously depended on the historical continuity of the political organizations. It is not by chance that the calendrical records that are oldest and continuous belong to the peoples who created stable, influential political organizations in their region: the Olmecs, the Mayas, the Zapotecs, the Nahuas.[29]

At the moment of their greatest power and cultural splendor, these societies were able to record in their calendrical systems events that went back several centuries, assigning a date to each of them. For example, Heinrich Berlin, on studying the dates relative to the dynasties that appear in the inscriptions of the Temple of the Cross in Palenque, found that these inscriptions can be classified into three groups. The first are so old that they can refer only to mythical ancestors, to a legendary era. The second have to do with dynasties and lineages that correspond to a more immediate time, while the last ones refer to contemporary historical events.[30]

This sequence of mythical, legendary events, followed by remote but less imprecise happenings integrated into a linear narration that goes from the most ancient to the most recent, is what we find in accounts such as the *Historia de los mexicanos por sus pinturas*, the *Anales de Cuauhtitlan*, or the *Historia Tolteca-Chichimeca*,[31] which are precisely narrations that give historical accounts of events relative to complex, lasting political organizations.

The *Historia de los mexicanos por sus pinturas* begins with one of the versions about the creation of the world, followed by an also mythical account of the founding of Tula, continuing with a chronological exposition of the migration of the Mexicas from Aztlán, to the founding of Tenochtitlan, and concluding with the narration of the Mexica conquests and expansions until the moment when they were interrupted by the arrival of the Spaniards. The *Anales de Cuauhtitlan* begin with a mythical narration of the Chichimeca migrations and the creation and destruction of the Four Suns, followed by an account of the happenings at Tula and by a more detailed and precise exposition, given in the form of annals of the arrival of those from Cuauhtitlan to the Valley of Mexico, of their kings, wars, and relationships with other ethnic groups. The *Historia Tolteca-Chichimeca* follows this same order. First, it gives accounts of remote facts, told in legendary language; it continues with the more precise narration of the Toltec-Chichimecas, although also mixed with mythic and legendary events; and it concludes with the settling of a group of Toltec-Chichimecas in Cuauhtinchan, and with the narration in the form of annals of the rulers, conquests, and wars that they had.

This last part follows the model of annals or counting of the years (*xiuhpohualli*). That is, in the text, all of the years that the account encompasses are also inscribed, but there is narration of the events only when in one of these years happenings worthy of remembering occur. These events are the ascension to power of their rulers, the death of the same and their genealogies, wars undertaken or suffered by the ethnic group, the boundaries and territorial possessions of the peoples, and other happenings related to these events.

The repetition of these characteristics in the majority of the Nahua historical accounts, especially in the annals, or *xiuhpohualli*, suggests that the need to remember the past and question the most remote origins was systematized when the ethnic groups managed to create complex social and political organizations. The oral memory of the band or tribe became written memory when the ethnic group was transformed into a more developed and cohesive political organization, owner of a territory and in possession of the technical instruments (writing, systems of chronological computation of time) capable of ordering and systematizing the shared past in a continuous manner.

In turn, the makeup of these political organizations created a subject of earthly, profane historical narration that from then on became the center and guide of the historical account: the development through time of the ethnic group is the principal subject matter of the chronology and of the historical account. Thus, the political organization simultaneously created the bases for accumulating and developing knowledge and a new historical subject: the politically organized ethnic group, whose origin, development, and destiny were the subject matter of the historical account.

The formation of long-lived political organizations also created a new definition of time and space. If in the cosmogonies and the creation myths time and space are two sacred realities, beginning with the organization of the ethnic groups in political units, time ceased to be exclusively sacred time to become also a profane time that recorded earthly events that were transforming the development of the ethnic groups. And by dedicating time calculations to recording the founding of earthly cities, ascensions and deaths of rulers, territorial battles and conquests, a change was also made in the conception of space. The space of historical accounts was now the space of the migrations and the geography where the life of the ethnic group took place, although there was still an insistence on making this earthly geography a replica of the sacred space of the cosmos.

The historical texts that exemplify these profound transformations in the subject, historical time, and space are the annals, or counting of the years (*xiuhpohualli*). In these texts the principal theme and subject of the historical account is the ethnic group, the avatars and experiences undergone by the group from the beginnings of its migration to the present. And the guideline of the account is the time-space relation, what happens to the group in a precise time and space. Furthermore, in opposition to primitive time, cyclical time, and circular time, the profane time-space relationship—by concentrating on the recording of human events that occurred in a time that is measured in temporal units that move from the past forward—created a continuous linear time that is the typical time of the *xiuhpohualli*, or counting of the years. This continuous, linear, profane time differs from the time of nature that recorded the incessant cyclical movement of the seasons and from the time that measured the annual movements of the sun. It is also a different time from the temporal record that measured the human passage of time by the succession of kings or dynasties. The *xiuhpohualli* and texts such as the *Historia de los mexicanos por sus pinturas*, the *Anales de Cuauhtitlan*, or the *Historia Tolteca-Chichimeca* include these archaic forms of recording the temporal passage of time, but introduce progressive, linear temporality, the continuous record, year by year, of human events. That is, the continuity of the political organization in time forced the creation of a form of temporal recording that collected the development of the group independently of the cyclical changes of nature, of the deaths and ascensions of chiefs, and of the catastrophes that appeared to announce the end of the world. In this fashion, the chronological system based on the movements of the sun was transformed into a calendrical system dedicated to accurately tracking the changes humans underwent in their social and political, earthly and profane development.

Both in the record of the events that shape the development of the state and in the accounts that trace the history of a politically organized ethnic group, the advance from a mythic and legendary history toward a more and more profane and earthly history is notable. It is constructed on the basis of events that definitely occurred and are thought to have transformed the lives of human beings. It is undeniable that these accounts are plagued with myths, legends, and supernatural explanations, particularly the ones that treat the origin and pilgrimages of the ethnic group. But it is also true that insofar as they describe territorial expansions, military conquests, political conflicts, imposition of tribute, and successions of power, they draw closer to what we today call the history of positive events. As has been observed in other ancient peoples, in Mesoamerica the journey from mythic history to earthly, profane history was determined by the acknowledgment of the social and political realities that conditioned the existence of human beings.[32]

The Codex Xólotl shows the new forms of defining time and space in the historical account. As is common in these documents, the Codex Xólotl gives an account of the entry into the Valley of Mexico of an ethnic group (the Chichimecas of Xólotl), their settling in this region, and their conversion into an important domain. Although much of the document is dedicated to establishing the genealogy of the descendants of Xólotl, the historical portion is notable for the lack of mythical and religious elements in the explanation of events and for the great concentration of pictographic elements dedicated to describing the material, social, political, and cultural changes that this group underwent from its entry into the valley until the death of Ixtlilxóchitl, lord of Texcoco, the kingdom to which the codex principally refers.

The historical account, which encompasses approximately two centuries, is coherent because it is all ordered around the same ethnic group and its area of domination. It is the development in time and space of the Texcoco kingdom that unifies the historical account. The plates that make up the codex all describe the same space, and the pictographs describe the principal events that occurred under the reign of each of the lords of Texcoco. Unlike the previously discussed texts, however, here it is notable that it is the succession of human events that creates the history, that human action is the agent that transforms reality, and that these actions modify physical space, converting it into human space.

Plate I of this codex shows the Chichimecas of Xólotl—their chief guides them—entering the Mexican basin in a semisavage state, almost naked, covered only with grass and rough skins, walking through the woods in search of game and living in caves. In their travels through the valley they discover "Toltec" groups with which they establish almost no relations. The *tlacuilo* who composed this plate, however, describes them with great precision as a culturally different group: they speak another language; they live off agriculture; they wear cotton clothing; they know the art of fine manufacturing; and there are temples of worked stone in their villages.

The same ethnographic precision is present in the following plates, which describe the Chichimeca expansion in the valley and the political and cultural transformation. Under the reign of Xólotl, the Chichimecas take possession of the valley and found the "Chichimecatlalli," or land in which the Chichimecas are strong and numerous. They reserve for themselves the realm of the woods and begin to surround the fields cultivated by the sedentary tribes, whose ownership they respect. Xólotl divides up the land for the new groups that arrive in the valley; he creates chieftaincies, the land and rule of which he grants to his sons; and the Chichimeca chiefs begin to marry "Toltec" women. Xólotl imposes tributes on the groups that settle in the valley, and the Chichimecas slowly convert to a sedentary life. The territory is divided ethnically and religiously. The left-hand part of the codex is identified as the region of the Otomíes and of the wandering tribes that continue to be hunters. The upper and right-hand part is the region of the Toltecs or Culhuas, while the Chichimecas from Xólotl concentrate around Texcoco and Cohuatlichan (Acolhuacan). Almost at the end of Xólotl's reign a war takes place between the northern hunting tribes and the already sedentary Chichimecas, perhaps because of problems arising from the different uses of the land.

The process of Chichimecan transformation continues during the reigns of Nopaltzin and Quinatzin. The fields of maize multiply in various parts of the territory. The land is divided in accordance with the new political organization: there are *tecpantlalli*, or lands of the palaces; *calpullalli*, or lands of the wards; and *teopantlalli*, or land of the temples. New Chichimecan groups enter the valley and several wars occur. The Mexicas are mentioned among the new arrivals, but no importance is accorded them. Under the rule of Techotlalatzin, the language of the "Toltecs," Nahuatl, becomes the official language of the Chichimecas, and the domain of Atzcapotzalco, with which Texcoco will go to war, becomes stronger. The last section of the codex narrates the murder of Ixtlilxóchitl, lord of Texcoco, by Tezozómoc, lord of Atzcapotzalco, and the presence of the son of the former, Netzahualcóyotl. These events are described with great precision and a multitude of details. Throughout the codex, the attention that is given to the genealogies of the ruling families is comparable to the precision with which the pictographs describe clothing, houses, temples, ethnic groups, personages, and characteristics of the territory. The Codex Xólotl, as are the final sections of some of the aforementioned documents, is a historical account that we could call profane and earthly. The technical resources of this document are concentrated in describing, with the greatest spatial and temporal precision, earthly events.[33]

In the last years of Mexica dominance, certainly the most generalized historical memory among the population comprised a mixture of myths, legendary accounts, and events that actually occurred. Nevertheless, along with the memory of mythical and legendary events appear the records of events that actually occurred. It can be said that the complex process that begins with the appearance of cosmogonic myths that reveal the creation of the universe, followed by the first dynastic accounts that gather the notable events of the rulers, and arriving at a culminating point with the apparition of accounts that describe the avatars of the ethnic group and the development of complex political organizations, marks a progressive break with the naturalistic and sacred paradigms that accounted for cosmic and human events. The appearance of a historical account centered on what happened to organized political groups that developed in profane time and space began to create a cultural world of its own, a subject and actor whose actions developed in a space and time of their own, more and more independent of cosmic and sacred order. This same world, constituted by the social, political, and cultural organization of the ethnic group, began to create a history of its own, progressively separate from the natural and sacred world, and began to define its own explanatory categories: a concrete geographic space, a continuous earthly time, and positive human events and actions. These, in turn, gave rise to an earthly, profane historical discourse. This was, without a doubt, one of the great cultural creations of the Mesoamerican peoples—an invention founded on social and political development itself, which brought with it the gradual development of a new system of knowledge for examining the actions of human beings in the world. The appearance of this profane history marked, then, a disruption, a breaking with the ancient mythical and sacred system that revealed the constitution of the universe and determined the actions and destiny of humans.

The Multiplicity of Forms for Representing the Past

Just as the tendency to assess the peoples of Mesoamerica using western criteria has distorted these societies' conception of temporality and the past, so has the custom of analyzing the representation of the past with criteria that explain western historical discourse prevented understanding the proper meaning of the Mesoamerican historical recovery and the forms by which that recovery was expressed. That is, while the majority of the studies on the Mesoamerican conception of history have been restricted to the analysis of codices and the oral texts that accompanied them (gathered by the missionaries in Spanish or Nahuatl),[34] the multiple seige of these cultures has shown that the pictographic text and the oral discourse, while they were the guiding texts for historical remembering, barely constituted one part of the representation of the past.

In western culture the written text is the principal means for recreating the past; in Mesoamerica the reactualization of the past put into play all of society's resources to evoke it and introduce it into the present. In the great ceremonies that celebrated the ascent to power of a new *tlatoani*, the dedication of a temple, or the warriors' victories, the oral discourse that explained those events by their mythic, legendary, or sacred origins was complemented and sublimated by the concurrence of music, dance, religious ceremony, sacrifice, and the presence of the gods through sculpture, painting, and collective rituals, in such a fashion that the gods and the sacred were as real a presence as the act that enveloped all of the celebrants.[35] Thus, the representation of the past implied more participation of the visual, acoustic, scenographic, and ritual media than of the written word; without exception, all of those resources were dedicated, from the distant past to the recovery of the past for the purpose of vividly incorporating it into the present.

The first mass manifestation of Zapotec sculpture at Monte Albán, the three hundred carved stones known as "the dancers," was a humiliating representation of ritually sacrificed captives. The stones' arrangement in a row along a great gallery can be considered "one of the most impressive works of military propaganda in all of Mesoamerica." In this era of ascension of the Zapotec chieftaincies, as later on, the records and representations of reality "are associated with political history."[36] The same thing occurs in the Maya area, where historical memory was for all intents and purposes an expression of royal power, and public art, a sum of the ideological creations dedicated to building and strengthening the kingdom.[37]

Among the Mayas, the stelae, bas-relief, painting, religious knowledge, and astronomical findings worked together to revive the outstanding events of the political history of each kingdom. The participation of all of these elements in reactualizating the past was fused with the manifestation of the sacred in the earthly world (*hierofanía*), one of the most powerful resources for reviving the past and presenting it surrounded by an aura of the sublime and impressive. In Palenque, because of the spatial arrangement of the buildings, during the winter solstice the sunlight fell directly on the Temple of the Cross only once each year. Like a spotlight, it illuminated for a few minutes the beautiful reliefs that represented Chan Bahlum's succession of Pacal. Likewise, in Yaxchilán, during the spring solstice, once each year, the sun's light illuminated the temple where the statue of the Bird Jaguar king was kept, and for brief minutes projected a light on its effigy. Thus, each year, this spectacular effect appeared to revive the person of Bird Jaguar in Yaxchilán. In Chichén Itzá, centuries later, the rulers of that city presented to the populace gathered in the enormous plaza that surrounded the Kukulkán building the moving spectacle wherein the sun traced on the steps of this pyramid the shining figure of the Plumed Serpent descending from the heights of heaven toward the earthly world and the underworld.

In this way, the rulers of Palenque, Yaxchilán, and Chichén Itzá combined astronomical, religious, architectural, sculptural, and scenographic knowledge to produce, one day a year, the spectacular effect of the movement of the sun ratifying the human acts implied in the political succession.[38]

The reactualization of the past, then, mobilized all of the expressive resources of these cultures and had as a goal the vivid reproduction of what had happened. It incorporated it as a past living and acting in the present reality. In the same way that the sacred burst forth in the cities of Palenque, Copán, or Chichén Itzá each year, consecrating the actions of humans, so also did the ritual of the great Mexica feasts periodically revitalize the past, fusing and integrating it with the present. Everything seems to indicate that the ultimate meaning of these reactualizations of the past was, as in the case of the cosmogonic myth or of the feast of the New Fire, to cancel the destructive effects of the passage of time and present the past as something fresh and vital on which the present could rest with the certainty that it in turn would also be perpetuated.

Value and Use of the Past

As in all complex societies, in the Mesoamerican societies multiple value was attributed to the past and the use that was made of it. The past served to give cohesion to the ethnic groups; it made remote origins common; it identified traditions and struggles as proper and constitutive of the idiosyncrasy of the peoples. In turn, being part of a common ethnic trunk promised, for those who worked to preserve the unity and strength of the group, messianic futures.

The remembrance of the past, by being lived as a reactualization of the constitutive origins of the cosmos, offered the double grace that human beings today do not have of a shared reliving of the beginnings of the world and of freeing themselves from the anxieties of the present. The continuous reactualization of the past inserted individuals into the group and fused them with the interests of the collectivity. In turn, the rite and ceremonies' constant revitalization of the past also served to exorcise the uncertainties of the present and the future. To bathe periodically in the primordial waters of the past was for men and women a means of reconstituting the origin, of uniting with the founding principles of the cosmos, and of reconstituting themselves. The collective catharsis signified by the mass ceremonies and rituals inserted individuals in their social origins at the same time as they infused them with new vitality and confidence to live the present.

The Prestige of the Past

As it had the quality of duration, the past was something that gave luster and prestige. It was constantly revitalized because its presence conferred value and meaning to present events, for like what was created at the moment of original creation, what happened in a remote past had the prestige of what had been able to resist the erosion of time without deterioration.

The Mayas, the Zapotecs, the Aztecs, and all of the peoples of Mesoamerica observed a fervent cult devoted to the past. What for these peoples was worthwhile and valuable, such as the origin of agriculture, the calendar, the arts or sciences, went back to a legendary time, wrapped in prestige and an object of veneration. [39] And also, everything that in the present had these good qualities or represented a value with which the populace was to be inculcated was made to descend from these prestigious antecedents, incorporating it into the lineage of charismatic, lasting foundations. But it must be noted that this cult of the past omitted both the erosion brought on by the flow of time and the transformation that temporal happening carried out on human events, thereby creating a direct connection between the mythic past and the present. By means of this artifice, which eluded the passage of time, the past arrived in the present with the luster of things that had resisted the passage of time, and the present was adorned with the prestige and strength of the what is lasting and almost immutable. This is why, unlike in the western historical tradition, which considers the past as something dead, distant, and separated from the present, as what is different from the current, in these societies the past is represented as a living past, as a reality that is profoundly integrated into the present. If in the western tradition the past appears to revive only by the incantatory art of the historian, in the Mesoamerican tradition the past is always a living past, a reality that is constantly reactualized in the present and a presence the evocation of which all of the arts and means of recovering what has happened have contributed to.

The Past as Sanctioner of the Established Order

Among the uses that the Mesoamerican peoples gave to the past, the use of historical memory stands out as an instrument for legitimizing power, sanctioning the established order, and inculcating in the governed the values that oriented the rulers' actions. This use of the past was very oppressive in that the ruling classes enjoyed a monopoly of power, such that the historical discourse this group produced was not only exclusive, but also imposed in an authoritarian fashion on the rest of the population.

The fusion between the dominant class and the ruling group and the weak presence of intermediary groups with their own economic and social base for generating a different interpretation of the past determined that the historical discourse elaborated by the group in power was exclusive and directed toward legitimizing the domination of the ruling group. This political structure co-opted the spread of a different discourse from that produced by the centers of power, monopolized in the ruling group the selection of the recovery of the past, and concentrated in the same group the means for effectively transmitting the historical message. The record of the past and the composition of the text that perpetuated it were carried out in the sovereign's own palace, and the spread of this memory of power was also done through state channels. In the great religious ceremonies, in the feasts that periodically reactualized the founding events of the social order, or in the ceremonies that celebrated the coronation of a new ruler, official history was converted into collective memory. As in Mesopotamia, Egypt, and China,[40] the rulers of the farming peoples of Mesoamerica made the recovery of the past into a powerful weapon to legitimize and sanction the established order. As in the ancient eastern civilizations, in Mesoamerica the first accounts that are not strictly mythical are dynastic annals, memory of the ascensions and successions of rulers, the record of the military triumphs of a chief over other peoples.

The news that the century-long effort to decipher Mayan writing has brought has been precisely the discovery that the famous stelae covered with inscriptions that were thought to allude to religious, astronomical, and calendrical themes are in reality monuments commemorating the ascent to power of a ruler, a record of the principal dates of his life, and a remembrance of his deeds.[41] (See figs. 20–22.) Another recent discovery—the reading and deciphering of the Mixtec codices—revealed the most extensive genealogical history known of Mesoamerica. The genealogies that Alfonso Caso presents in *Reyes y reinos de la mixteca* are a chronological record of the lords who ruled small kingdoms in that region from the year A.D. 692 to the sixteenth century. They gather the principal dates of these rulers—particularly those of birth, ascent to power, and death—and give an account of their deeds. These genealogies join the earthly lineage of the rulers with the divine—in this case, with Quetzalcóatl—and convert the coronation of the rulers into sacred acts, ratified by the presence of the gods themselves. Although they deal with human beings and earthly places and events, their purpose is to perpetuate the belief in the inextinguishable continuity of the ruling families and of the divine character of the royal office.

The Nahua peoples of Central Mexico and, in a unique way, the Mexicas, inherited and enriched this and other forms of utilizing the past to legitimize power. As we have seen, the majority of the historical testimonies that these peoples left us are a memory of power: annals collecting the significant events that made one ethnic group powerful; genealogies of rulers; records of the boundaries and territorial extension of a domain; monuments destined to record unperishingly the deeds of chiefs and caudillos.

Like all memories of power, those of the Mesoamerican peoples were selective: they retained what glorified and gave prestige to the rulers, excluded what affected the interests of the ruling lineage, and made a

Figure 20. Pacal's descent into the underworld. Stone sarcophagus lid
from the Temple of the Inscriptions at Palenque.

Figure 21. Pacal seated on the two-headed jaguar throne, next to his mother (Palenque).

systematic effort to adapt the past to the purposes of contemporary rulers. The fact that those who purified and transmitted the memory of the past were high-ranking members of the ruling class not only marked those tasks with great coherence, but also permitted periodic revisions of the historical memory that was transmitted to the present. Thus, when the successive conquests of the *tlatoani* Itzcóatl brought a political change to the Valley of Mexico and the Mexicas became one of the most powerful kingdoms in the Mexican basin, their rulers ordered the ancient histories destroyed and a new version of the past drawn up:

> Their history was kept.
> But then it was burned:
> When Itzcóatl ruled in Mexico.
> A decision was made,

Figure 22. Pacal wearing the informal dress of the Maya kings (Palenque).

the Mexica lords said:
It is not wise for all those people
to know the paintings.
The subjects (the people)
will become spoiled
and the earth will become twisted.
Because a lot of lies are kept there,
and in them many have been held as gods.[42]

The burning of ancient books and the appearance of other historical records that offered a new image of the past are tied to the new political position that the Mexicas occupied beginning with the victory of their *tlatoani* Itzcóatl over the Tepanecas in 1427. Prior to that date, the Mexicas were subjected to Tepanecan power, which had its center in Azcapotzalco, a power that they had served as mercenaries and allies. In

1426, the new ruler of Azcapotzalco killed the Mexica king, Chimalpopoca, and in response, the Mexicas allied themselves with Netzahualcóyotl, king of Texcoco and leader of the Acolhua group. Itzcóatl, successor to Chimalpopoca, also received the support of two cousins, Tlacaelel and Motecuhzoma Ilhuicamina, who were half brothers. They would later become famous in Mexica history. According to the historical revision that the Mexicas made later, Itzcóatl, Tlacaelel, and Motecuhzoma undertook a fierce war against the Tepanecas, and with their own forces—they do not mention their powerful allies from Texcoco—they defeated the Tepanecas.

The Mexica version of this episode states that Tlacaelel declared that all those who participated in the war would be raised in rank if they were triumphant. This decision signified an important change: henceforth, the Mexica political and social hierarchy was not exclusively based on lineage, for it was possible to ascend the social scale as a reward for military merit.[43]

Unlike Netzahualcóyotl, king of Texcoco, the three leaders who led the offensive against the Tepaneca power, Itzcóatl, Tlacaelel, and Motecuhzoma Ilhuicamina, descended from noble lineage only on the masculine side, not from both sides, as Toltec tradition required. For this reason, the new rulers of Tenochtitlan created other rules to eliminate the descendants of Chimalpopoca and accede to power themselves: Tlacaelel was raised to the rank of *tlacochcalcatl* (lord of the house of arrows) and later became *cihuacoatl*, main counselor of Itzcóatl. Motecuhzoma Ilhuicamina became *tlacateccatl*, a high military post equivalent to general of the Mexica army, and Netzahualcóyotl continued as ruler of Texcoco. In addition, the reforms introduced by Itzcóatl allowed these four persons to make up the Imperial Council of Tenochtitlan. These reforms also led to the lords who had aided Itzcóatl in the war's receiving new titles, and the conquered land's being divided among those who had been instrumental in the victory. So, to exclude the other lineages that aspired to power, principally the descendants of Chimalpopoca, who did fulfill the old requirements, these new rules were created and the old genealogical records and codices that supported the earlier traditions were destroyed.

The destruction of the ancient writings had, then, the triple task of ending the traditions that were not in agreement with the newly established rules of power, erasing the past that gave legitimacy and nobility to the ancient Tepanecan rulers, and creating a prestigious past for the victors. To legitimize their right to rule the ancient kingdoms and peoples of the Mexican basin, from 1427 on the Mexicas rewrote the past, and in this rewriting showed themselves as a people guided, of humble origins, and destined to become the greatest power that had existed in the

Mexican basin. The history we know of the Mexicas, the one that tells of their pilgrimage from the legendary Aztlán to the mythical foundation of Mexico-Tenochtitlan, is inscribed in the new codices, songs, and monuments. What we read in this version of the past is that the Mexicas were chosen by Huitzilopochtli to rule all the peoples, to impose tribute that would make them grow, and to sacrifice captives to keep the era of the Fifth Sun in motion.[44]

Another constant of these societies was the use of the prestige of remote civilizations to serve the ends of the present domination. The Mexicas, for example, while they systematically erased the memory that brought to mind their obscure origins or modified the events that opposed the political image that they sought to inculcate, also recovered the mythic tradition of Toltec dominance and converted it into an antecedent and cultural basis for their own dominance.[45] As Van Zantwijk has shown, the Mexicas specialized in what he calls "ancestor borrowing," and through this strategy they appropriated first the prestigious Toltec past and later the past of Teotihuacan and of other peoples.[46]

Because of these characteristics, because the historical memory of these societies was elaborated and kept by a restricted sector of the ruling class, the message that emanates from that memory is admonitory, imperative, intransigent, and authoritarian. Myth, ritual, religious ideology, painting, and pictographic and oral discourses explained the world, showed how it had been created, and highlighted the gods' participation in its creation and in the effort to keep it stable. And beginning with this "explanation," the burdens and obligations of humans were defined: to keep as unavoidable obligations the ritual, social, and political compulsion, and historical memory. The ruling class of these societies did not use the past simply as an instrument to sanction established power; it made of historical memory a powerful projector of social behaviors and practices that the oral tradition and ritual—aided by dance, music, painting, sculpture, and ceremonial staging—were charged with spreading among the populace. The reconstruction of the process that formed and characterized this social memory requires the analysis of all of its components, not just those texts that western tradition has qualified as historical.

3.

The Conquest:
A New Historical Protagonist
and a New Historical Discourse

Among the events that have done violence to Mexican history, none shook the foundations on which the indigenous peoples were based with as much force or was as decisive in the formation of a new society and a new historical project as the Spanish Conquest and colonization. Simultaneously with this vast transformation of reality began a new form of recording, selecting, and explaining past events, followed by the imposition of a new protagonist of historical action and narration: the conquistador. The Conquest expelled the indigenous people as a protagonist of history and established a new historical discourse in almost all aspects. In a violent, progressive fashion, the conquistador's discourse imposed a new language, postulated a new sense of historical development, and introduced a new manner of seeing and representing the past.

The Conquistador's Language

Spanish became the American language by becoming the vehicle that gave account of the discoverers, conquests, and Spanish settlements in the New World. Columbus's diary, Hernán Cortés's *Cartas de relación*, Gonzalo Fernández de Oviedo's *Historia general y natural de las Indias*, or Bernal Díaz del Castillo's *Verdadera historia* are several other examples of the new writing that the conquistador imposed by narrating his spread over the territories and peoples of America. In all these cases, language follows and completes the military process of the conquest, for it names, baptizes, and confers a new significance to nature, humans, and native cultures.

The American space lost its indigenous connotations as soon as the conquistador began to rediscover and classify it under his own geographic and cartographic concepts. The indigenous systems that ordered space, the cosmological and religious ideas that gave a basis to the relationship between human beings and territory, and the political and economic organization that permitted the exploitation of the physical space were suddenly displaced when this same space was transformed into a territory of the conquistador, tied to a distant homeland for which it was merely a peripheral portion, not the center of the world, as it had been for the Indians. Beginning then, the accidents of Mexican territory, the new routes that cut through it, and the relationship of this space with the rest of the world would be defined by the geography and the interests of the conquistador. It is true that indigenous toponymy managed to be preserved in thousands of places, but its indigenous roots would now be of interest only to those who would later inquire about the past, for those same indigenous names, contaminated by the presence of the conquistador, expressed a new relationship to the present. For thousands of those towns the new relationship with the present was made concrete in the Christian name that was placed before the indigenous name (San Juan Teotihuacan, Santiago Tlatelolco, San Juan Coscomatepec, etc.), a baptism that abruptly changed the traditions and identities of these towns. And the same thing occurred with the flora and fauna, which, like their territory, were the object of a process of discovery, description, and comparison with the European that culminated in a new classification and nomenclature that disturbed the native spirit.

The conquistadors' first descriptions were inhabited by fantastic, hyperbolic, or fabulous tales that mythified the American countryside and nature. Authors were inflamed by an imagination that sought in the new lands the confirmation of the riches and portents born in European fantasy. But from Columbus to Cortés, from the discoverer of the island profile of the New World to the effective conqueror of a considerable portion of solid ground, the description of the new land was converted into a realistic story and into a calculation of what the conquest of those territories would supply the Spanish monarchy. Thus, what in Hernán Cortés was a first draft of the economic potential of the new lands, in the work of Martín Fernández de Enciso (*Suma de geographia*, 1519) or Fernández de Oviedo (*Sumario de la natural historia de las Indias*, 1526) acquired the form of veritable geographic and natural treatises, which in a technical, detailed manner presented to the king the inventory of the extensive lands that his vassals had acquired for Spain.[1]

The mandatory description of the territory and nature of America in the works that made known Spanish feats is not explained only by the new nature of the Indies, or by the contrast of the latter with Europe. This diligent record constitutes an appropriation of nature by writing. The writing process, by describing, naming, and classifying this nature with another language and other concepts, converted it into a deciphered nature, assimilated and memorized in European terms. And this language, while it permitted the conquistador to make his a natural medium that was until then alien and mysterious, created an estrangement between that nature and the native peoples, to whom it would henceforth be incomprehensible in the language that names it, the system that classified it, and the use and exploitation imposed on it.

From Columbus to the discoverers of the northern lands of New Spain in the eighteenth century, no explorer or conqueror omitted an account of the geographical profile of the territories he traversed. The record of the territory and nature is also an instrument that reveals to the world the Spanish adventure. Spain was the country that discovers a new world for the old world. And this privileged mission, just as the discovery of an until then unknown humanity, became a historiographer and cosmographic mission. The king of Spain created the post of chronicler of the Indies in 1532 and, in 1571, that of chief chronicler and cosmographer of the Indies, for the purpose of receiving accurate information about the dimensions, riches, and possibilities of exploiting the world that had been discovered.[2] To name, describe, place, and precisely classify the physical American world was to appropriate it, to create the knowledge that would permit its strategic exploitation, and to transmit throughout that already colonized gigantic geography the epic, transforming character of Spanish actions. The history that western man began to write beginning then was written with western ideas and on the physical body of America.[3]

The first official chroniclers of the American reality and the more numerous ones who wrote without the backing of that title dedicated extensive parts of their works to collecting geographic novelties, to naming and classifying seas, coasts, islands, peninsulas, mountain ranges, rivers, plants, and animals. Gonzalo Fernández de Oviedo, in addition to writing his *Sumario de la natural historia de las Indias*, dedicated eighteen of the forty-nine books that form his voluminous *Historia general y natural de las Indias* to the description of nature. The same was done by Francisco López de Gómara, who, prior to treating the themes of the conquest of Peru and Mexico, forwarded his *Historia general de las Indias* with an account of his geographical discoveries. Juan López de Velasco, the first official cosmographer-chronicler of the Indies, systematized this interest in American geography in an exhaustive questionnaire that sought strategic information about the territory and its resources. From the responses to it came knowledge and experience that, accumulated, produced a veritable arsenal of data about geography, natural resources, history, and ethnography of the New World.[4] Later chroniclers, such as Antonio de Herrera (*Historia general de . . . las Indias Occidentales*, 1596–1615), took advantage of this information in works that included numerous books about American geography and nature. This double attention to the history of the natural world and the history of humans reached its highest point in the *Historia natural y moral de las Indias* (1590) by the Jesuit José de Acosta.[5]

But in all of these works, as in the more abundant ones that were written later, there is no true history of American geography or nature. With all the powerful attraction that the natural scenery provoked in the chroniclers, the interest they manifested in the new spaces turned out to be inferior to the history of the discoveries; instead of a history of the geography and nature, they wrote a history of the discoverers, of the men who for the first time walked on and described that splendid scenery.

They also made an effort to classify the prodigious American nature, with a profoundly strategic, utilitarian feeling, following the scientific molds of classical antiquity, that separated the natural order from the moral or social order. In these works, the classification of nature does not blend with the history of men. But this classification, at times extremely tedious and technically well carried out, came to be the geographic inventory, the memory and the practical knowledge that made the conqueror and the European settler into men in possession of a new world. By means of these writing practices, they converted the strange and alien American nature into a nature of their own, one that was known.

The Foundation of the New Historical Discourse

The new language that covered the vast body of the New World with new meanings also governed the account of contemporary reality and re-wrote the memory of the past. Few events reflect as clearly the automatic relationship between the exercise of power by a new social group and the production of a new historical discourse as the dramatic experience that the Mesoamerican peoples began to undergo beginning with the Spanish Conquest. The military conquest of the indigenous peoples was fol-lowed immediately by the annihilation of their historical memory. Beginning with the establishment of Spanish domination, the native peoples saw their past memory destroyed and made anathema. From leading actors in their historical environment, they turned into under-studies to other actors who rapidly transformed this medium into an alien scene, in which the Indians appeared as phantoms who lived and died without their actions seeming to have an effect on the historical reality of their time.

In the historical works that the conqueror wrote, the Indian was not a living subject of that history. He took on life only when he was a reflection of, a mirror of, or a witness to his material and spiritual conquerors. He lay vanquished and lacked a true role in the history of the victors. The actual protagonists of colonial history were, successively, victorious Spain, the winning nation of a new geographical orb and of a vast pagan humanity, and the direct agents of that epic, the conqueror, the evangelizing friar, and the new settlers of the land.

Simultaneously with the conquering action that repressed the reproduction of native memory and founded a new subject of history, the conqueror transferred to the New World the European cultural and ideological tradition with which he would interpret his own historical action and write the history of the vanquished. The conqueror did not invent a new interpretation of historical happening; he transferred and adapted to the American circumstance the ancient Judeo-Christian conception on the meaning of history, mixed with the eschatological, millennial, and providential ideas that proliferated in medieval Europe. He did not bring with him a single image of the past or one unique conception of historical development; he transported to American lands the accumulated burden of multiple pasts (pagan antiquity, primitive Christianity, the medieval heritage, the new horizons opened by the Renaissance), and disseminated various interpretations of the meaning of history and different means of comprehending time and recording it. And this was the accumulated burden of multiple pasts and conceptions of history and time that, when it crashed into American reality, provoked the rejuvenated appearance of ancient conceptions of history based on various European traditions, but animated by a new historical perspective, by a geographic and human reality that appeared as an open horizon capable of receiving and propelling new historical projects or ones that had been frustrated in the Old World.

American soil was not a passive recipient of the historical traditions of the Old World, but, rather, a powerful revitalizing agent of those traditions, a medium that, when these diverse traditions clashed and mixed with the native ones, created a cultural mixture that, like a new Babel, produced different historical languages, different ways of seeing and recording the past, and different conceptions of temporal happening and the meaning of history.

Hebrew and Christian Conceptions of Historical Development

The Hebrew tradition converted historical, profane, and worldly historical development into a revelation of God's plans. For the Hebrews, historical happening was a manifestation of the divine plan. The past and historical happening in general had a teleology, a final meaning and purpose that for the Jews resided in the fulfillment of God's promises to the chosen people and that, much later, was interpreted as the salvation not only of the Jewish people, but of the entire human race. Human history was conceived of as the stage where the will of God unfolded majestically, moving toward a final design: eternal redemption. In this teleological conception of history, time was seen as a linear process that always moved forward, from the creation of humanity to the final salvation. As Arnaldo Momigliano says, "the idea of a historical continuum initiated at creation ended up imposing itself and all other interests were sacrificed to it, including curiosity about non-Hebrew history. A privileged succession of events represented and signified the continuous intervention of God in the world that he had created himself."[6]

According to the oral and written tradition of the Jewish people, forged throughout a history of captivities, persecutions, and misfortunes, the salvation of the human race would take place through the intervention of a divine redeemer, a messiah who would be incarnated on earth, destroy the nonbelievers, and establish an earthly paradise in which the chosen people would live full of peace and enjoyment. In this way, the fulfillment of divine purposes acquired a messianic character because final salvation was made to depend on the arrival of a providential man and eschatological because the salvation was to be preceded by the catastrophic destruction of the world, in which were mixed vengeance against the enemies of the chosen people, punishment of the nonbelievers, and the prize of eternal glory for God's chosen ones.[7]

This messianic, eschatological conception of history had great influence among the early Christians. For the disciples and followers of Jesus of Nazareth, he was the Messiah announced in the prophecies, the awaited savior of humankind. Nevertheless, as Jesus was judged, crucified, and killed without his passage on earth giving rise to the establishment of the kingdom of the saints or the destruction of the world, his sermons and death were then interpreted as a manifestation in earthly space and time of the divine plan laid out for the salvation of humanity. The earthly life and death of Jesus, his historical passage through the world, his sermons, and the birth of his church were transformed into further proof of the divine plan and of the choice of the Christians as his divine people, chosen to anticipate the plan and carry it to fulfillment. The evangelists, principally Mark, Luke, and John, were the first ones to establish this new interpretation.[8]

The Christians of the first century continued to believe that the salvation of humanity would occur soon, when Christ in all his power and glory would return to earth for a second time to fulfill his eschatological mission. But as this return became delayed and the church turned into a temporal power, other explanations for the end of the world, the mission of the church, and the historical process began to appear. The end of the world and the day of eternal salvation were no longer imminent events because, as Mark had said, before this could happen the bearers of the word of Christ had to preach the Gospel among all nations. This idea conferred on the church an earthly mission: now it had to guide and give counsel to believers who were born and died awaiting the Final Judgment, and convert the nonbelievers. The church became, then, the mystic body of Christ, a divine entity founded on earth to fulfill in it God's plan for salvation. Henceforth, the care of the faithful, the preaching of the gospel, and the conversion of the gentiles became the tasks that were to be carried out year after year and century after century, until God decided to end the world.

And so as the earthly mission of the church became extended in the future, so also did the lives of the believers become extended in the future and divided into two phases. In the first, of unknown but brief duration, believers were to suffer during their earthly life for venial sins committed. In the second, inaugurated by the Final Judgment, believers were to receive eternal blessing, unless their sins merited perpetual condemnation.[9] These new interpretations supported a conception of temporal development also divided into two phases. The first began with the creation of the world and of human beings and ended with the birth of Christ. The second began with the year of our Lord and was to end in an unknown future with the Final Judgment. The tie that united these two phases was the birth and death of Christ, the earthly life of God's envoy, who had revealed to human beings the purposes of the divine plan. The Christians were thus the first to join past and future into a process that started with the origins of the world and took off into the future, encompassing the history of all nations and all races, without excluding, as the Hebrews had done, the non-Jewish or gentile peoples.

This new conception of the historical process was born from the pressure to justify the relative youth of Christianity in comparison with the pagan religions, and the need to justify the church's mission. The Old Testament not only served as a guide to Christians for revealing divine purposes, but it also incorporated into its beliefs and considerations a sacred text because it "made manifest the plans of the Christian God much before the birth of Christ and established therefore the superiority of Christianity in antiquity and its legitimacy over the entire pagan world. It is impossible to go back farther than Adam, as Tertulian said."[10]

The delay in the Second Coming of Christ and the distancing of the Final Judgment also forced Christians to reconsider the mission of the church, which since the sixth century had become an ever more complex and stable institution. At the beginning of the fifth century, it was clear to Christians that their church had grown, multiplied, carried out conversions, and become the official religion of the Roman Empire. The passage of time, then, appeared to Christians as an indispensable condition for the fulfillment of divine design, the conversion of the infidels, and the expansion of the community of believers.

The idea that the passage of time worked in favor of divine purposes was suddenly put into doubt by an unexpected event. At the beginning of the fifth century, in 410, Alaric's Goths invaded and sacked Rome, bringing about almost the complete unsettling of western Europe. Saint Augustine's *The City of God* was written precisely to combat claims by pagans who attributed the destruction of the city to Christianity, which had taken possession of the empire, and especially to show that no matter how catastrophic the ruin of the state might be, the city of God, that is, the church, would survive, triumphant, until the inexorable end of time. *The City of God* also fought the apocalyptic and messianic ideas that proclaimed the early coming of the Messiah and the establishment of a kingdom of saints on earth. According to Saint Augustine, "the Book of Revelation was to be understood as a spiritual allegory; as for the Millenium, that had begun with the birth of Christianity and was fully realised in the Church."[11]

Saint Augustine interpreted all of the history of humanity as a struggle between the Civitas Dei and the Civitas terrena. That is, he saw in the history of Egypt, Assyria, Greece, and Rome the inevitable ruin of the earthly city. The city that lasted and grew with the passage of time, was the city of God, the church.

Starting then, "the age of the church" was seen by Christians as the second phase of the divine plan. The first, which included God's relationship with the people of Israel, was that of evangelic preparation; it ended with the birth of Christ. The second phase, that of the church, had as its goal to increase the community of the faithful and take the word of God to all nations. The church in this sense, came to be the expression of God's purposes in history.[12] In this way, the missionary duty of the church, the preaching of the gospel, gave meaning within the history of salvation to the time between the Resurrection and the Second Coming of Christ. If the historical presence of Christ created the possibility of salvation, starting with the foundation of his church the responsibility for complementing it belonged to each and every one of its members.[13] By consolidating these ideas, Europe began to be

> dominated by a past that was in marked contrast to the past which had dominated earlier civilizations, the Greek and Roman worlds, or even the contemporary civilizations of China and India. It was, if one may use the term, a narrative past, a past with sharp and positive beginnings . . . a story of unfolding events, revealing the purpose of God and man leading up to the dramatic climax of

Christ's life and death; after this the pilgrimage of mankind to its final Doom, which would also come at a precise moment in time. And this narrative aspect of man's destiny was made visible; it was depicted on the walls of the churches, enshrined in rituals, enacted in miracle plays. This sense of narrative and of unfolding purpose bit deeply into European consciousness. It brought easy acceptance of the idea not only of change but also of development. . . . The past acquired a dynamic, almost a propulsion, which it did not acquire elsewhere.[14]

The time of the Bible and of primitive Christianity was a theological time. It began with God and was dominated by him. The unfolding of time was the necessary and natural condition of every divine act. Starting then and during the Middle Ages, the time of Christians was a linear time, provided with a meaning that tended toward God.[15] Christian's internal and external lives, their entire mentality, were flooded by the continuous, omnipresent perception of this divine time. The time of God, his Incarnation, Crucifixion, Resurrection, and the day of Final Judgment fused with the daily life of human beings, with their mission on earth, and with their hopes for the time that follows death. Time acquired a central significance at every moment in the life of humans: its passage was observed with fear and recorded in a solemn manner. The church's liturgical calendar marked the succession of days, not only reminding humans of the passage of the months and seasons, but also reminding them of each one of God's acts and the road to salvation.

The daily passage of time was introduced into the lives of humans in a heretofore unknown manner. In the countryside and in the city, the passage of time was marked by more than the passage of the sun and the tolling of the bells, which, since the seventh century, had tolled the canonical hours seven times a day and whose tones recalled the happy events or announced the death of a Christian soul, reminding everyone of their own.[16]

Thus, from the first century to the High Middle Ages, the church constructed a theological idea of history and of passage of time that impregnated all the acts of earthly life, but whose ultimate significance was beyond the earthly world. Nevertheless, if for the orthodox church the date that had changed the history of humanity was that of the Incarnation of Christ, for the poor and for dissident Christians, the most attractive date began to be the time when the apocalyptic prophecies would be fulfilled: the time when the Messiah was to destroy the power of the Devil and establish in its place the kingdom of the saints. That moment would be the culmination of history, because the kingdom of the saints would surpass all that preceded it in its glory and would have no successor.

This old Jewish and Christian tradition, although it was severely combated by the church, during the Middle Ages fed many messianic movements that sprang up among the oppressed, the dissidents, the unstable.[17] Starting in the twelfth century, the tradition took on new resonances and meanings as it combined with the dissatisfaction with ascetic and mystical movements that rejected the splendor and corruption of the secular church and proposed to live in poverty, as the apostles did, and to form a great Christian community similar to the one described in Acts: "And all that believed lived together, having all of their possessions in common . . . and nobody had anything of their own."[18]

Criticism of the church's growing profane orientation, the ascetic tendencies of monks and dissidents who aspired to restore the ideals of the primitive church, and the persistence of messianic and eschatological ideas among the masses found in the thought of Joachim of Fiore a surprising catalyst that disseminated throughout the world new types of eschatological prophecies. These were to be the most influential ones in Europe and in the Spanish colonies of America, where they resurfaced under new modalities in the sixteenth, seventeenth, eighteenth centuries, and even later.

Joachim of Fiore was a Calabrian abbot and hermit who between 1190 and 1195 confessed that while reading the Scriptures he had received "an inspiration that seemed to him to reveal a hidden meaning of great and original prophetic value." The idea that the Scriptures had a hidden meaning was not new. What was new was that these methods could be applied to understanding and forecasting the process of history, as Joachim of Fiore had proposed it. From his exegesis of the Scriptures, de Fiore drew an interpretation that conceived of historical development as a process divided into three successive and ascending phases, each of them presided over by a member of the Holy Trinity:

> The first age was the Age of the Father or of the law; the second age was the Age of the Son or of the Gospel; and the third age was the Age of the Spirit . . . [and] would be to its predecessors as broad daylight compared with starlight and the dawn . . . the first age had been one of fear and servitude and the second age one of faith and filial submission, the third age would be one of love, joy and freedom, when the knowledge of God would be revealed directly in the hearts of all men . . . In fact the world would be one vast monastery, in which all men would be contemplative monks rapt

in mystical ecstasy and united in singing the praises of God. And
this new version of the Kingdom of the Saints would endure until
the Last Judgement.[19]

De Fiore was not aware of the heterodox and subversive character of
his revelations, for he wrote them under the inspiration of three popes.
But it was evident that his idea of a third age clashed with Saint
Augustine's conception as stated in *The City of God*, according to which
the Kingdom of God had already been realized on earth from the moment
the church was born; consequently, there could not be a millennium that
was not the one initiated by it.

More subversive still were his interpretations dealing with the destruction of the church before reaching the age of the Holy Ghost. He
clearly identified that church with the carnal, hierarchized one of his era.
It would be replaced by the church of the religious, by the monastic
kingdom of pure charity. According to de Fiore, the millenary kingdom
could not be founded other than by the poor and the religious, who were
the chosen ones to live the millennium and contemplate the end of the
world.[20]

But his most disturbing ideas were the ones that explained when and
how that third age, which would bring love and happiness to the world
for a thousand years, would come to be. De Fiore calculated that the
culmination of human history would occur between the years 1200 and
1260; therefore, the road needed to be prepared. And this preparation
would be carried out by a new order of monks who would preach the new
gospel throughout the world. From them would be selected twelve
patriarchs who would convert the Jews, and the supreme master, *novus
dux*, who would separate humanity from its love of all worldly things
and lead it toward the love of the spiritual. During the three years
immediately before the third dispersal, the Antichrist would reign as a
secular king who would punish the corrupt, worldly church until it was
totally destroyed in its present form. After the disappearance of the
Antichrist, the spiritual age would arrive in all its abundance.

Although at first these ideas went almost unnoticed, they acquired an
unexpected subversive strength when they were adopted as doctrine by
the rigorist branch of the Franciscan order. Along with poverty, the
Franciscans adopted Joachim of Fiore's ideal of creating a monastic
church and were the most effective propagators of his eschatological
ideas about the end of the world and the establishment of the millennium. For many of them, the order's founder, Saint Francis of Assisi, was
the Messiah about whom de Fiore's prophecies spoke: the divine envoy
who would inaugurate the church of the religious and the age of the
spirit.

When this brotherhood of ascetic monks became an order similar to the others, its original ideals were weakened. But many Franciscans preserved the ideal of poverty and formed a minority group, inside and outside the order, known as the Spiritual Franciscans. Toward the middle of the thirteenth century, these Spiritual Franciscans unearthed the prophecies of Joachim of Fiore, edited them, commented on them, and thought up others that they attributed to Joachim of Fiore. These prophecies, when disseminated by them, turned out to be more influential than the originals. The group of spiritual Franciscans adopted the Joachite eschatology of the third age, or the age of the spirit, which would bring the end of the world, adapting it in such a fashion that they themselves "could be seen as the new order which, replacing the church of Rome, was to lead mankind into the glories of the Age of the Spirit."[21]

Three centuries later, when the first twelve Franciscans disembarked on the coasts of Veracruz to preach the gospel, Joachim of Fiore's ideas were forcefully reborn and nourished the hopes of many missionaries that this was the predestined land where the monastic ideal was to be carried out. Along with this eschatological tradition, the Spaniards transferred Hebrew and Christian religious traditions, the ideals of the orthodox church, and other providential ideas about the mission of Spain in the world to New Spain, so that the Conquest and the founding of colonial society were powerfully influenced by the medieval Judeo-Christian religious tradition, which was also the tradition that gave sustenance to the conceptions that appeared in America about the meaning of history and historical happening.

History as a Providential Mission of the Church-State

Spain inherited the universal, progressive, and providential conception of history that had elaborated Christianity and with it faced the unforeseen discovery of new lands and the no less unforeseeable contact with until then unknown civilizations. The confusion that the encounter with the American aborigine caused could be absorbed and explained by the Christian idea of human beings created in God's image and called, without regard to race, to eternal salvation. A creature of God, American man was one more member of the extensive human family. His rationality, however, could not be posed as an interdiction. As Bartolomé de las Casas demonstrated, the Christian idea of man did not support those who denied the human condition and the rational ability of the American aborigine; therefore, henceforth, the debate about American man concentrated on a discussion about his historical and cultural development, not about his rationality.[22]

The Christian idea of history also supported the imperial expansion of Spanish power, infusing it with a providentialistic and messianic sense. The medieval Christian church thought of itself as universal, but prior to the discoveries, Christendom was confined to a very small part of the world. It was the powerful impact of the discoveries of the fifteenth and sixteenth centuries that opened for the first time the possibility of expanding Christendom throughout the entire world and fulfilling the universal aspirations of the church. Among all of the nations of Christendom, few lived as intensely as Spain the privilege of feeling themselves predestined to carry out that ideal that all Christians clearly saw enunciated in the Holy Scriptures. The discovery of unknown lands and the conversion of pagan peoples appeared to the Spaniards as a clear sign of the providential mission that God had indicated for the chosen people.

Beginning with the Conquest, historical discourse develops within the margins of the Christian idea of history (which endowed it with its apostolic, messianic, and providential resonance) and runs immersed within the powerful current of Spanish imperialism, of which it becomes the herald and instrument of legitimization. Some protagonists in American history, such as Columbus and many soldiers and missionaries, acted under the conviction that they were the agents of Providence. And historians such as Pietro Martire d'Anghiera and especially Gonzalo Fernández de Oviedo and Francisco López de Gómara transmitted in their works the certainty that the successive discoveries and conquests were part of the providential plan aimed at unifying all the peoples and races of the world under the mantle of Christianity and the crown of the Catholic kings.[23] And for men with a mystical temperament, such as the first missionaries who spread the gospel in America, "this possibility appeared as a vision which was so blinding and radiant that its fulfillment must inevitably foreshadow the rapidly approaching end of the world. It seemed to these mystics that after all the races of mankind had been converted nothing further could happen in this world."[24]

Nourished by these ideas, missionaries such as the Franciscan Gerónimo de Mendieta believed that the principal duty of the kings was to extend the gospel among the infidels. According to the medieval theory of a Christian kingdom, they thought that the Spanish monarchs "derived the ecclesiastical nature of their kingship from their capacities as apostles among the infidels."[25] For these actors and writers of the Spanish action in America, the monarch and the church should unite their efforts in the attainment of those ends and act as one missionary state and church. From this and other sources came the idea that Spain was fulfilling a providential mission and the conviction that the Conquest and colonization of new lands was a work of civilization.

The Imperial Expansion as a Work of Civilization

What better or healthier thing could have happened to these
barbarians that to be subjected to the empire of those whose
prudence, virtue, and religion have converted them from barbarians
who barely deserved the name of human beings into men as
civilized as possible; from clumsy and libidinous to upright and
honorable; from impious and serfs of the demons into Christians
adoring the true God. They are already beginning to receive the
Christian religion . . . they have already been given public precep-
tors of humane letters and sciences, and most valuable of all,
teachers of religion and morals. For many things, and very serious
ones, these barbarians are obligated to receive the empire of the
Spaniards . . . because virtue, humanity, and true religion are more
precious than gold and silver.[26]

At the beginning of the sixteenth century, Juan López de Palacios
Rubio, Fray Bernardo de Mesa, and Juan Ginés de Sepúlveda, men of
letters in the service of the Spanish crown, unearthed Aristotle to affirm
the subjection of the imperfect to the more perfect, to justify the use of
force to establish the dominion of prudent men over barbarians, and to
hand down sentences such as this one: some men have such an advantage
over others in intelligence and ability that they seem born for nothing
but command and domination, while others are so stubborn and obtuse
by nature that they seem destined to obey and serve. From the very
moment they are begotten, some are masters and the others, serfs. Using
these ideas, Ginés de Sepúlveda concluded: "the Spaniards are perfectly
right to govern these barbarians of the New World and adjacent islands;
they are in prudence, ingenuity, virtue, and humanity as inferior to the
Spaniards as children are to adults and women are to men, there being as
much difference between them as that between wild and cruel and very
merciful persons, the prodigiously intemperate and the continent and
tempered, and I daresay from apes to men."[27]

The civilizing action that Spain carried out in the barbarian world was
then adduced as a justification for the Conquest. In addition, the
successive epics of the Spaniards seemed to demonstrate that Providence guided their acts and that they had a mission of salvation: the
Spaniards were the new Crusaders who had come to defeat Satan's most
extensive kingdom. Thus, Hernán Cortés, when he describes the favorable outcome of an armed encounter, says to his king: "As we had the flag
of the cross and fought for our faith and service of our sacred majesty, in
his very real venture, God gave us such a victory and we killed many
persons, without ours being harmed." And at the decisive moment of the

taking of Tenochtitlan, he tells his soldiers that they have on their side just causes and reasons to expect victory, "as we are fighting to increase our faith and against the barbarians."

The Spaniards had fought against infidels and by their own right had become, at the beginning of the sixteenth century, the champions of the Counter-Reformation; therefore, almost naturally, they saw in the discovery of the extensive lands of the New World and the conquest of the diverse and numerous peoples who awaited conversion the signs of a providential enterprise, indicated by God for the chosen people. Almost all of the historiography of the discovery and conquest of American lands is impregnated with this conception, which in turn is based on the idea that the ultimate goal of these grandiose events was the salvation of humankind under the unified command of Christianity and the Spanish monarchy. The novelty is that the transcendent mission of the church (the propagation of the faith) appears inextricably confused with the political goals of the Spanish state, which assumes in the Indies the character of a church-state.

An instrument of God, the Spanish are the people chosen, through the instrument of their kings, as conquerors and missionaries to implement the universal Catholic monarchy in the entire world, until the advent of the Final Judgment and eternal salvation. The historians' task was then to make known the sense and the importance of that highly providential mission, which was to conclude with the religious and political unification of the world under the Spanish crown.

Pietro Martire d'Anghiera, official chronicler of Castile and first reporter of the discovery of the New World, declares in his *Décadas* (pp. 1511–1530): "Spain deserves great praise in our time, for the many millions of heretofore unknown that our people have made known." Gonzalo Fernández de Oviedo, author of *Historia general y natural de las Indias* (1535–1549), which inscribes the American events in a framework of universal history, interprets the discovery, conquest, and evangelizing of the new lands as stellar episodes in the providential plan. And the fact that the Spaniards are the agents chosen to carry out this plan is proof for him of an alliance with God and of the inevitable advent of the world monarchy under Castile. "Just as the earth is one alone," he says, "praise to Jesus Christ that likewise there be only one religion and faith and belief of all men under the society and obedience of the Roman Apostolic Church and the high pontiff and vicar and successor of the apostle Saint Peter and under the monarchy of the emperor king Don Carlos, Our Lord, in whose venture and merit we see this soon carried out."[28] According to this providential interpretation, the Spaniards are the ones called to carry out the Catholic, universal sense of history. The discovery was the first notice that Providence guided the Spanish undertakings. Later, the conquests of Mexico and Peru did nothing more than corroborate the intention of divine purposes: the Spaniards had been chosen from all the peoples on the earth to broaden the geographic dimension of the world and to take religion to those souls deceived by the devil.

If Pietro Martire d'Anghiera and Gonzalo Fernández de Oviedo announce this messianic, evangelic imperialism, Francisco López de Gómara elevates it to the rank of an ideology:

> The greatest thing after the creation of the earth, excepting the incarnation and death of he who created it, is the discovery of the Indies: and thus they call them New-World . . . God wished, he told king don Carlos, to discover the Indies in your time and for your vassals, so that you might convert them to his holy law, as many wise, Christian men say. The conquest of the Indies began after that of the Moors, because Spaniards have always warred against infidels . . .
>
> All of the Indies have been discovered and their coast explored by Spaniards . . . and because the Spaniards found them, the pope of his own free will and purpose and with the agreement of the cardinals, donated and granted to the kings of Castile and Leon all of the islands and terra firma that they might discover to the west, as long as, when they conquered them, they sent preachers there to convert the Indians who worshiped idols . . .
>
> Our Spaniards in sixty years of conquest have discovered, explored, and conquered so much land, as I have said. Never has a king or a people explored and subjugated so much in so short a time as ours, nor done or deserved what Spain, in arms and navigation as well as in preaching the Holy Gospel and converted idolaters; for which the Spaniards are most worthy of praise in all parts of the world. Blessed be God who gave them such grace and power.[29]

In addition to serving as an explanatory principle of the events that at the beginning of the sixteenth century were exalting the name of Spain, this providential explanation gave basis to the relations that were established between the homeland and its colony during the viceroyalty; that is, it was the legitimizing principle of power in New Spain. The civilizing and missionary action of Spain in America impregnates the body of decrees known as *Recopilación de las leyes de Indias*. The task of civilizing and the mission of saving souls are the basic principles of the colonial pact: in exchange for receiving these goods, the colonies were obligated to give to the homeland their gold, silver, and men. In the colony itself, civilization and Christianizing were the principles invoked to justify the white minority's domination of the Indian majority, the castes, and the mestizos.

One effect of these providential ideas that legitimized the advance of Spanish imperialism was to transform the American land and people into a mere scene of Spanish action: Nature takes on life when it intervenes in that which is European; the indigenous peoples become the subject of history when they witness the conqueror's exploits; the indigenous past is revived when the victor's gaze illuminates it. That is, by its thematics, message, and effects, this manner of representing the historical reality is dedicated to exalting the work of the conqueror and to creating a colonial conscience and mentality: the conqueror is the agent of history and the colonized is the passive recipient of his action.

Mystic Ideas of the Religious

Together with the Christian idea of history placed in the service of Spanish imperialism, another conception of history—also of a religious character—also appeared that interpreted in a different fashion the discovery of the new lands and attributed a different meaning to the encounter with native humanity. This discourse, unlike that officially propagated by the crown, was disseminated by the members of the religious orders (principally by the Franciscans), but it was rarely recorded in print; nevertheless, it profoundly perturbed the minds of many mendicant friars and later was reborn with strength in the indigenous mentality, mixed with native eschatological ideas. In contrast to the characteristically political discourse of the crown, this was a mystical discourse, rooted in the salvationist, redemptionist ideas of primitive Christianity and in the messianic, regenerative ideas of medieval religious thought. It was a marvelous discourse; it barely touched reality but converted it into something different from the profane and worldly.

Men of mystic temperament read the succession of discoveries, conquests, and evangelizing in light of the ideas suggested to them by reading the books of the Old and New testaments. They were submerged in the prophecies that the Apocalypse described and excited by the mystic, medieval images that announced the imminent appearance of marvelous events: the establishment of a kingdom that would last a thousand years; the salvation of humanity by the arrival of a messiah who would redeem it; and the end of the world. Disturbed by these beliefs, Christopher Columbus, on his third voyage (1498–1500), when he found himself at the Orinoco River's mouth, thought he had discovered one of the four rivers of the Earthly Paradise. And on repeated occasions, he wrote that he had reached the new land announced by our

Lord in the Apocalypse of Saint John. Beginning in these years, Columbus was "firmly convinced that the world was rapidly approaching its end. . . . But before the awesome event could come to pass, all the prophecies had to be fulfilled. The gospel had to be preached to all peoples and to all races and in all tongues. . . . Secondly, Jerusalem had to be delivered from the unbelievers."[30] So convinced of this was Columbus that he thought of himself as predestined to open "the door of the Western sea" so that the missionaries could enter through them and reach all the Gentiles of the world. He thought that fulfilling the other prophecies—among them the freeing of the Holy Sepulcher—had been reserved for him. For men touched by these ideas, "The discovery of the Indies, the conversion of all the Gentiles, and the liberation of the Holy Sepulcher were considered the three culminating events that announced the end of the world."[31]

Similar ideas, but more articulated and persistent, peopled the imagination and writings of Gerónimo de Mendieta (1525–1604), a member of the Franciscan order, the first order in medieval Europe to welcome and disseminate Joachim of Fiore's ideas, and the first one to send friars to preach the Gospel in New Spain.[32] Influenced by these ideas, Mendieta composed a new interpretation of the Conquest: he conceived of the friars' evangelizing mission as an emulation of the primitive church of the apostles; he saw in the indigenous peoples the ideal material for establishing an earthly paradise; and he infused the American historical process with a mystic, eschatological meaning.[33]

In his *Historia eclesiástica indiana*, written between 1571 and 1596, but not published until 1870, Mendieta converted Cortés into the central figure of the history of the New World. For Mendieta, Columbus's discovery was merely the prelude to the real event, the Conquest of Mexico, which permitted the entry of the gospel into new lands. In his interpretation, Cortés appears as the one chosen by Divine Providence to conquer the Aztecs and to "open the path for the preachers." In Cortés, Mendieta saw a new Moses. The conqueror of Mexico was born in 1485, in the same year as eighty thousand Indians were sacrificed during the inauguration of the temple dedicated to Huitzilopochtli. That is, on "the day that the 'slavery of the Devil' was reaching its bloodiest climax in Tenochtitlan," in Spain the new Moses came into the world "to liberate the Aztecs from their bondage and to lead them to the Promised Land of the Church."[34]

Cortés was also the inspired one who requested that the king of Spain send friars, the personnel who were really going to carry out the conquest of the new lands through preaching of the gospel. Mendieta recalls, emotionally, the reception that Cortés gave the twelve Franciscan friars when he went out to receive them at the entry to Tenochtitlan and humbly knelt before them and kissed their hands. For Mendieta, the arrival of the twelve Franciscans in Tenochtitlan converts this city into the New Jerusalem, and the friars into apostles.[35] In other words, "Mendieta was responsible for formulating what must be considered the mystical interpretation of the conquest."[36]

This interpretation led Mendieta to see transcendental purposes in the actions of the crown and the church in the New World. Inspired by the apostolic ideas in the Old Testament, he interpreted the Spanish crown and church's goals as exclusively directed to fulfilling the apostolic mandate to preach the gospel and convert the infidels. He thought that the function of the Spanish princes in the New World was that of being missionary-kings, apostle-kings. He saw the sovereign as a messiah, and the Spanish sword as the instrument necessary to demolish the infidels' resistance and to establish political unity of humankind in the world.

In one paragraph he set forth how this apocalyptic mission was to be accomplished:

> I have figured out that just as these Catholic kings were entrusted with removing the three diabolical squadrons indicated above . . . so also was it granted that the kings, their successors, would finish this business; so that just as they cleansed Spain of these bad sects, so also should the universal destruction of them on the earth and final conversion of all peoples to the brotherhood of the church be done by the hand of the kings, their descendants.[37]

But once the sword had accomplished its task of scourge and domination, it should leave the field free to the missionaries' evangelizing action. Like many other friars, Mendieta did not accept the intrusion of the crown or of the secular church in his task of planting the gospel and re-creating the primitive church of the first apostles. For Mendieta, the Indies were literally a new world, a world without the burden of the corrupt tradition that had destroyed Europe. He thought that if this world were left to the care of the friars, it "could attain angelic perfection, while Europe, apocalyptically speaking, would go to Hell."[38] That is why he said that "our Lord God did not discover this New World of the Indies, nor did he put it in the hands of our Kings of Castile to take the gold and silver from here to Spain, but to cultivate and farm the mines of so many souls that have been lost and are lost by not paying attention to this spiritual farming that God himself came to the world to practice."[39]

Mendieta saw Adam-like qualities in the Indians' condition: they were meek, docile, simple, humble, obedient, and lived in harmony with poverty. "The Indians were the creatures of the Lord," frequently mentioned in the New Testament. They were innocent, simple, and the pure "who would inherit the kingdom of Heaven." They were the ideal material for re-creating the apostolic asceticism and poverty that had characterized the founders of Christianity. Since for Mendieta those ideals were shared only by the friars and the Indians, he concluded that "the friars of the mendicant orders and the Indians constituted the soul of the population of the celestial city."[40]

According to Mendieta, only in this part of the world could the dreamed-of prophecy be fulfilled. John L. Phelan, the best investigator of Mendieta's ideas, indicates that for "centuries the observant Franciscans in Europe had dreamed and demanded a return to evangelical poverty, but the idol Mammon had not been overthrown in the Old World." Nevertheless, "when the friars and the Indians encountered each other on the other side of the Atlantic, the possibility opened that the promise of three centuries was about to be fulfilled. The often-voiced claim of the mendicants that they should have exclusive jurisdiction over the Indians . . . did not spring only from a desire to protect the natives from exploitation by laymen or even from a concealed lust for power. The mendicant program was also nourished by the conviction that after the friars had experienced three hundred years of frustration in Europe, the Indians presented them with the unique opportunity of applying on a large scale the doctrine of evangelical poverty. No wonder that a mystic such as Mendieta would think that a terrestrial paradise in America was both possible and practicable."[41]

The passion that led Mendieta to conceive of this paradise led him also to lash out against everything that delayed its realization. Mendieta saw in the Audiencia, in the judges, royal officials, and tribunals of the viceroyalty "the image and figure of hell itself";[42] for him those functionaries were worshipers of the idol Mammon, greedy searchers for riches, corrupt exterminators of the Indian. He was a censor of the tributes that the crown imposed on the Indians and, together with Alonso de Zurita, was the harshest critic of the allocation of indigenous workers among Spanish farmers and miners (the Repartimiento), indicating that the only thing they sought was "to fatten and enlarge themselves in order that they can have more and more for their vanities and superfluities at the cost of the sweat and blood of the Indians. They wish to keep the natives in perpetual captivity."[43] He saw in the functionaries of the viceroyalty, in the members of the secular church, and in the Spanish colonizers men possessed by worldly greed and therefore natural enemies of the paradise that the friars strove to build. He opposed all Spanish policies that aimed at Hispanicizing or civilizing the Indian, because, for him, they were corrupt policies that would destroy the Indian's Adamic simplicity. For Mendieta all of these policies tried to say that "the City of Man peopled by the avaricious Spaniards was trying to destroy the City of God that the friars and Indians together were beginning to build."[44] Mendieta identified the European customs and practices with the worldly city, the city dominated by the beast of avarice, contrasting it with the celestial city, which for him was the one formed by the friars and the Indians.

The indispensable assumption for this celestial city was that the Indians be kept apart from the Spaniards. Without this condition the millenary kingdom could not occur in the New World. Mendieta imagined it as a kingdom where the Indians, guided by the friars and preserving their Adamic virtues, would devote themselves to glorifying God. The friars would assume the role of protective parents. For the friars, the Indians were soft wax that only required good fathers and teachers to educate them. Those fathers could only be the friars, who would administer justice in the indigenous community itself, "in the form, manner, and license that fathers and teachers have by natural, divine, and human right to rear, teach, and correct their children and disciples."[45] Mendieta conceived of an indigenous community organized as a "large monastery or a large school."[46] In this great classroom, under the exclusive care of the friars, the Indians could come to be "the best and healthiest Christianity and police of the world-universe" and manage "an otherworldly perfection never before realized by any race on earth."[47]

Nevertheless, during 1595–1596, years of great mortality and calamities for the Indians, Mendieta ended his *Historia*. He had to recognize, greatly disturbed, that the battle between the lambs of the city of apostolic poverty and the wolves of the city of greed had been won by the latter. He said at the end of his *Historia*: "Great evil and evil of evils, that are without number and that cannot be related, and all of them proceed from having let in the fiery beast of greed, which has devastated and exterminated the vineyard, making itself worshiped (like the beast of the Apocalypse) by universal woman, by making men bind all their happiness and hope on black money, as if there were no other God in whom to put one's faith and to confide in."[48]

Mendieta started his book overcome by an apocalyptic optimism and concluded it by forecasting dark apocalyptic catastrophes. His apocalyptic, mystical interpretation divided the history of New Spain into four stages of different meaning. The first, the pre-Hispanic, was the period of the Egyptian captivity of the Indians, the time in which men fell into the slavery of idolatry. Cortés ended that slavery by liberating the indigenes from the Egyptian captivity and, like a new Moses, leading them to the promised land of the church.

The second stage, the 1524–1564 period, marked by the date of the arrival of the twelve Franciscans and the death of viceroy Luis de Velasco, was the golden age of the Indian church, a time in which the friars were dedicated to preaching the gospel, supported by Cortés and Emperor Carlos V.

The third phase, from 1564 to 1596, was the period of decadence of the Indian church, the time of calamities that announced the Apocalypse, the period in which, according to the Old Testament, the people of God and their church would fall under Babylonian captivity. Babylonian captivity was interpreted in Europe as the time when the great calamities would occur that would precede the millennial reign on earth. Translating this to New Spain, Mendieta saw the years 1564–1596 as the time of the fall of the Indian church. And, in fact, those were the years in which a new system of tributes was imposed, the allocation of Indians for Spanish activities increased, epidemics and starvation that decimated the indigenous population proliferated, northern silver mines were discovered, and the monarch, the Audiencia, and the viceroys adopted a policy against the friars and favorable to the secular church. Mendieta concluded his *Historia* "with a prayer that God would send the Messiah who would kill the beast of avarice."[49] This could be the fourth and last age, which is equivalent to the third of Joachim of Fiore.

What is impressive in Gerónimo de Mendieta's eschatological message is not that it reproduces at a three-century distance the prophecies of Joachim of Fiore, but that these ideas were so fundamental in the social and religious project that the missionaries, especially the Franciscans, proposed to carry out. Today we know that behind the mystical and eschatological resonances of this message was hidden a project aimed at establishing in the earthly world the primitive church's ideals of evangelical poverty and purity. The Franciscan order's founder, Francis of Assisi, elevated these ideals of original Christianity to the condition of basic principle. He considered poverty as the necessary condition for the fulfillment of the promises contained in the Scriptures. And for Joachim of Fiore, the prophet of the spiritual Franciscans, the millennium was above all the kingdom destined for the poor, for the most humble, for the last among all people.[50] As Georges Baudot has shown, these ideals were the same ones that guided the twelve first Franciscans, who in 1524, disembarked in Veracruz, for they came from the Spanish Franciscan order that had managed to preserve the purest principles of Saint Francis's rule.

Under the impact of the American discoveries, this radical faction of the Franciscans thought that the discovery of the unknown lands and the presence in them of a vast gentile population were an announcement that the end of the world was near.[51] In this sentence Gerónimo de

Mendieta synthesized the vigor of the apocalyptic belief: the New World is the end of the world.[52]

This ideal of poverty that the Franciscans began to practice so enthusiastically in New Spain, however, provoked a radical confrontation with the principal interests of the Spanish crown and with the aspirations of the majority of the social groups that directed the process of colonial transformation. For the crown, the spiritual conversion of the indigenous population was a second-order objective within its political and economic strategy and, beginning with the discoveries of the silver mines in the north, this objective was subordinated to that of extracting silver, an activity that transformed the colonial economy and society in a mercantile and capitalist sense radically opposed to Franciscan ideals. Thus, while the Franciscan ideal exalted poverty and disinterest in material goods, historical reality marched at an accelerated pace along the path of the commercialization and monetarization of society. This new orientation, which, beginning in 1560, dominated colonial society, converted enrichment, profit, usury, and the acquisition of material goods in the principal objectives of earthly life. Hence, beginning in those years, an increase is seen among the religious of irritation and apocalyptic certainty in the coming of the Antichrist who will hasten the disaster of the earthly city. In addition, their criticism of Spanish greed and corruption becomes more violent. That is, while in the Europe of the time the interests of the church had adjusted to the interests of the new economy,[53] in New Spain the religious, dominated by their mystic aspirations and submerged in theological time, embraced the European messianic and eschatological prophecies to propose an ideal world, a society that was the reverse of the Europe of the time. Their ideas were profoundly subversive in this sense.

The Franciscan missionaries transported to New Spain another Joachite ideal that distinguished their eschatological and millennial ideas from other, similar, ones; their obstinate pursuit of it brought them into confrontation with the secular church and widened their differences with the crown and the Spanish colonists. Joachim of Fiore imagined the last age of the world, that of the Spirit, as "a vast monastery, in which all men would be monks in contemplation, in mystic ecstasy praising God." The missionaries, in turn, dedicated their best effort to the proposition that the preaching of the gospel should culminate in the creation of a gigantic monastery, in which the Indians, guided by the friars and segregated from the secular church and from the Spanish colonizers, would be dedicated to the glory and praise of God. Bartolomé de las Casas had proposed keeping the Indians separated from the Spaniards, but the missionaries considered this separation indispensable for the realization of their mystic fantasies.

The discovery of an ideal state of simplicity and purity in the Indians was a revelation that was so overwhelming and charged with apostolic significance, that men guided by other motivations, such as the judge Vasco de Quiroga, on seeing the Indian barefoot, with long hair and bareheaded, "in the manner of the apostles," was convinced, as of 1531, that it was possible to set up in New Spain "a kind of honest Christian, like the primitive church." But unlike the missionaries, Quiroga combined these Christian ideals with the Renaissance ideal of the search for human perfection, so that the mixture of the apostolic ideals and his reading of Lucian's *Saturnalia* about the golden age, and especially Thomas More's *Utopia*, gave him the guiding ideas to organize the indigenous population into communities separate from the Spaniards and directed at the perfection of the human condition.

Excited by the Indians' naïve, humble, and simple disposition, in 1531 Quiroga proposed to the Council of the Indies a vast plan to congregate the populations, "where working and tilling the soil, they will maintain themselves by their work and be ordered in all good order of police and with holy and good and catholic ordinances . . . until through time they make a habit of virtue and their nature is converted." His idea was that all the Indians of New Spain were to be organized in this fashion. In 1532, even before he had a reply to his proposal, he founded the República y Hospital de Santa Fe de México; in 1533, when he had already been named bishop of Michoacán, he created a similar establishment on the banks of Lake Pátzcuaro, in a natural, splendid, and idyllic setting.

Quiroga organized his Hospital-Republics following the principles that governed More's *Utopia*, as Silvio Zavala demonstrated some time ago. As in the kingdom of Utopos, in the Hospital-Republics there was no place for private property: land and belongings were held in common and were worked and enjoyed communally, without anyone's being able to own them. Society was organized by family units that lived together and rotated agricultural and manufacturing tasks. The fruits of their labor were divided among all of the members of the community, according to their needs, and surpluses were targeted for poor Indians and works of charity. All the inhabitants of the Hospital-Republics were to practice useful tasks, in six-hour workdays. The administrators were to be chosen by direct, secret ballot and were to hold office for one, three, and six years, "so that the rotation includes all eligible married persons." Quiroga completed the organization of his Hospital-Republics with Christian doctrine and practice, so as to introduce in the Indians "the mixed faith and police" that they lacked to make of "this primitive, new, and reborn church of this new world, a shadow and picture of that primitive church of our known world of the time of the Holy Apostles."

The search for the perfect community, an aspiration that was shared by believers in the primitive apostolic church, believers in the primitive communism of the Golden Age, and Renaissance men who yearned for a society free of impurities, was an ideal also shared by many religious and by some of the Spanish functionaries, who, like Vasco de Quiroga, came to found a new society in New Spain. For Quiroga, the task of civilization in the New World did not consist in transplanting the old European culture to the discovered peoples, but, as Silvio Zavala has said, in elevating them "from their natural simplicity, to the ideal goals of humanism and primitive communism."[54]

The difference between this earthly utopia that Vasco de Quiroga managed to make material in small spaces in New Spain and the mystic project of the Franciscan missionaries resided in the latter's not accepting the "mixed police" that Quiroga set up in his Hospital-Republics (a spiritual government directed by the Catholic faith side by side with the indigenous republic governed by indigenous and Spanish alcaldes). The ideal of mystics like Mendieta was to create the church of Christ in New Spain, an earthly paradise founded on the Adamic qualities of the Indians, such as he evoked in the following passage: "The Indians are not good as teachers, but as disciples, nor as preachers, but as subjects, and for this the best in the world. Their mass/body/flesh is so good for this, that I, a worthless little thing . . . make me with little help from companions of having a province of fifty thousand Indians so well set up and organized in good Christianity, that they would say naught but that it was all a monastery."[55]

Whereas in More's thought the utopians would make up one great family, in Mendieta's plan the Indians would form one great monastic classroom. Whereas the highest end for humankind in *Utopia* was self-improvement and human perfection, the highest goal of Mendieta's earthly paradise was to praise God.[56] And it was precisely this mystic radicalism of the missionaries' project that frustrated its realization and set them into a confrontation with the secular church (which distinguished perfectly between this world and the eternal one, between secular time and eternal time), with the crown, and with the ruling groups in society. To return to the primitive church's ideals of apostolic poverty, as the missionaries proposed, was to condemn the corruption that had taken over the church beginning with Emperor Constantine and, more concretely, the Spanish secular church. Because of this, Mendieta proposed a special ecclesiastical regimen for the Indians, administered by the poor and disinterested friars, for the miserly bishops and the worldly secular priests only served to adulterate the faith of the neophytes.[57] The perspective of a vast monastery of Indians dedicated to the adoration of God and governed exclusively by the friars was also unacceptable to the Spanish crown, which in the mid-sixteenth century had started a policy of Hispanicizing the Indians that was persistently rejected by the missionaries. Finally, what made the missionaries' project unbearable to the men of that time was their intention of creating a world free of material goods in a medium won by the fever of earthly riches and power.

Subversive in its final goals, this mystic project of the missionaries was revealed to its critics (the crown, the secular church, and the Spanish settlers) as an immediate danger, for both the missionaries' obsession in maintaining the Indians apart from all contact that was not with the friars and their obsessive interest in knowing the traditions, the religion, the dialects, and the history of the indigenous peoples. As soon as the friars saw in the Indians the ideal material for making an earthly reality of their mystic project, inquiries about their origin and past history became an irresistible attraction. They signified, for men such as the missionaries who interpreted history through the Scriptures and the prophecies, the clarification of the link between the American peoples and the generation of Adam, the discovery of why the Indians had fallen into idolatry and why the task of eliminating it and leading them to the true church had been reserved for the missionaries. That is, the interest in the indigenous past had a transcendental meaning for the religious: to know God's design. But for the crown and the members of the secular church, this obsession with digging up the indigenous past, with giving value to pagan customs, with interpreting the demoniac idolatries with patterns that could be applied only to civilized nations, and with preserving and even exalting their way of life, came to be, more than a means of catechizing the Indians, a way of giving hope to their autonomy and fostering a rebellion, especially when the pacification of the land had not yet been completed, and when the conquerors and their descendants showed themselves dissatisfied with the crown's policies. This is why it is understandable that the crown began openly to combat the missionaries' project and, beginning in 1570, forbade any investigations into the indigenous past and prevented the publication of works that the missionaries had prepared on indigenous religion and traditions.

The Creators of a Realistic and Profane Historical Literature

Alongside the crown's providential-imperialist interpretation of history and the religious' mystical-apocalyptic one, there was a third interpretation that explained the American reality in another manner. Hernán Cortés and Bernal Díaz del Castillo were the founders of a realist, profoundly earthly historical literature. They shared, with other civil and religious chroniclers of their age, the providential and messianic ideas of their time, but their interpretation of the historical events was not guided principally by these ideas. They were soldiers and they wrote in the first place to give detailed accounts of their exploits. What has surprised the successive generations of readers of the *Cartas de relación* that Cortés wrote to Charles V is the composed spirit, the austerity and realism that impregnate those accounts. Cortés does not interpret the events, he describes them. He is an amazed and attentive observer of the new reality that he is discovering, but, instead of looking for hidden, transcendental purposes, he observes it and explains it in a realistic way, accepting it just as it is presented to him. He accepts naturally that Motecuhzoma believes that he and his Spaniards are descendants of Quetzalcóatl, the legendary hero who, according to Toltec and Mexica traditions, would return one day from the east to recover the domains from which he was expelled. In addition to accepting this interpretation as a circumstance favorable to his purposes, however, he concentrates all of his effort on the political and military strategies that will really assure him the conquest of the land. He tells his soldiers, at crucial moments, that they should neither fear nor doubt their victory, for, as they are fighting against the infidels, they have Providence on their side, but he focuses his chances of success on the timely handling of men, arms, and allies, in the strategic planning of all of his military resources. Unlike Columbus, he does not see himself as predestined nor does he make mystical or eschatological interpretations of his deeds. Instead, he is seen as obsessed in reproducing with precision the indigenous reality that is conquering him. His descriptions of the cities of Tlaxcala, Cholula, Iztapalapa, and Tenochtitlan, or his impressions of the court of Motecuhzoma, the markets, and the richness of the earth, are, along with those of Bernal Díaz on the Conquest of Mexico, the most expressive pages that we have of that unique moment of encounter and discovery of two different civilizations.[58]

Of the three incentives that took so many Spaniards to seek their destiny in the New World—to serve God, to serve his Majesty, and "to have fame and fortune"—Cortés and Bernal Díaz del Castillo were typical examples of the last. But while Cortés satisfied this ambition in spades, Bernal spent half his life stating that his captain had swindled the other participants out of their glory in the conquest of Mexico. Bernal spent a great deal of time demanding prizes and rewards for his multiple merits, which according to him were never well recompensed. The resentment is so strong in Bernal for the little glory that Cortés left for his companions, and so imperious and bare, his request for recompense, encomiendas, and material rewards, that for Ramón Iglesia these two forces are the ones that gave rise to the *Verdadera historia de la conquista de México* that Bernal wrote at the end of his life. According to Iglesia, "this environment of dissatisfaction . . . this resentment, and this avidness of the conquerors . . . this formidable and very long fight that they have with the crown over the matter of interests, in the sharing of the lands and the Indians, forms the basis, the root of the *Verdadera Historia* by Bernal."[59]

Just as the chronicler Cortés that we know is the result of the *Cartas de relación* that the conqueror had to write to give an account of his merits, so also is the origin of the work written by Bernal the compulsion to make his merits and services known and to demand his due through the "memorial of the wars" in which, according to him he had participated. "The germ of Bernal's work has to be sought, then, in the fight for encomiendas and in the accounts of merit and services" and in his aspirations to glory and immortality. "Bernal's ambition for notoriety, this desire for glory and riches, this feeling of continual postponement and dissatisfaction, is what moves his pen. His book is an unrestrained list of merits and services."[60]

The motivation that converts Cortés and Bernal into chroniclers is, then, worldly. But they are also distinguished from the other chroniclers of American discoveries and conquests by their straightforward, direct style, by evoking what was really lived by the actors of history without complicating the account with speculation about the meaning of the events, and, in Bernal's case, by his narrative virtues. Both are notable and precise observers. But while Cortés is exact and austere and writes his *Cartas* almost like military dispatches that contain what is essential for the Spanish monarch to understand the scope of his deeds, Bernal has the culture of the jongleurs and medieval reporters of history. He cannot put an end to his chronicle because his prodigious memory takes him from one episode to another, and for him all of them have equal rank and all are worth remembering. Both, but especially Bernal, inaugurate in American literature the account of what was really experienced; they make of writing a means of bringing readers close to the events experienced, so that they see or imagine they see beings of their own size acting in exceptional historical circumstances. Bernal introduces to American historiography the richness of the life; he combines in his chronicle small details and everyday anecdotes with the dazzling events that transformed the direction of history. He complains, recalling Gómara, of his rough style, without polish, but he has the gift of a storyteller; he possesses a memory that recovers the details and knows how to narrate. He knows how to tell a story well that he has lived, and he has the gift of transmitting the freshness of life to his account.

On the Plurality of Forms to Record the Historical Reality of the Official Chronicle

Together with those diverse forms of interpreting and writing history, Spain introduced into America the extensive variety of literary techniques and styles developed in Europe to re-create the past. Some of these forms, such as the travel diary and the accounts of discoverers and captains, reached moments of great plenitude in America (Columbus's *Diary*, Hernán Cortés's *Cartas*), by combining the impact of a dazzling reality with the consciousness in their authors of being the first heralds of an unprecedented historical experience. The chronicle, an old genre that in Europe had become rigid and formal, in the hands of soldiers, captains, and missionaries became a fresh, ingenuous, and amazed account that vigorously expressed the direct experience of great and small actors of the Spanish exploits in America. At this time, the epic style dominated the tone of the majority of the chronicles.

The progressive domination of American soil gave way to the generation of official chroniclers of the Indies, who introduced in American culture models from classical antiquity and from the medieval chronicle. In this way, the remembering of the past became a bookish experience, technically and socially monopolized by the professionals of letters and subject to the rules dictated by the guild.[61]

As this was the genre that was officially protected by the Spanish crown, it soon came to be imitated in the American colonies. During the process in which it managed to assert itself, it devalued the impressionist accounts of the actors of history and converted candor in perceiving the minor aspects of life and the use of direct, colloquial language into historians' sins. Instead of these simple rules, it proposed and succeeded in having history books become dense works, loaded with quotations from Greek and Latin authors and from doctors of the church, written in an inaccessible language for persons without book learning.

Supported by the monarch's power and the institutional and monopolistic character of their charge, the official chroniclers of the Indies set down the bases for the ordered accumulation of historical knowledge: the concentration of information and the creation of archives ran parallel to the office of official chronicler. In addition, the chroniclers created the obligation for the historian to document the events he narrated; they turned this activity into a specialized, remunerated art; they disseminated the methods and styles of classical historians and raised the historical work to the category of cultured genre, both by the requirements henceforth demanded for their composition and for the recherché style that was adopted as a model.

With all the variety of forms, techniques, and styles that the narrators of human actions and the describers of nature introduced, the most important expansion of historical knowledge of the era was due to men who were captured by the novelty of American peoples. As had happened to Herodotus on discovering the eastern civilizations, the Spanish missionaries were transformed into ethnographers on facing the recognition of strange people and cultures. In contrast to the accounts by the conquerors and chroniclers, the works of the missionaries constituted a veritable inquiry into the language, history, culture, traditions, and religion of the indigenous peoples. The change between one way and the other of seeing the Indian was determined by the transcendental ends that inspired the missionaries. The conversion of the Indians, the mission of establishing on American soil a church like that of the primitive Christians, and the millenarian ideal that inspired the friars converted the Indian into prime material for their projects and transformed the knowledge of their culture and their history into a requirement, as Father Bernardino de Sahagún clearly confessed.[62]

With these purposes, Andrés de Olmos, Toribio de Benavente (Motolinía), Diego Durán, Juan de Tovar, Gerónimo de Mendieta, José de Acosta, Bernardino de Sahagún, and other missionaries began the rescue and translation of the Indians' hieroglyphic paintings and oral traditions, they composed grammars and vocabularies of their multiple tongues, and composed the first historical and ethnographic texts of the Meso-american peoples. This vast exploration opened the road to rigorous knowledge of the indigenous world and laid the bases for all future research on the history, ethnography, languages, customs, and religion of the native peoples of America.

Nothing better distinguishes the different European attitudes toward the Indians and their culture than the testimony of the conqueror, the official chronicler of the crown, and the missionary. While the first two made use only of their direct personal impressions to compose their works, or the second-hand accounts, the missionary undertook an extensive and profound investigation that had the Indian as its primary source of knowledge. The missionary made the Indian into his principal informant and, starting with that source, composed scrupulous questionnaires that, as in the paradigmatic case of Sahagún, permitted the reconstruction of the global image of a culture.[63] This attitude was responsible for the history of the aboriginal peoples of America surviving the destruction of the Conquest[64] The first image of the complexity of the indigenous civilizations, and the creation of methods and techniques especially directed at the recovery of these strange cultures, is due to the missionaries who saw in the indigenous humanity the ideal material to construct a new society. Their interest in indigenous history and culture surpasses the material and strategic interest of the conquerors and goes beyond the bookish interest of the official chroniclers. It is an interest provoked by the need to know the historical process that shaped a human being different from the European.

The Chronicler of the Corporate Society

The time when the heroic cycle of the great discoveries and conquests concluded, when historical agents themselves were at the same time the actors and the narrators of their actions, coincided with the years in which the crown acquired complete dominion over its possessions and established a centralized colonial order. Parallel to the destruction of the power of the conquerors, encomenderos, and friars, and the creation of a political-administrative apparatus managed from the distant homeland, the crown imposed rigid control over historical and literary production. Henceforth, the only works published would be those approved by the king, his representatives, or the corporations and authorities specifically appointed for that purpose.

At the same time as the press became the principal propagator of ideas, the new states imposed strict vigilance on everything that was published. In Spain, a country that was fighting against the powers that had designs on its newly acquired possessions, against disrupters of the unity of the church, and against infidels, this vigilance became strict censorship. In the open dominions of Spain in America, the impression, publication, and circulation of books was limited by such an oppressive number of restrictions, censures, permissions, and approvals that, except for contraband, nothing was disseminated that was contrary to the interests of the state or the church.[65] In the case of historical works, these restrictions were particularly severe, for, in addition to propagating political and religious ideas and conceptions, these works contained geographic, economic, and political news that at that time was considered the equivalent of state secrets.

A first measure to control the diffusion of American news was the creation of the chronicler and cosmographer of the Indies, a position similar to that of the official chronicler of the kingdoms of Castile. Henceforth, this chronicler came to be the only one authorized to write the general histories of the Spanish dominions in America, and the only receptor/receiver of the American news and reports requested by the crown or sent by its overseas functionaries.[66] Later, the viceroyalties, the religious orders, and the capitals of these kingdoms had their own official chroniclers, so that the writing of history becomes one more function of the political and administrative regime of the ruling strata of colonial society. Not only was a virtual monopoly of historical reconstruction created by limiting the practice of this activity to one single person, but interpretation and explanation of the events were subjected to the dominant interests of the corporation, the religious order, the viceroyalty, or the homeland's government, the last link to which, by general political principle, the other private interests were subordinated.

This monopoly of historical production affected the liberty, the plurality, and the social representativeness of the historical discourse. Nothing says this better than the historical production itself. In contrast with the vitality, plurality, and inventiveness of the historical discourse of the sixteenth century, the works of the seventeenth century are drowned in rhetoric and more dedicated to repetition or synthetic compilation than to creation. The monumental works of Father Juan de Torquemada—*Monarquía Indiana*—and of Juan de Solórzano Pereira—*Política Indiana*—are representative of this tendency. The official chroniclers of the Indies, previously obsessed with the extensive recording of the American novelty, in the seventeenth century became dense compilers of data and apologists for Spanish works in America.[67] Of all of them, only Antonio de Solís shines. His *Historia de la conquista de México* became a classic description of this event and the most widespread work among all the ones that treated this subject. But the fame of this work rests on its capacity for synthesis and on its elegant, harmonious style, not on its strictly historiographic qualities.

The decadence of the official chronicle is tied to various factors that worked on its deterioration. The institutionalization of the office of chronicler, the selection of these from among the monarch's favorites, the reduction of the soil that inspired the plurality of historical creation, the rigid control exercised by the crown and the church over everything that was printed, and the penalty imposed on the works of dissidents, are the principal causes of the decadence of the official chronicle.

What we know today as "historiography of the sixteenth century" is, in great part, a result of the presses of the nineteenth and twentieth centuries. With the exception of the works of the official chroniclers of the Indies, Cortés's *Cartas* and the *Crónica de la conquista de México* by Gómara, the principal works of the best historians of the New World were not published during the authors' lifetimes. Las Casas saw only his *Brevísima relación de la destrucción de las Indias* published; his longer writings, the *Historia general de las Indias* and *La Apologética historia sumaria*, were not published until 1875–1876 and 1909, respectively. The first publication of what has been preserved of Motolinía's *Historia de las Indias* is from 1848 and the first edition of his *Memoriales*, from 1903. Joaquín García Icazbalceta attributed the nonpublication of

Mendieta's *Historia eclesiástica indiana* to the virulent attacks it contained against the Spaniards.[68]

The most unfortunate case of this chain of censures and repression is that of Bernardino de Sahagún. In the fifty years that Sahagún dedicated to the compilation of his grand sum of knowledge of indigenous culture, the work successively suffered from the contradiction of the friars themselves and of the high ecclesiastical authorities of New Spain, the haggling for financial support to carry the work forward, the dispersal of his work, and finally the confiscation, by order of Viceroy Enríquez, of all his papers, which were sent to Spain to be examined by the Council of the Indies. He died without knowing what fate had befallen the work to which he had dedicated his greatest energy.[69]

The seizure of Sahagún's work was an act tied to the crown's decision to prevent knowledge of the indigenous past from serving interests different from its own. When the crown's power was still weak in New Spain and that of the conquerors and encomenderos vigorous and defiant, the authorities prohibited the circulation and reprinting of Hernán Cortés's *Cartas de relación* in 1527, and in 1553, they ordered the seizure of the history of the conquest of Mexico written by Francisco López de Gómara, a work praising the merits of the conqueror of Mexico and centered on his person. Later, this policy was affirmed. According to Georges Baudot, "the forgetfulness/forgetting that buried the works of the first chroniclers had been decided, ordered, and prepared with the express desire to conceal forever the remembrance of their writing and the themes that they had treated."[70] In 1577, Philip II instructed Viceroy Enríquez to seize the work of Sahagún, ordering him: "as soon as you receive this royal decree, with much care and diligence seek to have those books and without there remaining any original or copy of any, send them safely as soon as possible to our Council of the Indies, so that they can be examined by it; and be advised not to consent to any person's in any manner writing things that touch on the superstitions and way of life that these Indians had, in any language."[71]

Thus, simultaneously with the creation of the official chronicler and cosmographer of the Indies (1571), the crown prohibited the religious community, its most constant critics, from continuing to collect, study, and transmit the history of indigenous peoples. This decision attacked the almost subversive posture that the missionaries had adopted, particularly the Franciscans, who continued to insist that the Indians be kept separated from the Spaniards, that only they intervene in the administration of the Indians, and that the Spanish functionaries were corrupt and perverted. In addition, they proclaimed the idea of the coming of a Messiah who would establish the millennial kingdom, the time when the friars and the Indians would found a celestial paradise on American soil, a paradise dedicated not to the exploitation of the mines and people, but to the glory of God.[72]

The seizure of the written works of the religious also ratified the decision adopted in 1550 to weaken the power of this group and to strengthen that of the secular church. The support that the crown provided the secular church beginning then considerably reduced the administrative authority and the legal capacity of the religious to intervene in the social and spiritual organization of the Indians and diminished their legitimacy to speak in the name of the Indians as their spokespersons.

What was decisive about the 1577 prohibition was that, from then on, no one wrote about the history of the Indians or their culture without first requesting permission from the proper authorities. Nor was it possible to publish any book about those topics without first submitting it to the censorship of the specialized corporations and functionaries (the Council of the Indies and the Spanish Academy of History were the organizations in charge of fulfilling these functions in Spain). This ruling was extended to the viceregal chroniclers, to the historians of the religious orders, and to the chroniclers of the capitals of the viceroyalties. Henceforth, an author who wanted to see a work published had to take the precaution of dedicating it to the monarch himself, or to a notable person close to the same, and eliminating from it any opinion that might lead the censors to condemn it. In this way, the chronicler ended up tied to the prince and to the church by the double chain of appointment as official chronicle, which could be granted only by them, and by the net of censorship.[73]

Beginning then, the condition of the colonial chronicler was that of an "organic intellectual" of his group. First his education and upbringing and then his relationship with the estate that kept him in his post as official chronicler made him an individual conditioned by the interests of his group, obligated to serve it and to be its public propagandist. In that way, taken as a whole, the chronicles of this period turn out to be uniform in the chronicler's exaltation of the order, the city, or the viceroyalty that had designated him its panegyrist. They are more descriptive than analytical, and the majority, rather than works of historical creation, have been considered as "sources," as vast warehouses of data by succeeding generations.

The lack of imagination and invention is one of the typical traits of the official chroniclers of the Indies of the seventeenth and eighteenth centuries. Another, more significant trait is their distance from the events that at that time were transforming the American world and their inability to reflect them in their works. The majority of these chroniclers continued to be obsessed by the spectacular successes of the Conquest, which were considered the great feats that had changed the destiny of the recently discovered lands. Nevertheless, those chroniclers were witnesses and actors in a more profound transformation: the conversion of the land of the Conquest into a new society. More than blindness to these changes, what would have to be considered is the social and political limitation imposed by the post of chronicler as one of the factors that made such a chronicler, instead of a historian of his society and his time, a chronicler of and for his estate. There cannot be a historian of society when the latter is hierarchically divided into groups and estates that, instead of opening the historian to the life of his time, lock him into the narrow limits of group interests.

4.

Transformation of
Indigenous Memory and
Resurgence of Mythic Memory

The Conquest befell the Indians like a cataclysm that dislocated the bases on which were seated their relations with the gods, the cosmos, and temporal happening. Suddenly, the energy that had maintained the power of the gods ran out; they fell, conquered, and on their ruins was raised the god of the Christians.

For the indigenous mentality, the destruction of their gods was a catastrophe of cosmic proportions. The conquest and destruction of Tenochtitlan represented not only the loss of the Mexica capital, it was the demolishing of the center of the cosmos, a disruption of the sacred order that, beginning in Tenochtitlan, the navel of the world, united the celestial powers with those of the underworld and established the relationship with the four directions of the universe. The demolishing of Tenochtitlan appears, then, as a dislocation of the forces that endowed the cosmos with energy and organized territorial space, as a general destruction of the cosmic balance. The indigenous witnesses who give accounts of the effect produced by the Conquest express this sensation of cosmic disaster with great drama:

> This is the face of Katun, of 13-Ahau: the face of the sun will break. It will fall breaking on the gods of now. Five days will the sun be bitten and it will be seen.

> A signal that God is giving that it will happen that the king of this land will die.[1]

> Castrate the sun, that is what the foreigners have come to do.[2]
> The tearful lament is extended, the tears drop
> there in Tlatelolco
> ... Where are we going? Oh friends?
> Later was it true?
> They are already abandoning Mexico City:

the smoke is lifting; the fog
is spreading . . .
Weep my friends,
understand that with these events
we have lost the Mexican nation.[3]

Leave us then to die
leave us then to perish,
for our gods have already died![4]

After the fall of the gods and the upsetting of the cosmic order came the disruption of the human order, the violent transmutation of the masters of the land into servants of the conquerors, and change in their customs, traditions, and ways of life. Violence and incessant change replaced the stability of the old order, so that the daily eruption of violence accentuated the sensation of living a derangement of time, a "crazy time"; it was a total cataclysm, as the following text expresses vigorously:

Only by the crazy time, by the crazy priests, was it that sadness
entered us, that Christianity entered us. Because the very Christian
arrived here with the true God; but that was the beginning of our
misery, the beginning of tribute, the beginning of begging, the
reason for the hidden discord to reveal itself, the beginning of
fights with firearms, the beginning of the outrages, the beginning
of the plundering of everyone, the beginning of slavery by debt, the
beginning of debts stuck on one's back, the beginning of the
continuous struggle, the beginning of suffering. It was the beginning of the work of the Spaniards and the priests.[5]

The Indians attempted to rationalize, in terms of their own logic, this destructive invasion that reaped everything that before had been strong, ordered, and sacred, this sudden intrusion of chaos. Among the Mexica, the arrival of white men was interpreted as the fulfillment of ancient prophecies that had supposedly announced the return of Quetzalcóatl, the return from the east, in a Ce Ácatl year, of the master who had been stripped of his kingdom and who had promised to return to recover it. The Maya attempted to explain the commotion that the arrival of the white men produced with the idea of the completion of a temporal cycle and the inauguration of a new time, and with the custom that had been established by priests of trying to predict what would happen in a future year by means of the knowledge of what had happened before in a similar cycle.

The Katun 11-Ahau first counted is the initial Katun . . .
it was the record of the Katun
when the red-bearded foreigners arrived
    Oh! Let us be sad because they arrived![6]

    It will be our twilight when it comes! . . .
    Its God's face has a menacing appearance.
    Everything it teaches, everything it says is "You are going to
        die."[7]

    Oh! Let us be sad because they arrived!
    Oh Itzá, warlock of water,
    your gods will no longer be worth anything!
    This True God that comes from Heaven
    only of sin will he speak
    only of sin will be his teaching.[8]

Until the arrival of the conquerors, the calendrical system, the techniques for collecting historical events, and the indigenous procedures for discovering their meaning worked in a regular manner. Until that moment, events were dated and inscribed in the codices and an explanation was sought for each of the actions that marked the advance of the Spaniards. But after the conclusion of the siege of Tenochtitlan, with one city after another of those that exercised power in a territory falling, that all disappeared suddenly. The fall of the cities brought the destruction of the person who articulated the account of the past around an ethnic group whose actions were manifested in a space and unfolded in a specific, concrete time. Then the murder and persecution of the ruling class and the priests followed, and with them disappeared the group and the institutions that had possessed the techniques and knowledge to order and record the historical facts in the painted books.

Suddenly, there were no more painted books to explain the succession of events according to the indigenous point of view and techniques, nor was there further accumulation of knowledge that precisely articulated and stored the old with the new in a succession of significant facts. Hieroglyphic writing disappeared and was replaced by that of the conqueror. The calendrical system that dated the most distant in time and sacred events, incorporating them into the present through the feasts and ceremonial rituals, was abolished by the conqueror, and those who knew it were exterminated for being necromancers and possessed by the devil. The precise indigenous recording of time ended with the arrival of the Spaniards: "This year the katun was through being kept; that is, they stopped placing upright the public stone that was put upright for every twenty tuns that came . . . before the foreign gentlemen, the Spaniards, arrived here in the county. After the Spaniards came, that was when it was never done again."[9]

Perhaps nothing marked for the defeated the sensation of abandonment and derangement of the world that followed those events more than the proscription of the calendrical system. The Tonalpohualli, or 260-day divinatory calendar, and its relation to the 365-day calendar (Xihuitl) and to the 52-year "century" was not only a chronological ordering of the succession of the days, months, and years, an arrangement of the feasts and ceremonies that fell on these dates, and a means of knowing which were the auspicious and unlucky days in an individual's fate,[10] it was a system that articulated time with space and both of them with earthly happenings, with the life and destiny of humans. Time was the result of the combined action of the divine powers that ruled the high and the low and the four quadrants of the universe, that became concrete in each of the space-time moments that formed in the temporal succession. It imbued each of those moments with a specific force, meaning, and symbolism so that each of the acts of humans, by the mere fact of their happening in a temporal occurrence, immediately acquired a relationship with the presiding gods and divine powers that was both time and space. According to this idea of temporal happening, each act of humans in time related them to the cosmic balance and to the divine forces that ruled it. To destroy this relationship was equal to setting human beings loose from the cosmos, throwing them into space and time without support.

In addition, the calendrical system was the vehicle that unified the past and the present; it functioned as a device that set historical memory into motion through the ceremonies and rituals that celebrated the founding and outstanding events of the ethnic group. Hence, when it was proscribed, the Indians felt that they had simultaneously lost their relationship with the cosmic forces that sustained the world and their connection with a past that filled the present with meaning. Thus, because they were disconnected from that current that endowed the group with identity, cohesion, and vitality, the Indians ended up dismembered, disarticulated, disconnected from the thread of strength that until then had incorporated the past into the present continuously and in turn had projected the present toward the future. With the system that activated historical memory extinguished and the priests and chiefs who had put it in motion dead, the Mesoamerican peoples lost the unifying and systematizing center of collective memory and the majority were reduced to the use of oral memory, a memory without the capacity to continuously and in an orderly fashion collect historical facts and without the strength of written memory to perpetuate those facts.

The first effect of the Conquest on indigenous historical memory was the destruction of the state-run system that collected and organized the past in order later to actualize it in the present by bringing into play all of the resources created by those cultures to evoke it as a living, acting tradition. The second was the repression of all attempts by the defeated to express and to articulate their memory. Beginning with the Conquest, the recollection and transmission of the Indians past was produced in a field of tension created by the presence of the conqueror; it developed in a climate of generalized repression that drowned all forms of remembering that clashed with those imposed by the conqueror. Hence the majority of the systems the Indians conceived to preserve and transmit their past became hidden, underground networks, often disguised in Christian clothing, or hermetically sealed in the language and secret practices of the peoples loath to come in contact with the Europeans.

In this sense, the Conquest introduces a collision between different pasts, a clash between cultures vitalized by antagonistic conceptions of time, the past, and temporal happening. This initial clash was what inspired, over the course of three centuries, an asymmetrical struggle between those two conceptions that during that entire time battled incessantly, one of them to get control and the other to survive.

The pages that follow about the reconstruction and transformation of indigenous memory in the viceregal centuries, more than a systematic exposition of this process, are a collection of scattered, fragmented images that can help scan what the process of recomposition of indigenous memory was like in the setting of Spanish domination. There has not been enough research to attempt an organized reconstruction of that process. Spanish ethnocentrism first and then Mexican ethnocentrism, which are responsible for the rescue and study of historical memory, have concentrated on the dominant group, ignoring, obscuring, and declaring nonexistent the memory of the vanquished. Nevertheless, the Indians adapted various procedures for preserving and transmitting their past to the situation of the Conquest. They did not conceive of one, but of many, ways to recover their past and put it at the service of their current situation. This diversity of forms is at the same time a chart for understanding how they managed to preserve their ethnic and cultural identity and an exceptional window for perceiving the complex process created by the clash, the mixture, the adaptation, and the transformation of different cultures that coexisted in a commonly disputed territory and developed in the same historical time, but were nourished by different conceptions of time and historical development.

Golden Age and Nativist Insurrections

If the indigenous testimony on the Conquest collected by the first friars, and particularly by Fray Bernardino de Sahagún, is excluded,[11] we note that no other documents have been found that express the Indian point of view on the facts that followed the introduction of Spanish dominion. Apparently, the terrible years from 1521 to 1540—years in which the Spaniards' boundless ambition brought to its climax the breakdown of the structures that organized the indigenous society—lack native historical accounts, but it is unlikely that there were none. What is more certain is that, by expressing a point of view contrary to that of the conqueror, the indigenous would have hidden it or that these accounts were destroyed by the conquerors themselves, preserving only texts that did not contain unacceptable criticism of the Spaniards. Above all, testimonies written by the indigenous peoples themselves would have been rare, given the destruction of their centers of power and of the specialists who recorded historical facts. But, although the institutions, the specialists, and the techniques that were used in ancient times for collecting events through hieroglyphic writing disappeared, the oral tradition was maintained, and it was a millennial knowledge generalized and deeply rooted in the Mesoamerican peoples.

The Book of *Chilam Balam of Chumayel*, a text that the Maya kept hidden until the nineteenth century, was written in Maya with the Castilian alphabet and dates from at least the beginnings of the seventeenth century.[12] It provides this idealized vision of the time prior to the arrival of the Spaniards:

> Then everything was good
> and then [the gods] were knocked down.
> There was in them wisdom
> There was no sin then . . .
> There was no sickness then
> they had no aching bones then
> there was no fever for them
> there was no smallpox . . .
> Standing straight was their body then
> It was not thus that the Tzules did
> [the foreigneres]
> when they arrived.
> They taught fear,
> they came to wilt the flowers.
> So that their flower would live,

they harmed and sucked in our flower . . .
They Christianized us,
but they pass us around from one to another
like animals.
God is offended by the suckers.[13]

The indigenous transmitter of the past offers here an idealized image
of the time prior to the arrival of the conqueror ("when everything was
good") that is contrasted to the illnesses and servitude that the Spaniards
introduced. And this was apparently the common image that the priests
and chiefs who escaped the first campaigns of extermination tried to
inculcate in the population. It was a representation quite close to what
had happened to them, and, by being spread at the moment when the
indigenous world was threatening to sink, it made the lost age more
intimate. Remembering the lost world in an idealized manner was a
means of enlarging it in contrast to the present and making the latter an
even more detestable time. This double movement of violent rejection
of the present and almost magical restoration of the old rule, when
"everything was good," was the substratum that characterized the two
most important indigenous insurrections of the sixteenth century.

A Nativist Millenarianism: The Mixtón Insurrection, 1541–1542

The return of that mythical native age "when everything was good"
inspired the most violent indigenous insurrections [14] that the Spaniards
faced after the taking of Tenochtitlan.

In New Galicia, one of the peripheral areas of New Spain, adjoining
the Chichimeca frontier of fierce Indians, Governor Nuño de Guzmán
had left a trail of depredation, slavery, and mistreatment of the Indians
that the encomenderos broadened. The destructive presence of the
Spaniards in this region taught the Indian groups the sequence of their
advance: conquest, friars, persecution of the "sorcerers," removal of
idolatry, encomienda, slavery, and loss of autonomy. The response of the
indigenous groups in this region, who had until then been isolated from
each other and who lacked the complex social and political organization
of the peoples of the central-south, was to unite before the intrusion of
the conqueror to create an alliance that proposed to destroy the Spaniards and restore the Indians' own traditions.

According to Spanish sources—no direct indigenous testimony is
known—insurrection was instigated by some "sorcerers" or "emissaries
of the devil" who came from the north (from the mountain range of
Tepeque and Zacatecas, that is, fierce Indians, unconquered) to spread
the news that their god had proposed expelling the Spaniards among the

peoples of New Galicia (Cuitlán, Huele, Coltlan, Tepeque, Tlatenango, Suchipila). For this purpose, this god had formed an immense army composed of all the Indians who had died and whom he had resuscitated: "[This indigenous god] brings with him all your resurrected ancestors with great riches in jewels of gold and turquoise, feathers, mirrors and bows and arrows that never break and many clothes in which to dress us and many beads and other things for the women." To those who would join this army and abandon "the doctrine of the friars," the Indian god offered immortality, freedom from all need, eternal youth, and a paradise where, without effort, they would enjoy goods and pleasures. The preaching of the Indian god promised those who would repudiate the religion preached by the friars the restoration of their ancient traditions and magical weapons to defeat the Spaniards:

> You will never die nor will you be in need, and the old men and old women will become youthful, and conceive, no matter how old they may be, and the lands will be sown for you without anyone putting their hands to them and without it raining, and the fire-wood from the mountain . . . will come to your house without anybody bringing it [. . . and this god will order men to have as many] women as they want, and not one like the friars said . . . and know that the Indian man or woman who believes [in the Christian God and not in the Indian god] would no longer see light and would be eaten . . . [by] the wild animals.[15]
>
> Then Tecoroli [the Indian god] will go to Guadalajara, to Jalisco, to Michoacán, to México, to Guatemala and to all the places where there are Christians from Spain and will kill them all. Once they are finished, he will return to his home and you will live happily with your ancestors without knowing what work or pain is.[16]

The actions of this insurrection were, like their message, profoundly religious and anti-Christian. In the populations where the uprisers entered, they concentrated their fury on religious symbols. They burned the monasteries, churches, and crosses. They profaned the objects of the cult and religious objects, made sacrifices and performed pagan dances, and gave themselves to sacrilegious ceremonies, as in Tepechitlán (Zacatecas), where they parodied the mass, simulating adoration of a tortilla. The Indians who had accepted Christianity but who joined the insurrection, before being added to the ranks of the rebels, had their heads washed to erase the trace of Christian baptism and were obliged to do penance for the number of days that they had adopted the foreign religion.[17]

One of the most notable characteristics of the Mixtón insurrection was its insistence on removing all vestiges of Christianity, restoring native religions and customs, and expelling the Spaniards from indigenous land. The message and the procedures for reaching these goals, different from the other insurrections that will be discussed later, were profoundly nativist. The paradise that was offered to the followers of the indigenous god and the magical arts that he offered to the rebels in order to defeat the Spaniards were characteristic of the indigenous cultural substratum. That is, the device that activated this insurrection was the force of its historical memory, the conviction of having one's own past based on autochthonous forms of living and customs and the violent rejection of the Spanish invasion, which threatened to suppress these traditions. The message that this insurrection spread was that of finishing off the foreign invader and restoring one's own ancestral traditions.

The Maya Nativist Insurrection of 1546–1547

In 1546–1547, the Maya east of the peninsula of Yucatán, particularly the *cacicazgo*s and peoples of Cupul, Cochuah, Sotuta, and Uaymil-Chetumal, headed an insurrection similar to the Mixtón uprising. Like the latter, the Maya insurrection involved an extensive territory and joined various peoples and *cacicazgos*. It was inspired by a profound religious sentiment and proposed exiling Christianity and expelling the Spaniards from Maya land. It also had as its setting a peripheral region in relation to the Spanish dominion (concentrated around Mérida-Valladolid and Campeche) populated with indigenous peoples who had offered a strong resistance to the first Spanish invasions and by groups who had not been completely dominated. Its leaders were also priests, men imbued with the cultural tradition that blended political organization with religious knowledge. The province of Cupul was the center of inspiration for this movement.

The priests of Cupul began this insurrection, passing themselves off as messengers of the ancient divinities. The most influential of them, Chilam Anbal, presented himself to the rebels as the son of God. Under this identity, the Maya priests announced to their followers that the desire of the gods was for the Spaniards to die to the last person, without a trace of them being left in Maya land:

> The Indians rebelled "because of some Chilams that they called gods. One of them intimated that he was the Son of God, while the others [said] that they had been sent by God. [These] Chilams told their people that they should let the Spaniards go to the towns where there encomiendas were, and that they should kill them all there. [This should be done] because God had said that all of the

Spaniards had to die and that none should be left on earth. . . . The principal [Chilam] . . . was the one who said that he was God, and he was called Chilam Anbal.[18]

Surprised by the silence that surrounded the preparations for the insurrection, by the number of towns participating, and by the religious furor that ignited the spirit of the rebels, the first Spaniards who fell prisoner were crucified under the blazing tropical Maya sun and then shot with arrows. Others were tortured and burned with the copal that served as an incense to the Maya gods. The rebels did not distinguish between men, women, and children: all the Spaniards who fell into their hands were sacrificed. Several of these had their heads, hands, and feet cut off, and each of these parts was sent to other provinces to publicize the Indian victories. Similar punishment was inflicted on the Indians who lived with the Spaniards; more than five hundred were killed.

The deep sense of the contrary presence of the white man and his culture is revealed by the fact that, along with the physical destruction of the Spaniards, the insurrectionists proceeded to uproot the trees and the plants that the settlers had brought from Europe. To this same end, the Indians killed horses, cattle, chickens, dogs, cats, and every animal of European origin.[19]

The Zapotecs of Titiquipa in that same year of 1547 began another insurrection motivated by similar ideas. According to the interrogations that the Spaniards carried out after quelling the insurrection, it was instigated by a principal Indian of Titiquipa named Pece, who traveled through the villages of that region telling the indigenous peoples to gather together *chalchihuites* (green precious stones), gold and feathers, because three lords had been born, one in Mexico, another in the Mixteca, and the third in Tehuantepec, to whom they should pay tribute, and not to the "king or to the Spaniards." This rebel Indian announced that there "was to be a great storm in a week during which the earth would shake and the Spaniards would die and that they should not be afraid of the Spaniards, whom, upon their arrival there at Miaguatlan, he would kill."[20]

What distinguishes these insurrections is their decision to erase all traces of the presence of the invader and restore the old order and traditions. The leaders of these movements of repelling-restoration were, as in the old times, priests, the men most informed about the ancient traditions and the best trained in organizing and handling of the people. To unite distant and separate peoples, they used the idea, traditional in their culture, of a message from the gods—the announcement that it was an order from the gods to destroy the invaders. The spread of this message, in a situation of foreign occupation in which the indigenous peoples knew beforehand the results for their old way of living was a unifying element in this sacred war against the conqueror. As in the past, prior to the arrival of white men, the Indians went to war stimulated by the call of their gods, armed by magical weapons (arrows that did not break), protected by powers that would revive them in case they fell, certain of expelling the enemy who threatened to destroy the bases on which they had built their lives and that of their ancestors. The prize was not only the elimination of a terrible menace but the restoration of the old Indian order, a prize sublimated by the arrival of a happy era in which everything would be obtained without effort—a blessed age that the Indians would share with their revived ancestors, living together "without knowing what work or pain is." The goals of the insurrection, its leaders, its strategy, and the mythical thinking that inspired it were, then, genuinely indigenous and were concentrated on the purpose of expelling the presence of the foreign invader. In these tragic experiences, the indigenous past participated as principal sustenance and inspiration of the rebels' struggles.

Pulverization of Ethnic Memory and Development of Local Memory and Cultural *Mestizaje*

In the peoples of south-central Mexico, those who had developed under the domination of complex centralized political organizations, there is no report of a reaction similar to that of New Galicia or the Maya area, regions where the existence of multiple ethnic groups (New Galicia) or of autonomous, dispersed chiefdoms (Yucatán) delayed their conquest and permitted the organization of indigenous resistance. On the contrary, among the Mexicas and Tarascans, the fall of their centers of power was followed by the simultaneous surrender of the small lordships and towns subject to that central power. In turn, the destruction of the gathering centers of the ethnic group's collective memory brought with it the destruction and pulverization of the global ethnic memory and, much later, the appearance of a memory concentrated on recalling and recording local events.

One of the changes that most affected the indigenous culture was the destruction of the larger political institutions, "the transformation of the independent indigenous kingdoms into indigenous farming communities."[21] The Conquest broke the political framework that unified the towns spread throughout an extensive area and broke the command that articulated the economic interchanges and military, religious, and cultural solidarity. The disintegration of the large political units broke off the interchanges between one town and another so that there was no longer any social solidarity among towns that belonged to the same ethnic group; not the Mexicas, the Tarascans, or the Zapotecs spoke during the viceroyalty of a Mexica, Tarascan, or Zapotec nation. Only the political units called independent "city-states," such as Huexotzingo or Cholula, were preserved as separate administrative units. The majority of the old local lordships, the towns, were cut from the larger political units and converted into independent units, into tiny *repúblicas de indios*, as they were called. Beginning in 1530, these *repúblicas* were gradually organized into a system of government based on the Spanish municipality, with common rights to land, their own government, and a collective obligation to pay tribute and supply labor to the conquerors.

The creation of the *repúblicas de indios* caused a triple separation of the Indians with regard to the global society: territorial and ethnic in the first place, because the republics or communities were considered private residences of the Indians, excluding the Spanish, blacks, and "castes." In the cities that were the centers of Spanish population, the Indians were also forced to live in special neighborhoods separate from the white and mestizo population. The separation was legal because the Indians and their republics were separated from the rest of the population by special laws, judges, and courts dedicated to protecting their rights in a private and paternalistic manner. Finally, the separation was economic because all these divisions derived from the principal division between conquerors and the conquered and ratified the economic subordination of the indigenous population to the dominant economic interests that guided the settlers.[22] This multiple ethnic, territorial, legal, political, social, and economic segregation closed off the possibility of developing a historical global memory and conscience and inspired the formation of social memory and solidarity reduced to the local area.

Uprooting and Recomposition of the Indigenous Communities

When the Spanish municipal model began to be used to organize the Indian towns, a succession of demographic catastrophes hastened the decomposition of the indigenous population and its violent adaptation to a foreign model. Today we know that the terrible death tolls caused by the epidemics of 1545–1548, 1563–1564, 1576–1581, and 1587–1588, along with the need for charging tribute, extracting the work force from the towns, and evangelizing the population, were the arguments the viceregal authorities used to decide on a radical reorganization of the indigenous population. This population, with the exception of the former centers that were capitals of larger political units, lived dispersed in small towns or scattered among the cultivated zones.

From the initial years of colonization, the pattern of traditional indigenous settling characterized by farmers' huts scattered among the cultivated fields without forming compact nuclei had been counter to the Spaniards because it made it difficult to control the population, collect tributes and workers, and carry out the task of evangelization. Nevertheless, when the disappearance of millions of Indians and the conversion of thousands of hectares of cultivated land into abandoned fields was added to this . . . Viceroy Velasco (1550–1564) decided to concentrate all the Indians in organized towns and to divide the remaining lands among the Spaniards. Between 1550 and 1564, this vast program, which encompassed the entire agricultural zone of the country, was carried out from New Galicia to Yucatán and introduced radical changes in the landholding and the political and social organization of the aboriginal populations.[23]

From 1576 to 1580, another devastating epidemic wiped out half the indigenous population. Once again, between 1595 and 1605, the viceregal authorities promoted a new congregation of the indigenous population into towns. Thus, between 1550 and 1605, the policy of congregation of peoples radically changed the ecological localization, the political organization, and the social and cultural physiognomy of the indigenous peoples. By virtue of this policy, the former capitals of the indigenous populations, were brought down from the rocky hills and skirts of the hills where they had been settled, and resettled on lowlands, joining them at times to towns or *estancias* that were subjects of the former capital These new populations were organized Spanish-style: in the center a Christian church was erected, along with the government buildings, and on the outskirts the farmers' residences. The farmers who lived in the dispersed towns were compelled to move to the neighborhoods, to the new populations, or to establish *estancias* or gatherings of towns subject to the principal *cabecera*. Thus, obligated by force, the Indians had to leave the sites where for centuries they had been protected by their gods, where their common divinities were and their ancestors rested, and where they worshiped the founders of the town.

Chalcatongo cave in Oaxaca exemplifies the religious, historical, and community symbolism of these sacred places. It is the site in which the Indians buried their caciques and that they managed to keep hidden for several decades after the arrival of the friars. Fray Benito Fernández, a legendary Mixtec missionary and persecutor of idolaters, found out about this place and immediately went in search of it, accompanied by a multitude of terrorized Indians. Here is what he did, according to the chronicler Francisco de Burgoa, when he discovered this site , which he saw as diabolical:

As soon as the servant of God recognized the place, he discovered an extensive square with light from some small windows that had been opened above and on the sides and some stone urns and on them an immensity of bodies arranged in rows shrouded with rich clothing and a variety of precious stones, strings of beads, and gold metals, and drawing closer, he saw some bodies of caciques who had recently died . . . and whom he held as being good Christians [and] burning with rage for divine honor, he attacked the bodies and threw them on the ground, stepping on them, dragging them as spoils of Satan [then he saw] further inside, like a chamber, another station and entering inside he found little altars and niches that had an immense number of idols of various figures and a variety of gold, metal, stone, wood materials, and canvas paintings [and] here his holy fury began to grow fiercer, breaking with blows everything he could and throwing the rest underfoot, cursing them as spirits of darkness, and the Indians, seeing how long it was taking him, were certain that he was already dead [and] avenged by the gods for that disrespect when they heard him coming out tired and sweaty, in the skirts of his habit the idols that were most venerated, and throwing them before him, he stepped on them again and again and to mock them cursed them . . . and began to preach to that numerous gathering [of Indians and] so great was the efficacy of his reasoning, so fired his spirit, that it softened those hardened hearts as if they were of wax, it reduced them to where they built a huge bonfire there [obliging them to throw into it] the idols and bodies of their dead lords . . . and with this frightful triumph he left them so confused and embarrassed about the deceit that they had lived that it was followed by numerous conversions. [24]

Sometimes the transfer of the peoples from one site to another implied only a change of place, but in many cases, the population obligated forced to congregate in a new site had to live with other ethnic groups with different languages and traditions. If in ecological terms this massive transfer of the population created a global readjustment to a different medium, in political and cultural terms, this change signified the uprooting, the brutal removal of a group of traditions that had accumulated for a long time, and the violent imposition of a new way of life. Suddenly, the Indians were torn from the places that were protected by their divinities, uprooted from the towns where they had formed traditions that gave them a past and an identity, and thrown into a strange environment where everything was organized according to the commands of foreign men and gods. Seen in historical perspective, this gigantic displacement of the population is one of the most violent acts of social and cultural uprooting of which there is memory in the history of Mexico, especially from the indigenous perspective, because in the pre-Hispanic tradition, the conquest of one people by another was rarely accompanied by the destruction of their gods and traditions. Once a people was dominated and forced to pay liege money and tributes imposed by the conqueror, the vanquished people continued with its own customs and gods. Its past was not disconnected from the present.

But beginning with the Conquest, what the indigenous peoples experienced was a continuous and inexorable break with their past. The process that the friars began with the removal of the ancient idolatry and the imposition of Christianity was completed by the congregation of towns, because in these reductions, the ancient fortifying and revitalizing past was progressively cut off from the present and replaced by a new social and cultural situation in which remainders of that past were combined with European traditions and customs. A new identity and new forms of social solidarity were formed in the congregations around the communal lands and the Christian church, which was erected in the middle of town. The majority of the hundreds of towns congregated were baptized with the name of a Christian saint, which was placed before the old indigenous name. In many of these towns, the Christian foundation was mixed with traditional indigenous practices. For example, the ancient religious custom of organizing the territorial space of the towns in accordance with the four cardinal directions of the universe was continued, indicating each one of those points with a cross.[25] In other towns, the Indians tried to make the dates of the old ceremonies coincide with those of the Christian ritual or with the feast of the patron saint until the friars discovered what they were doing and modified the calendar of the festivities.

The vitality of this ancient cultural substratum as a basis for new forms of indigenous life is perceived in all those practices that the anthropologists and historians call syncretisms. These revitalizations of the ancient culture sought to incorporate the old into the present through the procedure of covering it over with a Christian veneer that permitted it to be accepted in the dominant culture. Such is the case of the enthusiastic reception that the Indians gave in their towns to the cult of the saints. According to Charles Gibson, "The community of the saints was received by Indians not as an intermediary between God and man but as a pantheon of anthropomorphic deities,"[26] just as the cult of their various deities was in the past. The same can be said for other practices, such as the very extended one of ceding part of the communal lands of the towns to the saints so that, as in pagan antiquity, the cult could be maintained from the production of those lands.[27] The cult of the dead should also be mentioned along with a multitude of agricultural rites that, under Christian forms, continued pre-Hispanic rites. Conversely, the transformation of European rites, as the Dance of the Moors and Christians, which celebrated the reconquest of the peninsula by the Spaniards, becomes the Dance of the Conquest, a setting of the historical moment when the Spaniards clashed with the Indians.[28]

Oral tradition, ritual, and myth, the ancient instruments that, from the oldest times, served the Indians to transmit the past, were the principal channels of indigenous memory under Spanish domination. Without the support of writing and calendrical systems, however, and in the repressive conditions that the Spanish domination created, both the ritual and the oral transmission of the past lost efficiency for preserving the authenticity of their traditions and the power to transmit them with the multiplying force and effect that they had prior to the arrival of the conqueror. Myth and ancient indigenous ceremonies had to hide behind Christian masks to pass a message that grew ever more separate from the nourishing strength that used to make it a transmitter of profound ethnic identities. The impossibility of articulating a message with autochthonous indigenous content opened, then, an irreparable fissure between the pagan past and the colonial present. These fractures, which progressively debilitate the transmission of the indigenous past, are observed in almost all of the mechanisms that served as transmission lines of that memory.

Toward the middle and end of the eighteenth century, the majority of the indigenous populations congregated in the towns had lost the notion of belonging to a broader ethnic community, with the exceptions of the principal caciques and Indians, who were more integrated into the exterior world, particularly with Spanish civil and religious authorities. Only the Maya and other isolated peoples continued feeding their present with the secret reading of the traditions contained in their sacred books. In the others, only agrarian rites and oral traditions deformed by or screened by Christian ceremonies and practices survived. The destructive effect of Spanish domination and the "spiritual conquest" on the memory of these peoples is revealed by a simple fact: in the eighteenth century, the majority of these peoples lacked an articulated account that united their present with their past. Not a single indigenous text is known that treats the history of one of these newly founded towns from its pre-Hispanic ancestors until the colonial present. Nevertheless, these towns invented a new form of transmitting the past, a mixture of indigenous and Spanish traditions that, without having the coherence of the ancient historical annals, was a powerful vehicle for maintaining the social cohesion of the peoples.

This is the case that is exemplified by a series of indigenous documents called "primordial titles" that, although they were written in Nahuatl at the end of the seventeenth century, during the eighteenth and

later, they undoubtedly rest on prior oral traditions and documents
already lost at the time the titles were composed.[29] A first reading of
these documents, whose central theme is the original adjudication and
partition of the towns' lands, seems to confirm that it is a disjointed and
confused memory that lacks an exact chronological record of events.
Thus, in a document related to the town of Zoyatzingo, it is said that the
Spaniards arrived in the year 945. In another one, it is stated that
Christianity and the Spaniards came to the town of Zula in 1907 or 1909,
even though in another part it states that the people of Zula were
baptized in 1532. It is common in these documents for events that
occurred at a specific time and place to be superimposed or for mythic
narrations to be mixed in with actual events. There is no trace in these
accounts of the ordered narrative sequence, which is typical of the
ancient indigenous annals or *xiuhpohualli*. Finally, seen in the light of
western criteria, these and other similar documents appear to deserve to
be clarified as "patently inaccurate, poorly informed, false and . . .
deliberately falsified."[30] The latter is due to the very justified reason that
many of them are clumsy falsifications of official Spanish documents
that formally assigned the land to the indigenous peoples.

But, in truth, are these indigenous versions of the division of the land
and of their history false? A reading of the internal contents of this
discourse shows that it is not a matter of falseness, but of an account of
historical events that actually occurred, and were written from the
indigenous point of view, not that of the conqueror. The careful analysis
that James Lockhart made of these texts indicates that in them historical
memory, although fragmented and incoherent to non-Indian eyes, re-
tains the crucial facts of the history of the towns and unites its members
around fundamental values: the property of the communal lands, the
ancestral possession of these, external dangers, the need to remain
united and to defend their traditions.

Significantly, several of these documents include a historical account
that ties the primordial adjudication of the land and the foundation of the
city to pre-Hispanic times. In several, remote indigenous personalities
are cited, surrounded by a mythical aura acting as founding figures or
participants in the act that established the original distribution of the
town's lands. In some cases, these remote indigenous persons, with
Christian names, are represented as alive in the immediate period of the
Conquest, and these are the persons who received the lands from the
Spanish authorities. That is, these persons appear as immune from time,
perhaps to symbolize the unity between the indigenous tradition and the
new Spanish customs. In any case, the delimitation and distribution of
the lands, the division of the neighborhoods, the naming of the authori-

ties of the town, the baptism of the population, the construction of the church, and the cycle of acts that accompanied the establishment of a town are presented with an aura of primordial foundation that, as in the pre-Hispanic era, established the sources of legitimacy of the community.

Also common in these documents is a recollection of the ancestral defense of the land in the face of external invaders or enemies. In several of them, land conflicts are mentioned that took place with neighboring peoples in pre-Hispanic times and from which the people emerged victorious because they knew how to make their rights prevail through argumentation founded on the legal procedures introduced by the Spaniards or through myths that corresponded to the pre-Hispanic tradition. That is, again, in defense of the land, ancient and contemporary procedures are mixed without paying attention to the temporal extrapolation, because everything serves the same goal: preserving the tradition of the defense of the land.[31]

The indigenous "primordial titles" also preserved memory of a remote time when people did not live grouped in villages but wandered dispersed among the mountains. Along with this recollection, they retained the memory of the Chichimeca invasions in the area of the settled peoples and the memory of the congregations of peoples under the Spanish domination. But frequently, these three events situated at different historical junctures appear confused as only one: "before the faith came, they all went scattered about, hiding among the wilds and crags."[32] The notion of a settled life and of the founding of towns appears tied to the traumatic fact of the congregations in the same way that the pagan era is identified with the nonsettled, and Christianity and the presence of the religious and the Spanish authorities are identified with the congregations. The people of these towns knew that in a far-off and imprecise time, their ancestors were pagans, that their towns lacked saints, persons with Christian names, and caciques with the title of "don." But this historical consciousness no longer distinguishes between the properly indigenous and the Spanish, for both roots are evoked in a mixed manner, forming a single past.

The progressive symbiosis between the pre-Hispanic and the colonial past is also present in the manner in which the inhabitants of these towns interpret the elements of Spanish culture closest to them. In these primordial titles created by the indigenous peoples themselves, there is no trace of incredulity with regard to Christianity nor resistance to this previously repudiated faith. There are no attitudes of disloyalty with regard to the Spanish king, as well. On the contrary, Christianity, Spanish authorities, and procedures appear in these texts as a new form of legitimizing the traditions of the town. The Conquest is hardly mentioned at all in the titles, nor is any painful memory of it recalled. Rather, these facts have the quality of cosmic events that do not merit explanation. They are seen as new arrangements of the world that have their justification in and of themselves:

> When the señor Marqués brought the Catholic faith, the fathers of the order of our father St. Francis came carrying a Holy Christ in front, and the Spaniards, those with white hides and with tubs on their heads, carrying their swords under their armpits, said they were called Spaniards and that they had given license to establish all the towns formally, and they [the Sula people] should think what saint they wanted to be their patron, because the Catholic faith was in Mexico City already.[33]

Cortés, the friars, the viceroy, and the archbishop are mentioned not as usurpers or enemies but as sources of legitimacy for the new order that rules in these towns. The primordial titles of each town always mention a high representative of the Spanish government (Cortés, the king, the viceroy, the archbishop), as a kind of god who intervenes in the founding and laying out of the town, and grants it legitimacy. True, knowledge of the ranks and functions of these authorities is inexact and imprecise: the viceroy is confused with the king, Cortés is identified with Don Luis de Velasco ("our great lord, the viceroy emperor Charles V," "Cortés and Don Luis de Velasco, the Marqués"). But for the people of these towns, it is clear that these names are or represent the power on which possession of their lands and continuity of these towns depends, although they ignore the exact rank of that authority. This does not matter; what matters is that these authorities, which are now recognized authorities, confirm and legitimize the right of the towns. The same occurs with the European calendar dates that appear disarranged, giving the impression that the indigenous scribe did not master the European calculations of the counting of years. The indigenous scribes show ignorance of the precise rank of the Spanish authorities, of the exact meaning of the European legal procedures, and of the meaning of the European calendar, but they are not unaware that these authorities, procedures, and dates are legitimizing signs essential in European documents. Because of that, they use them in theirs, although in these they appear as if magical imprecations, as elements that, by the very fact that they are mentioned, will give access to eternal and irrevocable titles of possession of the territory.

In contrast to this attitude of assimilation of the basic elements of the Hispano-Christian domination system in the indigenous primordial titles and in the general attitude of the peoples, there is a rejection, a repulsion, a connotation of danger in relation to the Spaniards specifically and to strangers to the village. Lockhart, who has studied these documents, indicates that significant parts of these texts are dedicated to warning the inhabitants of the towns not to show the documents to anyone, particularly to the Spaniards. "The Zoyatzingo title warns people to watch lest Spaniards coming in the future should make friends with their descendants, eat with them and become their *compadres*, then force them to sell them land or give it to them for friendship."[34]

These documents show that the historical memory of the towns had been concentrated in the preservation of the territorial rights, in the essential factor that permitted the existence of the town and cemented the social cohesion of its inhabitants.[35] The form and use that were given to the primordial titles also reveal their character as instruments for collecting the historical memory of the towns and of warning of the principal dangers that threaten their existence. All the titles Lockhart found denote by their style that they were made by the ancients of the town for the benefit of the young and generations to come. The rhetorical declamatory style of the primordial titles is very similar to the *huehuetlatolli*, or discourse of the ancients, which in the pre-Hispanic era transmitted to the young the precepts that had regulated the life of their ancestors. "Oh, my children," "Oh, my young brothers," are common formulas in the primordial titles but apart from the style, the use given to these documents shows that they were new vehicles for transmitting memory of the old to the new generations. Their composition in Nahuatl, the password, the admonition to keep them hidden from the Spaniards, and the warning call that constantly springs from them to defend the lands, made of these titles preservers of the vital memory of the indigenous peoples: it was the memory that recalled the rights that the indigenous peoples thought they had to the land.

For the Spaniards who found out about these documents when they were presented at some point as reliable proof of the indigenous rights to the land and to many historians who judged them from the point of view that authenticates the historical documents of the victor, these documents are false because they lack the formalities that distinguish titles issued by the conquerors. But this "falsification" of land titles by the Indians is the strongest proof of their authenticity, a sample of their great capacity for adaptation to the situation of the Conquest. What the Indians did by "falsifying" the land titles was to attempt to legitimize with Spanish procedures and uses their ancestral rights to the land, expressing them in the forms imposed by the conqueror. For whoever might want to see colonial history from the point of view of the Indians, the "false" primordial titles are indicative of the other side of this history: the hidden side. And for the purposes of this essay, the Indians' primordial titles demonstrate with a force that is not found in other documents how the indigenous peoples reconstructed their historical memory under the oppressive conditions of domination.[36]

The Historical Reconstruction Elaborated by the Indigenous Nobility and Their Mestizo Descendants

The only indigenous sector that preserved part of the old memories and techniques for gathering historical facts was the reduced group of principal Indians descended from the ancient ruling class. The extermination campaign that finished off the priests and chiefs excluded a small group of principal Indians who collaborated with the Spaniards in the Conquest (Tlaxcaltecans, Texcocoans, Cholultecans, etc.), and by curious coincidence this group, together with the missionaries, was the one that directly transmitted to the new colonial situation the pictographs and the most remote indigenous memory, adapting them to the European historiographic tradition. We owe the appearance of a mestizo historical literature to this group, for their status as allies of the conquerors and as heirs of the genealogies and historical texts of the ancient ruling families permitted them to preserve this past in the new colonial situation and led them to use the European techniques and styles to transmit it.

In the first decades that followed the Conquest, the indigenous nobility allied to the Spaniards was the principal conservator of the codices and texts that stored the memory of their ancestors. These genealogies and historical texts served the principal Indians to prove the antiquity of their lineage and to affirm the political and territorial rights for which they argued with the Spaniards. As in the pre-Hispanic past, the historical texts here served the old task of supporting the continuity of the group in power and of legitimizing the particular interests of the caciques and principal Indians.

This indigenous usage of the ancient historical texts was stimulated by the Spanish administration itself. In order to grant privileges and political posts to these Indian nobles who continually requested them, the viceregal authorities insisted that the petitioners prove their claims with historical documents. Thus, the first viceroy of New Spain, Don Antonio de Mendoza (1535–1550), ordered that a history of the governing families of the Chalco-Amaquemecan province be drawn up to serve as a reliable guide for granting positions requested by their descendants.[37] The charge of gathering this proof of merit fell on a certain Andrés de Santiago Xuchitotozin, who in 1547 was the judge of the village of Amaquemecan. This was the origin of an extraordinary compilation of historical documents about the Chalco-Amaquemecan, which later, at the beginning of the seventeenth century, was systematized by another Indian: Domingo Francisco de San Antón Muñón Chimalpahin Cuauhtlehuanitzin.

For Chimalpahin, who descended from the old families of Chalco-Amaquemecan, these documents legitimized the rights of the heirs of the old ruling class to political "appointments" that the colonial administration offered. This is why one of his concerns was to authenticate the antiquity and veracity of the historical texts that fell into his hands. He states that "these old histories . . . of royal lineages that are reported here . . . are not imagined or pretend things. This is not any kind of a fable; rather all the data have been reconciled one with the other according to the oldest versions of the old men and women of nobility . . . our ancestors . . . whose grandchildren and great-grandchildren we are." He repeatedly indicates that the historical accounts he offers are a faithful copy "of five parts of books of ancient painted papers made by the beloved old nobles."[38]

Like the ancient Tlacuilos, Chimalpahin undertakes the task of collecting the pictographs moved by petition from the indigenous governor of Amaquemecan, who requested that "he arrange the paintings and the book of antiquities called Nenotzallis" (original accounts). But Chimalpahin goes beyond that mandate: he undertakes a meticulous investigation in order to obtain the greatest number of documents; he submits his doubts on interpretation to the sages of the region; and after organizing the various historical accounts that he obtains, some of which were in an advanced state of destruction, he reconciles them with each other and proceeds to put in letters the ideographic message that appears drawn in the pictographic codices. His task is the ordering, translation, and recovery of a historical memory on the point of extinction, dispersed and, until then, inaccessible to the majority of the people in his region. Thus, with a purpose different from that of the missionaries, this indigenous man educated in Spanish schools, master of Spanish and Nahuatl, turns into letters the blurry language of the pictographs and delivers to his compatriots a collection of writings in Nahuatl that gathers the history of the Chalco-Amaquemecan region from the most remote past to the end of the sixteenth century.

As the original texts that Chimalpahin used have disappeared, it is difficult to discover the innovations or changes he introduced in the version that appeared by his hand. But it can be stated that he did not propose to recreate original materials or to forge with them a personal account. The six historical accounts that have been translated from Nahuatl to Spanish show that he was quite faithful to the original pictographs of the annals, or *xiuhpohualli* genre. In this annual succession of outstanding events that happened to the ethnic group, the most notable alterations are interpolations of Christian chronology of some biblical accounts and of contemporary news of the history of Spain and Europe.[39] But that is what they are, mere interpolations, insertions of sentences and paragraphs in the old text, distinguishable at first sight but not modifying the original version.

The *Crónica Mexicáyotl* reached us in a like manner. It relates the origin and greatness of the Mexica people. This is also a "chronicle" based principally on the annals, or *xiuhpohualli*, and on other old historical texts. Its conservator and transmitter was likewise an indigenous noble: Fernando de Alvarado de Tezozómoc, who transcribed it to Nahuatl around 1609 with the collaboration of Chimalpahin.[40] Modern and contemporary historians have disputed much about the authorship of these and similar texts, but it is clear that it is a senseless discussion. The *Crónica Mexicáyotl*, the *Historia Tolteca-Chichimeca*, and the other historical accounts of indigenous ascendance were not drawn up by individual authors in the style of the western tradition. They were made, modified, and rewritten by the chiefs who governed these peoples. Fernando Alvarado de Tezozómoc, Chimalpahin, and other noble Indians who had access to the ancient pictographs did not write these texts; they simply inherited them. Their job was that of preservation and translation of the ideograms and oral traditions to written Nahuatl.

Without intending to, the indigenous nobles and missionaries who converted the contents of the ancient pictographs to written Nahuatl or to Castilian introduced a radical mutation in the indigenous historical tradition: they separated the indigenous text from its oral interpretation. From the moment when the ancient indigenous traditions were put into Nahuatl or Spanish, they lost their multiple significance, the interpretive richness and coloring that illuminated them when they were declaimed and explained by specialists in indigenous pictographic reading. Starting with the putting into letters of the ideographic message of the codices, the indigenous historical text acquired a univocal meaning that it did not have before. This new writing of history broke the old relationship between the ideograms of the indigenous text and their explanation by the interpreters of them, which was a combination rich in decipherment, gloss, and oral commentary, an incessant give and take between the contents of the pictographs and the creative digression always renewed and changing, of their oral explanation. The introduction of the European alphabet in this way converted the polyvalent ancient Indian text into a text with a *single* meaning, because the new writing, by choosing a single interpretation among the various that the ideograms of the codices permitted, established a single sense of the content of the text. It defined a single interpretation of the historical tale and, besides, converted this interpretation into the only authorized one. The text created authority. Henceforth, what was established in the text took precedence over any oral interpretation. This was another way—perhaps the most important one—in which the new historical discourse imposed its supremacy over the old one. Beginning with this fundamental rupture, the Indians could no longer read, recall, or explain their texts according to their own written and mental categories, but their own historical tradition began to be explained in a strange language governed by other mental categories.

The conversion of the ancient Indian ideograms into written letters signals, then, a crucial moment in the history of the acculturation and domination of the American peoples. Before these ideograms were transferred to the European alphabet, their reading was another, indigenous; but as soon as they were transferred to the new alphabet and transformed into texts with a univocal meaning and explanation, they acquired the categories and the values of western culture. This fact demonstrates another poorly studied phase of the drama of the Conquest: not only is the history of the conquered written by the conqueror, but the conquered's own historical tradition is first suppressed and then expropriated by the conqueror, who converts it into a reading that only the victor can carry out.

The appearance of a reinterpretation of the indigenous historical tradition based on ancient indigenous texts but carried out with other criteria and attributable to individual persons occurs almost at the same period in which the ancient pictographs were transferred to written Nahuatl, but its authors were not ethnically or culturally pure Indians. Diego Muñoz Camargo (born around 1529 and died in 1599), Juan Bautista Pomar (who must have been born shortly after the Conquest), and Fernando de Alva Ixtlilxóchitl (1578–1648), the creators of this new historical literature of indigenous themes, were mestizos. The three descended on their mothers' side from old Indian ruling families. Muñoz Camargo was related to indigenous families from Tlaxcala; Bautista Pomar was a descendant of the family of Nezahualpilli, lord of Texcoco; and Alva Ixtlilxóchitl from the same family of Nezahualpilli and Ixtlilxóchitl, ancient rulers of Texcoco. The three had Spanish fathers and all wrote what we could today call "regional histories," accounts of a region and of an ethnic group. In this they carried on the tradition of their indigenous ancestors, who built their accounts around the politically organized ethnic group. But their manner of approaching this history and their style mark a deep break with this tradition and an affirmation of the Spanish historiographic tradition. In contrast to their predecessors, these authors do not limit themselves to being mere compilers and systematizers of old indigenous texts. The three use old annals and oral indigenous traditions, but compose their accounts according to the models and styles of the European chronicle.

Juan Bautista Pomar wrote his *Relación de Tezcoco* by order of King Philip II, who mandated the preparation of geographical accounts of the dominions of Spain in America. Under this constraint, Bautista Pomar drew up one of the first local histories made by mestizos. His work fulfills the requirement of presenting a geographic description of the region, but the historical information that he adds on the lordship of Texcoco is more important: an account that encompasses the description of its rulers, gods, ceremonies, customs, forms of war and government, nourishment, and so on. That is, it is a historical-ethnographic account made as if the author were outside the indigenous world. It is an account that no longer follows the indigenous models of telling: it imitates the composition and style of European historical accounts.[41] These new tendencies in the content and form of the historical accounts are expressed with greatest force in the *Descripción de la ciudad y provincia de Tlaxcala* and in the so-called *Historia de Tlaxcala*, both written by Diego Muñoz Camargo, and in the historical works of Fernando de Alva Ixtlilxóchitl. Muñoz Camargo composed his descriptions and his *Historia de Tlaxcala* based on old Indian annals and traditional histories. But in contrast to Chimalpahin and Tezozómoc, who faithfully transcribed the indigenous model of narrating the facts year by year, Muñoz Camargo adopts the model of the European chronicle. Instead of presenting some annals in the strict sense, he offers a continuous account of the events to which he adds at the end of a chapter or throughout the text, the indigenous account of the years.[42] In fact, the greatest part of his work, although based on old indigenous texts and oral traditions, reveals a progressive distancing from the strictly indigenous and a very accentuated proclivity toward seeing the indigenous from the Spanish side.

In one place, Muñoz Camargo says that he is writing the history of the lordships and kingdoms of Tlaxcala so that "their memory is not lost because of the coming of the Christians and first Spaniards."[43] Probably this same purpose was what led Juan Bautista Pomar to undertake the many steps that he reports having taken to find "old, intelligent Indians" and "very old songs" and to compose with that information a faithful account of the antiquity of Texcoco.

Reading these works, one cannot doubt that their authors wrote them with the desire of preserving that memory that so many other factors contributed in their time to destroying. But in their pages, that memory and that indigenous tradition appear distant and even alien, as if they dealt with a tradition that is no longer fully theirs. Both authors express this feeling of detachment. Juan Bautista Pomar establishes a measured but unbreachable distance between him, the narrator, and the indigenous world he describes. In his text, the indigenous world is the other, something alien and distinct from his own person. In the case of Muñoz Camargo, the separation between the narrator and the world he describes is even more definitive for, although he comes from Indians, he identifies with the Spaniards, whom he calls "our people."[44]

Another expression of the distance that is being created between the narrator and the subject of the narration is the evaluations that determine it. For example, Juan Bautista Pomar only considers in his account the governors of Texcoco, whom he calls "virtuous," because "they converted their vassals in good customs and an honest way of living." Besides, he erases from history all those who do not meet this ideal of good ruler taken from the European models. When talking of the old religion, the thorniest subject that could be treated by a chronicler of the era, he makes a distinction between the mass of the population, which practiced idolatry and human sacrifice, and "some principals and lords" who doubted that their idols were gods and conjectured the idea of a single god, creator of everything in existence, similar to the Christian God.[45]

Diego Muñoz Camargo goes further still, for, in his writings, the sacrifices, the witchcraft, the superstitions, the idolatry, and other perversions that he observes in the indigenous peoples are works of the devil, a result of their ignorance of the true God.

These and other criteria that Bautista Pomar and Muñoz Camargo use to judge the Indians demonstrate that these mestizo historians had ceased to understand Indian values. Not only had they become culturally strange persons from their ancestors, they thought and judged the Indians by the conquerors' values.

Another notable case of this powerful process of acculturation induced by the Spanish Conquest is exemplified by the ruling indigenous nobles of Tlaxcala. In these initial and close collaborators of the conquerors is observed one of the first examples of adaptation of the old indigenous historical tradition to the goals of Spanish domination. Following the old indigenous tradition, the rulers of Tlaxcala had painted, certainly since the decade of 1550, a group of allegorical illustrations of the discovery and conquest of American lands. These were hung in the chamber and hearing room of the Tlaxcalan Council and in another principal house of the rulers. True, on these walls were maintained alive the indigenous tradition and techniques of collecting historical facts by means of paintings, but what was represented here was a series of allegorical and realistic scenes of the Spanish discovery and conquests that transmitted the message of domination: the power of the Spanish kings, the discovering deeds of Columbus, the expansion of

Spanish dominion, the catechizing and civilizing job of the missionaries, and, in more detail, the great epic of Hernán Cortés, and the decisive participation of the Tlaxcalans in the conquest and colonization of New Spain. That is, the universal history and the history of New Spain flow together for the first time in an indigenous space, expressed in the old indigenous pictorial tradition, but transmitting the message of the Spanish conqueror.

The finding of a lost work of the Tlaxcaltecan mestizo historian, Diego Muñoz Camargo, demonstrates the continuity and the strength of this process of acculturation. The descriptions of the paintings that decorated the chamber and hearing room of the Tlaxcalan Council and the murals of the principal house of the Tlaxcalan governors coincide precisely with the paintings that Muñoz Camargo added to his *Descripción de la Ciudad y Provincia de Tlaxcala*, which are none other than the very well-known ones that illustrate the famous *Lienzo de Tlaxcala*, published by Alfredo Chavero in 1892—that is, the indigenous nobility who ruled Tlaxcala, having joined a few decades after the Conquest the indigenous historical and pictorial tradition with the message of Spanish domination to express the Tlaxcaltecans' collaboration in the conquest of New Spain and to affirm their tie with the new dominators of the land.

Juan Bautista Pomar, Diego Muñoz Camargo, and Fernando de Alva Ixtlilxóchitl affirmed to the Spaniards the Indian blood that ran in their veins, taking care to point out that it was noble blood. But culturally, they were not nor did they feel like Indians. They lived among the Indians, making them note their strong ties to the world of the Spaniards, and on those ties they based their superiority to the indigenous masses. Their most notable difference from the indigenous population was that they, in addition to speaking and writing Spanish, thought like Spaniards. Their histories written in Spanish were not directed at the indigenous population but at the conquerors. Like their indigenous ancestors, they are historians of one ethnic group of one Texcocoan Tlaxcatecan town, but their interpretation of that history is not identified with the interests of the Texcocoan or Tlaxcaltecan peoples but with the interests of the caciques and Indians allied to the Spaniards. The *Descripción* and the *Historia de Tlaxcala* by Muñoz Camargo are an unadorned and often false apology for the Tlaxcaltecan contribution to the triumph of the Spaniards, whose ultimate purpose was to obtain rewards for the indigenous caciques who aspired to rule the Tlaxcaltecans.

The work of Fernando de Alva de Ixtlilxóchitl, the most complete and elegant historian of this group, is also a elegiac account of the Texcocoan nation, principally of its most distinguished rulers: Netzahualcóyotl, Ixtlilxóchitl, and Netzahualpitzintli, from whom Alva Ixtlilxóchitl himself was descended. In the majority of the works by this historian, but especially in *La historia de la nación chichimeca*, the decisive participation of the Texcocoans in the conquest of Mexico-Tenochtitlan is stressed. The political meaning of this recovery of indigenous history is exemplified by the very life of the historian who created it, for Fernando de Alva Ixtlilxóchitl was rewarded by Spanish authorities with the appointment as *juez gobernador* of Texcoco, Tlalmanalco, and the province of Chalco, and later he held the post of interpreter of the Juzgado de Indios.[46]

Nevertheless, there is in these works something more profound than the immediate use of the historical recovery for the purposes of domination. All of them exemplify a process of "disindigenization," of loss of the Indian qualities and values to interpret the historical development and the indigenous society. In none of them are the indigenous categories used to interpret and measure historical time, a characteristic of the old pictographs and traditions that served as sources for all these accounts. In their place appears the Christian chronology and conception of the passage of time. Fernando de Alva Ixtlilxóchitl makes a unique attempt among these historians to incorporate into these chronicles the cyclical conception of the four creations and destructions of the world, but he ends up by twisting this conception and adjusting it to the Christian interpretation of history.

In one of his first works, the one that is most faithful to its sources and to indigenous tradition, he indicates that the Indians had the idea of the creation of the world and expounds the cyclical conception of creation and destruction in this order: the first age was that of the Water Sun (*Atonatiuh*), which was destroyed by a deluge. Some people survived this catastrophe, building a kind of ark, then they built a *zacuali*, or very high tower. At the same time, the languages they used multiplied and changed, which forced them to disperse.

The second age was that of the Air Sun (*Ecactonatiuh*), which was destroyed by hurricanes. The third was that of the Earth Sun (*Tlachitonatiuh*) in which giants lived and which was destroyed by an earthquake.[47] In this work Ixtlilxóchitl does not mention either the fourth or the fifth sun, which other indigenous versions do include.

In two later versions of the same account, Alva Ixtlilxóchitl changed the order of succession of the ages, or Suns, also adding a fourth age to his scheme. In the new version, the second age was converted into the third.[48] The explanation of the alteration of this succession of the Suns does not appear to be any other than that of accommodating the indigenous account to the Christian conception of the historical process.

In the first version of the creations of the world, there is already a clear intent to relate the indigenous conception of the creation of the first Sun to the biblical account, for he introduces three biblical elements foreign to that mentality and to the indigenous, autochthonous texts: the idea that some people were saved from the deluge by building an ark; the idea that they built a *zacuali*, or tower, similar to that of Babel; and the idea that the dispersion of this first humanity was caused by the confusion of tongues.

In the version of the four Suns that appears in the *Historia de la nación chichimeca*, which is a much later, personal, and finished work by Alva Ixtlilxóchitl, he goes further with his intent to relate the indigenous version of the creation of world with the Christian conception of history, but now centering on the figure of Quetzalcóatl. In this version, what occurred in the first and the second ages is related rapidly and not connected with the biblical narrations. The third age, however, the Air Sun *(Ecactonatiuh)*, which in the first version appeared as a second age without importance, acquires an unusual relevance. Everything occurs as if the destruction of the first two worlds was a mere preparatory antecedent to the third age, which for Alva Ixtlilxóchitl is without a doubt the most important because of the space that he gives to it and the content that it reveals. According to this version, in the third Sun, Air Sun, lived the Ulmecas and the Xicalancas, who "came in ships or boats from the Oriental parts." When they peopled the land, there arrived "a man they called Quetzalcóatl . . . due to his great virtues, holding him as just, saintly, and good." Quetzalcóatl taught the Indians, through his deeds and words, the path of virtue,

> avoiding the vices and sins, giving laws and good doctrine; and to break them of their crimes and dishonesty he imposed fasting on them and [was] the first who adored and placed the cross called Quiahutzteotlchicahuializtéotl by some and Tonacaquáhuitl by others, which means God of the Rains and Health and Tree That Sustains Life . . . [After Quetzalcóatl had] preached the aforementioned things in all the other cities of the Ulmecs and the Xicalancas and especially in that of Cholula, where he was most often, and seeing the little fruit that had come of his doctrine, he returned to the same place from which he had come, which was toward the east, disappearing along the coasts of Coatzacoalco; and at the time he was saying good-bye to these peoples, he said that in coming times, in a year to be called Ce ÁCatl he would return and then his doctrine would be received and his children would be lords and possess the land and that they and their descendants would live through many calamities and persecutions; and many other prophecies that later were seen very clearly.

Alva Ixtlilxóchitl finishes his interpretation of this third age in the following manner. Once Quetzalcóatl left the earth,

> a few days later followed the destruction and devastation of the third age of the world and then that building and tower so memorable in the city of Cholula, which was now like a second Tower of Babel that these peoples [built] almost for the same purposes, the wind destroying it. And afterwards, the ones who escaped the consummation of this third age, in the ruins of it they built a temple to Quetzalcóatl, who they placed as Air God . . . And it appears from the aforementioned histories and by the annals, the aforementioned occurred some years after the incarnation of Jesus Christ, our Lord; and from that time to now came the fourth age, which they said was called Tlétonatiuc, which means Fire God . . . Quetzalcóatl was a well disposed man with a serious appearance, white and bearded. His clothing was a long tunic.[49]

By placing in the third age of his invention the historical presence of Quetzalcóatl and the diffusion of his doctrine, Alva Ixtlilxóchitl joins a group of Spanish chroniclers, who since the Conquest, had tried to explain some indigenous religious and cultural traces, adducing the preaching of Christian faith prior to the arrival of Hernán Cortés. That is, he follows the interpretation that Motolinía and Father Las Casas only insinuated but, at the end of the sixteenth century, Fray Diego Durán expressed without hesitation by affirming that Quetzalcóatl was "probably . . . some apostle that God brought to this land." Alva Ixtlilxóchitl thus took the side of those who, beginning then, tried to explain indigenous history outside of its own categories, beginning with the Christian conception of history.

The introduction of the Christian conception of history simultaneously created a negative assessment of indigenous culture and an idealized historical paradigm into which they forcefully attempted to fit the rescue of the indigenous past. Alva Ixtlilxóchitl is a man crushed by the weight of the new interpretation of historical development. In fact, on the one hand, he condemns in his work the idolatrous and barbarous history of his ancestors and refrains from explaining it based on its own values. On the other, he proposes an interpretation of that history in light of Christian conception. His Quetzalcóatl is not the indigenous cultural hero or the wizard necromancer that other chroniclers describe; rather, he is a "just, saintly, and good" gentleman, the preacher of a new doctrine, and the man who revealed the future to his people, the time when he would return accompanied by other white, bearded men to establish the true religion and become lords of the land. It is clear that

Alva Ixtlilxóchitl's rearrangement of the order of the ages obeys the purpose of situating this third age, in which Quetzalcóatl preached, as a continuation of the age of Christ; this is why he says, "And it appears from the aforementioned histories and the annals, the aforementioned occurred some years after the incarnation of Jesus Christ, our Lord."

Compelled by its requirement to legitimize indigenous history based on the values of Christian history, Alva Ixtlilxóchitl goes to the extreme of converting his Chichimeca ancestors into white men, into Spaniards: in some of his chronicles, the Chichimeca kings are represented as tall, white, bearded men.[50] According to this interpretation of the history of the Spanish invasion, it is then not a catastrophic break of the autochthonous history but the restoration of a situation experienced and announced in the past that will continue in the future.

There is no doubt that in this peculiar recovery of the past by the descendants of the ancient indigenous nobility, their condition as collaborators of the Spaniards played an essential role, as did their assimilation of the Christian conception of history. As a direct instrument of the conquerors in the domination of the *macehuales*, the indigenous nobility could not undertake a recovery of the Indian past based on the interests of the native population. In their works, not only do they not identify with the traditions of this population, but there is a distancing first and then a rejection of the categories in which the indigenous people were accustomed to perceive and evaluate historical development. Unlike what occurs in Peru with the indigenous historian Felipe Guaman Poma de Ayala, who recovers the indigenous past and sees the colonial reality through authentically indigenous categories,[51] the Mexican indigenous nobles establish a clear separation between themselves and the past and present indigenous world. Their link with the political and mental structures of domination is so strong that they see indigenous history exclusively from the Spanish side. So complete is their acculturation to the values of the conqueror that they do not show the ambivalence observed in another famous mestizo historian, el Inca Garcilaso de la Vega. Garcilaso recovers the history of his ancestors beginning with the categories of western history, but he also constructs an elegiacally idealized and nostalgic vision of the lost world of the Incas.[52]

The drama of these mestizo historians is not only the impossibility of identifying with the history and interests of their ancestors but also their inability to create their own authentic discourse. The raw material of their chronicles is the indigenous sources and historical traditions, but no indigenous discourse of history flows from them because the categories that rule their discourse are European. In addition, they write in

Spanish and compose their accounts modeled on the European chronicle, and they attempt to explain historical development in light of the Christian conception of history. But this great effort to assimilate strange categories and concepts does not conclude in a discourse of their own, but in a mediated and forceless transposition of European conceptions. In the same manner as the social position and power they hold in colonial society is not their own but delegated by the Spanish authority so also is their discourse of history a hybrid text without its own substance that is neither identified with the indigenous society nor is it the real discourse of the dominator.

In Search of Lost Identity: Indigenous Religious Movements and Insurrections

One century after the Conquest, in many of the new Indian towns, there began to be felt a subterranean tremor that later exploded in various parts of the country. The cause of these shakeups was not the direct rejection of political subjugation or economic exploitation established by the system of domination. In the majority of cases, these upheavals had as their origin the search for an ethnic and cultural identity that had been broken by the Conquest and then radically disturbed by the process of Spanish domination.

At the beginning of the seventeenth century, Spanish domination of the indigenous peoples was so well established that it was not questioned. In almost all of these peoples, there were claims to land, water, forests, withdrawal of workers and tributes, or protests against the abuses of the Spanish proprietors and functionaries or against the exactions of the church. But these protests did not question the system of domination as such: they were direct allegations aimed at persons, authorities, or concrete corporations, individualized, that almost never adopted the form of unified claims due to the same fragmentation that burdened the towns. Against a system of integrated and coherent domination, the indigenous peoples reacted individually without the capacity to extend their protests to other towns and regions.

The same Spanish strategy that had broken the Indian groups' old ethnic and political identities, however, the same action that had striven to remove the old religious practices, created a serious social and cultural identity problem in the new towns. Each of the new towns had a form of government, well-established rules to accede to the land that sustained them, fixed rules for relating to the exterior, and a new religious and social center. Around the church and the patron saints of the towns now spun all the rights, ceremonies, feasts, and principal acts of the life of the community. Although all these new forms of constructing the life of the community were well established, however, in essence they were strange forms that lacked legitimacy inside the communities. The new gods, ceremonies, and rites had very little that was Indian in them. They continued to be foreign gods, alien to the internal pulses of the community.

This deep uprooting of the peoples gave rise to intense religious movements that sought to give an indigenous meaning to the gods, to the saints, and to the conquerors' ceremonies. What is new about these movements is that they did not propose, as was the case of the nativist movements of the years immediately following the Conquest, to restore the force of the ancient gods or to return to the traditional religious practices. The best proof that the "spiritual conquest" had been consummated is that these movements did not question the legitimacy of the new gods or the new cult. On the contrary, instead of rejecting the Christian religion and cult, these movements sought to make these values truly theirs by converting them into indigenous divinities, saints, and rites.

Origins of the Tonantzin-Guadalupe Cult

The first account of the new cult that the Indians made to the image of the Spanish Virgin of Guadalupe at a site where it had been their custom to adore a pre-Hispanic deity comes from an *información* that the second archbishop, Fray Alonso de Montúfar, ordered prepared in 1556. It had as its origin a sermon that was given by the provincial of the Franciscans, Fray Francisco de Bustamante, before the viceroy, Don Luis de Velasco, the members of the Real Audiencia, and the principal representatives of the religious communities. Halfway through the sermon, Bustamante attacked the cult that was made to the image of the Virgin of Guadalupe, saying that "it seemed to him that the devotion that this city had taken in a hermitage and home of Our Lady that they have entitled of Guadalupe is a great harm to the natives because it leads them to believe that that image painted by the Indian Marcos performs miracles . . . and to tell [the Indians] that an image that was painted by an Indian performs miracles, would be great confusion and undo good that had been planted there."[53]

Bustamante added that the Indians "adored" the image, taking alms and offerings and, among these, donations of food, an act that appeared idolatrous to him. The provincial criticized Archbishop Montúfar, himself, reproaching him for protecting this cult and speaking in favor of the miracles of the image without verifying its truth. Montúfar responded with weak arguments, for he explained that he only preached "leading to understand how reverence is not given to the board or to the painting but to the image of Our Lady because of what she represents."

The data of the *información* indicate that toward the middle of the sixteenth century in Mexico City a new cult to the Virgin of Guadalupe had developed, that this cult was to a painting, board, or image of this Virgin, and that the Indians practiced this cult, believing that the Virgin had been painted by an Indian and that the image performed miracles. Bustamante states that "the Indian Marcos painted" the image of the Virgin of Guadalupe, that is, he notes that it was a human work, not a miracle. In his defense, Archbishop Montúfar lets it be understood that he did not favor the cult to the painting by the Indian Marcos or "to the board," "but to the image of Our Lady [of Guadalupe] because of what she represents." It is also evident that at this time only the archbishop, the representative of the secular clergy, seemed to favor the cult to the Guadalupe while the religious, particularly the Franciscans, were against this new devotion.

A later text also opposed to the new devotion shows a deep nexus that this devotion had with the pre-Hispanic cults. Bernardino de Sahagún, the friar who was best acquainted with indigenous traditions, wrote the following around 1570 about the cult to the Virgin of Guadalupe in Tepeyac:

Around the hills there are three or four places where [the Indians] used to make very solemn sacrifices and they came to these places from distant lands. One of these is here in Mexico, where there is a hill that is called Tepéacac and the Spaniards call it Tepeaquilla, and now is called Our Lady of Guadalupe; in this place they had a temple dedicated to the mother of the gods, whom they called Tonantzin, which means our Mother; there they made many sacrifices to honor this goddess and came to her from distant lands from more than twenty leagues, from all the regions of Mexico and they brought many offerings; men and women and young men and young women came to these feasts; there was a great gathering of people on those days and they all said let us go to the feast of Tonantzin; and now that the Church of Our Lady of Guadalupe was built there, they also called it Tonantzin, taking this from the preachers who called Our Lady the Mother of God Tonantzin.

Sahagún adds,

Where the [pre-Hispanic] basis of this Tonantzin was born is not known for certain, but what we truly know is what the word signifies from its first imposition, to that ancient Tonantzin, and it is something that should be remedied . . . this appears to be a satanic invention to lessen the idolatry under the equivocation of this name Tonantzin and they come now to visit this Tonantzin from far off, as far off as before, which devotion is also suspicious because everywhere there are many churches of Our Lady and they do not go to them and [but they do] come from distant lands to this Tonantzin as in olden times.[54]

What worried Sahagún about this new cult to the Virgin of Guadalupe was its link with the place where the pre-Hispanic cult had been celebrated. The confusion between the cult to the Virgin Mary and that of the ancient Tonantzin seemed to him "a satanic invention to lessen the idolatry under the equivocation of this name of Tonantzin." He was convinced that the Indians who, at that time, were mostly devotees to the new cult, adored their ancient deities in the guise of a Spanish religious image. For Sahagún the cult to Guadalupe was not a Christian cult but an indigenous, idolatrous one, which he states in precisely these terms in another place when he says that the "idolatrous dissembling is taken from the names of the idols that were celebrated there, that the names with which they are named in Latin or in Spanish mean what the name of the idol that was adored there in old times meant, as in the City of Mexico, an idol that formerly was called Tonantzin and it is understood by the old and not by the new."

But precisely this "idolatrous dissembling," this procedure preserving the ancient by dressing it up with new and foreign form and content was what was done with the Guadalupan cult, a proper cult rooted and extended among the Indians of Mexico. In this way, the pre-Hispanic Tonantzin, our Mother, began to be fused with the Christian cult of the Virgin Mary. Years later this strange fusion would produce one of the most extraordinary religious myths of the American world and a national symbol that identified Indians, Creoles, and mestizos in one same and celebrated belief. But this transmutation of the simple Guadalupan cult of the first half of the sixteenth century into a religious and cultural symbol generalized throughout New Spain was not a work of the Indians but of the Creoles, another ethnic group characterized by uprooting and lack of its own identity.

Between 1550 and 1600, the Guadalupe cult was controversial, poorly articulated from the religious viewpoint, practiced especially by the indigenous population of the surroundings of Tepeyac hill and Mexico City without the apocalyptic, prophetic, providentialist, and patriotic charge that the Creole preachers would infuse in it later in the seventeenth and eighteenth centuries and without the marvelous history of the Virgin's appearances to Juan Diego. What is known for sure is that in these years the ancient cult that was paid to the pre-Hispanic Tonantzin had become confused with a new cult of the Virgin of Guadalupe, for whose picture or image a simple hermitage had been built on Tepeyac hill. It is unknown what type of image this was, although the Franciscan Bustamante stated in 1556, without anyone's contradicting him, that it was "an image painted by an Indian," and in 1582 English traveler Miles Phillips described it as a full-sized silver statue.[55]

The news that the Virgin of Guadalupe performed miracles spread in the second half of the sixteenth century. At that time, the Spaniards themselves and the Creoles began to visit the shrine on Sundays, encouraged by Archbishop Montúfar, who made an effort to convert the visit to Tepeyac into a kind of visit to the country combined with mandatory mass in the shrine of Guadalupe. But in those years worship of Guadalupe was mostly indigenous. As various witnesses indicate, from many parts of the Valley of Mexico Indians came to Tepeyac hill to worship the image of Guadalupe and to present offerings according to their ancient customs. This alarmed the Spanish religious as much as the ancestral practice of offering food and drink to the gods. In this manner, the worship, the offerings, the periodic visits to the old indigenous Tonantzin, and the mythic burden of the ancient Mesoamerican religions were transferred to the image of the Virgin of Guadalupe of Tepeyac.

This appropriation by the Indians of the Spanish Virgin of Guadalupe through worship and religious ceremony was accompanied by progressive distancing of the Mexican image in regard to the Virgin of Guadalupe of Extremadura. It has been said that the Extremeño origin of many of the first conquerors, particularly Hernán Cortés, favored the development in New Spain of devotion to the Virgin of Guadalupe of Extremadura, which at that time enjoyed such great prestige on the peninsula. Martín Enríquez, himself a viceroy, said in a letter dated 1575 that "they named the image Nuestra Señora de Guadalupe to say that it resembled Guadalupe of Spain."[56]

But the image of the Guadalupe of Tepeyac presents the disconcerting paradox of being completely different from its presumed peninsular model. These differences between the two images have not been explained well. It is supposed that at the beginning of the worship to Guadalupe there was in the shrine of Tepeyac a copy of the image of the Extremeña Guadalupe on an engraving or a banner, for it was forbidden at that time to reproduce the Spanish Guadalupe as sculpture. What is certain is that around 1556 the primitive image of the Guadalupe of Tepeyac was replaced by a painting made by an Indian named Marcos against which, as we have seen, the provincial of the Franciscans, Francisco de Bustamante, spoke out. Many years later, probably around 1575, the Indian Marcos's painting was replaced in turn by the current image, which is likewise very different from that of Guadalupe of Extremadura.[57]

Along with these changes in the image that Mexicanize Guadalupe, there was a change in the date of the celebration of the birth of the Virgin, which in Spain was on September 8, the same as in Mexico, until the end of the sixteenth century. But around 1600, the Feast of Guadalupe of Tepeyac was changed to September 10 and later to December 12, deepening in this way its separation from the Guadalupe of Spain. All these changes express an irrepressible desire to "nativize" the Virgin, a process that will end up by turning Guadalupe of Tepeyac into an emblem of those born in New Spain.

The intellectual materialization of this collective urge was a series of accounts that narrate the appearances of the Virgin to the Indian Juan Diego. In the sixteenth century, there are no express mentions of the appearance of the Virgin or discussion about it. Only one Creole chronicler, Juan Suárez de Peralta, on describing the visit that Viceroy Martín Enríquez made to the Shrine of the Virgin of Guadalupe, indicated that this was "a very devout image that is some two leagues from Mexico City and that has performed many miracles." And he added this laconic note: "She appeared among some cliffs and all the land comes to worship her."[58]

The creation of a literature dedicated to giving a foundation of the appearances of the Virgin of Guadalupe was the work of a group of priests and Creole scholars obsessed by the need to give roots and identity to those born in New Spain. This spiritual movement manifested itself as a powerful impulse, as a sentiment of affirmation of a rootless social class that lacked the place and identity needed in the new society that had formed in the territory of New Spain. What is significant is that this spiritual movement, guided by Creoles, had its first and strongest affirmative expression among the religious in the field that was the unifying element of the ethnic, economic, cultural, and political diversity that at that time was New Spain. In this fertile field of religion, the Creoles managed to integrate in a single spiritual current the repressed indigenous religiosity with the rich Christian tradition. The encounter of these two traditions will make of Guadalupism a deeply indigenous and Creole spiritual phenomenon anchored in the Christian tradition and in the orthodoxy of the scriptures but also penetrated by the legacy of the prophecies of messianism and apocalyptic millenarianism that mobilized populist groups, sects, and religious orders in the Christian Middle Ages.

The Appearances of the Virgin of Guadalupe and the Creation of the Mexicans' First Great Unifying Symbol

Francisco de la Maza discovered in the work of Miguel Sánchez the first coherent foundation of the appearances of the Virgin of Guadalupe to the Indian Juan Diego and a new and durable interpretation of the meaning of the appearance of the Mother of God in Mexican lands.

Born in Mexico City in 1594, Miguel Sánchez was a priest, a recognized theologian, a famous preacher, and a Creole obsessed by the desire to extol the goodness and principles of those born in Mexico. In 1640 he published a sermon entitled *Elogio de San Felipe de Jesús, hijo y patrón de México* in which he eulogizes this famous Creole missionary, whom he calls "Indian Jesus." A little later, in 1648, he published his most important work, *Imagen de la Virgen María, madre de Díos de Guadalupe* . . . In the prologue he states that he looked for and did not find the documents that describe the appearances of the saintly image; therefore, he based himself on the traditions preserved by old men. Thus, based on the oral tradition, he published for the first time the appearances of the Virgin in the following fashion:

First Appearance

> Mexico, the populous city, imperial court of this new world, in its time of heathens, barbarity, and diabolical idolatry, a city today truly fortunate . . . received the light of the gospel from the hand of MARY, Virgin mother of God . . . Around the beginning of December of the year 1531, it occurred at the spot that today is called *Guadalupe* . . . and then Tepeyac . . . Here one Saturday [day to be consecrated to MARY] an Indian was passing by . . . recently converted [who at this spot heard] sweet music, chords, harmony, uniform modulations . . . and as the harmonious choir had paused . . . he heard a voice that called him by name . . . Juan Diego heard the voice and felt the echoes of it in his soul [and] discovered [on the height of the hill] a lady who ordered him to come up . . . being in her presence astonished without fear . . . contemplating a beauty that makes him love without danger, a light that illuminates without dazzling him, a pleasure that captivates him without flattery. He hears a sweetly pronounced language, easy to understand, unforgettably lovely, that all this is placed in the VIRGIN MARY, who said to him: Son Juan, where are you going . . . He, grateful and compelled by the tenderness of the words, replied. Lady, I am going to a teaching of gospel in obedience of the religious fathers who teach us in the town of Tlatelolco. Most holy MARY continued speaking, revealing herself and stating to him,

"You know, son, that I am the VIRGIN MARY, mother of the true God. I want a house and a shrine to be founded here for me, a temple in which I, pious mother, can reveal myself to you and to my devotees, who will seek me out for remedy of their needs. So this proposition of mercy can take place, you are to go to the palace of the bishop in Mexico City and in my name tell him that I have a [private] wish for a temple to be built on this spot for me, reporting to him what you have heard . . . Juan, humble, venerates and adores her [and] obediently hurries [to comply with her wishes]. He walks to the city, seeks out the bishop's palace [and] the messenger Juan finally arriving with the VIRGIN MARY's request to the consecrated prince of the church, D. Juan de Zumárraga.

Second Apparition

That same day he returned with the reply and, climbing up to the indicated site on that hill the messenger [found] the VIRGIN MARY, who awaited him piously, and humbling himself in her presence with all reverence, he said: I obeyed, Lady and Mother of mine, your command. Not without difficulty did I enter to visit the bishop. At his feet I knelt: he accepted me piously . . . listened to me attentively, and indifferently replied, saying: Son, another day when there is space you can come. I will listen to you more slowly . . . I will find out the root of this request of yours. I judged from his appearance and his words that he was convinced that the request for the temple that you are asking for . . . was born in my own imagination and not from your request. Therefore, I beg of you to entrust this business to another person who is given more credence. There will be no lack of them, replied the holy Virgin, but it is proper for you to request it and . . . I ask you, entrust you, and beg you to return tomorrow with the same care to the bishop and on my behalf again . . . advise him of my will that a house I have asked for be built. . . My lady, said Juan, with great pleasure . . . and punctually I will obey the order you have given me. I will see you tomorrow when the sun sets.

Third Appearance

At the indicated time, as the sun was setting, he arrived at Mount Guadalupe, a new Mount Tabor, with the assistance of the VIRGIN MARY, who was waiting . . . he said, My lady, I repeated my voyage, your request, my visit to the bishop in his palace, and I proposed [for] the second time your request. I stressed that you sent me. I assured him that you were asking for a house and temple in this place . . . all this with insistence, tears, and sighs, fearing that the angered priests would either have me beaten as being inopportune, or dismiss me, seeing me as stubborn. The bishop, somewhat severe and . . . somewhat rudely, examined me curiously [asking me] what I had seen in your person and what I had understood of your conduct; as best I could I painted you with humble knowledge. I described you with my limited ability and I think that it worked, for between doubtful and persuaded, he resolved that in order to believe me and to know that you are MARY, the true Mother of God . . . that I ask you for a sign . . . that would certify your will and would convince him of my request . . . with a pleasant appearance and grateful caresses, the purest Queen of Heaven replied: Tomorrow, my son Juan, you will see. I will give you the sign.

Fourth Appearance

The following day passed when Juan was supposed to return to take the sign and he was unable to because when he arrived in his town he found an uncle of his sick and passed his time in finding medicines for him, which did not help because they aggravated his illness . . . The third day after he had been with the VIRGIN MARY, he left his town very early for Santiago Tlatelolco to call a religious to administer the sacraments to the sick man and, reaching the place . . . of Mount Guadalupe [he took another path to shorten the trip] and did not stop to talk to MARY [but she] came out to the path to meet him. Juan . . . sad or embarrassed . . . greets her saying good morning. And replying likewise, the pious mother lovingly listens to his excuse . . . the VIRGIN MARY, satisfied in the simple truth of his statements, reprimands him compassionately [and asks him] why he would be afraid of danger, afraid of illness, or be upset with work, having her as his mother . . . and protection . . . that his uncle's illness should not embarrass him for he . . . she assured him was already at that point entirely well. [And to keep her promise], the VIRGIN MARY, without delay, said: Climb up this mount to the very place where you have seen me. . . From there cut, pick up, and put away all the roses and flowers that you find and bring them down to me. Juan, without retorting about the weather—it was December, cold winter . . . without arguing about the nature of the mount . . . that all of it was flint stone . . . without saying from experience that the times he had been up at her calling he had seen neither roses nor flowers, with all haste . . .

climbed up . . . to the indicated point where instantly before his
eyes several flowers bloomed miraculously or prodigiously, blos-
soming marvelously, the roses combining with white lilies . . .
carnations . . . violets, jasmine . . . rosemary . . . irises . . . and
broom . . . and gathering up that spring from the sky . . . in his
rough, poor, and humble blanket . . . he came down from that
sacred mound to MARY's presence to whom he presented the roses
and flowers . . . the holy Mother, taking them in her hands so that
for the second time they would be reborn miraculously, . . . gave
them back to him . . . telling him that those roses and flowers are
the sign that he has to take to the bishop, to whom he is to say on
her behalf that with them he will know the will of the one who is
asking and the faithfulness of he who is taking them; warning Juan
that only in the presence of the bishop should he let go of the
blanket and uncover what is in it. Juan took his leave then . . . sure
and confident walking to Mexico City to the palace of his illustrious lordship.

Last Appearance

Juan Diego entered with the flowers into the palace of the illustrious lord D. Juan de Zumárraga. He found his steward and some
servants, whom he asked to advise the prelate that he would like
to see him. None of them bothered to do so . . . He waited a long
time and, noting his patience . . . and that he showed he had
something covered in the blanket, they became curious and asked
him . . . and since then no resistance would be of any use to Juan
. . . he could not prevent them from seeing the roses. They, not
without admiration when they saw them . . . covetously each one
attempted to take one of the flowers and, having persisted three
times and not being able to, it occurred to them that they had been
painted, engraved, or knit into the simple blanket [finally] the
admirable novelty of what they saw hastened them to advise their
master. [When Juan was in the bishop's presence he told him]
everything that had happened in his comings and goings and
visions and he said, Sir and father, in faith of what you sent me . . .
I told my Lady, MARY, Mother of God, that you were asking for a
sign so that you would believe me . . . the lady without difficulty
offered me these roses, which I bring you, which she gave me by
her own hand and placed on this blanket . . . She told me to offer
them to you in her name, as I do, and that in them you would have
enough signs of her continued desire and of my repeated
truths."He revealed the clean blanket to present the gift of heaven

to the fortunate bishop; he, anxious to receive it, saw on that blanket a holy forest, a miraculous spring, a small garden of roses, lilies, carnations, irises, broom, jasmine, and violets, and all of them, falling from the blanket, left painted on it the VIRGIN MARY, Mother of God, in her holy image that today is preserved, guarded, and venerated in the sanctuary of GUADALUPE in Mexico City.[59]

Thus, with this naïve flavor was shaped forever the miraculous account of the appearances of Guadalupe to the Indian Juan Diego. From this founding text begins the inexhaustible later literature, the very rich iconography and multiple theatrical representations that made this happening popular until it became the most celebrated by the majority of Mexicans. But Miguel Sánchez, who in addition to integrating a dispersed and certainly varied oral tradition, produced an interpretation of the Guadalupan miracle that converted that religious happening into the keystone of Creole patriotism into the irrefutable proof that New Spain was the country chosen by God himself.

Miguel Sánchez saw in the miracle of the appearance of the Virgin the redemption of all the ills that afflicted his homeland and the sign of its privileged destiny. For him, the manifestation of the Virgin in Mexican lands washed away the idolatry prior to the arrival of the Spaniards, it explained the transcendent meaning of the Conquest, and instead of the horizon without hope that weighed on the children of this land, it converted the Mexican land into a symbol of pride and optimism for those born in Mexico. He says in his book: "Let it be understood . . . that all the work, all the suffering, all the troubles that Mexico might have are forgotten, remedied, rewarded, and relieved by the appearance in this land and the coming out of it as from her mysterious and accurate drawing the semblance of God, the image of God that is Mary in her holy image in our Mexican Guadalupe." That is why he explains that "if God, for the first image of him that was to appear on earth," created Adam, "we can agree and say: that as the Virgin Mary is the most perfect copied image of the original of God . . . and as in our Mexican Guadalupe hers is so miraculous in circumstances and so unique in this land, prepared, ordered, and carried out the beautiful line in this her Mexican lands, conquered for such glorious purposes one so that in it would appear an image so of God." Persuaded by his own arguments, he concludes in exaltation that "the conquest of this land was because in it was to appear the Virgin Mary in her holy image of Guadalupe."[60]

These radical new interpretations about the deep meaning of the appearance of the Virgin signal a new phase in the Creole process of assertiveness, of what is theirs, and of progressive separation from Spain. By affirming that the deep meaning of the conquest of this land was "because in it was to appear the Virgin Mary in her holy image of Guadalupe," Sánchez devalues the epic of the Conquest that had been created by the Spaniards and at the same time makes the apparition of Guadalupe the central event of the history of New Spain, precisely because this founding event has nothing to do with Spain but is a special privilege of God to those born in Mexico. The actual presence of Spain in the carrying out of the Conquest and the founding of the society of New Spain is erased by this apocalyptic interpretation that makes God himself intervene in the appearance of Mary and converts Mexico into a new Promised Land, into a place where the miraculous prophecies announced in the Scriptures will take place. To give basis to this interpretation, Miguel Sánchez takes recourse in Saint Augustine and states that Augustine led him to read in the Apocalypse of Saint John the prophecy of the appearance of Guadalupe, a theme that he develops in a chapter of his book entitled "Prophetic Origin of the Holy Image of Guadalupe Piously Foreseen by the Evangelist Saint John in Chapter 12 of the Apocalypse." In this part of the Apocalypse, Sánchez reads sentences such as these: "And there appeared a great wonder in heaven; a woman clothed with the sun, and the moon under her feet, and upon her head a crown of twelve stars"; "And to the woman were given two wings"; and so on. On interpreting this reading, Miguel Sánchez deduces that the apocalyptic woman is the Virgin of Guadalupe, and he composes a tortuous disquisition to prove that the appearance of the Virgin of Guadalupe in Tepeyac was prophetically foreseen in the Holy Scriptures.

These Creole college graduates, priests, and theologians not only believe in the Guadalupan miracle and are its prime propagandists, but they give a theological, apocalyptic foundation for it based on the same religious culture that they inherited from the Spaniards. But instead of this tradition's invoking Spanish interests, as had been common before, now these Creoles use it to create a distance between Spain and their homeland and to raise the prestige of the Mexican land to the highest level.

Motivated by his patriotic fervor, Miguel Sánchez sets to deciphering the passage of the wings of the apocalyptic woman and reaches the conclusion that these are the Mexican eagle's wings to which the foundation of Mexico, Tenochtitlan, alludes. He recalls that the Aztec capital took as "device and coat of arms . . . a royal eagle on a cactus," and from there he deduces these surprising statements: "Observe that when she was on land, the apocalyptic woman dressed in eagle wings and feathers to fly: *that was to tell me that all the feathers and genius of the Mexican eagle were to be shaped and formed into wings so that that prodigious, sacred Creole woman could fly.*" Thus, Sánchez is the first, as indicated by Francisco de la Maza, to present Guadalupe as a standard of Mexico, mixing into that standard the Christian apocalyptic prophecies and the symbols of the ancient Mexicans. In a vignette that Sánchez put in his book appears the Virgin, but not on the angel, rather, on a cactus. Behind can be seen two eagles whose wings are posed in such a manner that de la Maza interpreted them not as representing the Austrian coat of arms but as the wings of the Mexican eagle. Instead of the eagle's standing on the prickly pear cactus, as Mexican traditions establishes, Sánchez has it be Guadalupe who rests on the cactus (fig. 23).[61]

The profound meaning of these surprising interpretations is stated simply by the author himself: "I became a painter of this holy image describing it; I put all possible care into copying it; *love of my country drawing it.*" And at the end of his book he states the reasons that led him to take on the job as artist and basis-giver of the appearance of the Virgin: "*I was moved by the homeland, by my companions, those of this New World,* having as best to discover myself, I daringly ignorant of such an enterprise for such a purpose that I presumed all would forget how guilty I was with such a relic and such an image *originated in this land and its primitive Creole roots.*"[62]

This interpretation that Miguel Sánchez makes of the appearance of Guadalupe as a prophecy and symbol of the Creole homeland will have a lasting influence on the movements for identity and assertiveness that will be put into practice both by indigenous groups and populist and Creole sectors. His account of the appearances of the Virgin will be the model to which so many learned versions will be adapted, as well as popular oral iconographic and theatrical versions. In Sánchez's account, the religious, messianic, and apocalyptic European traditions blend with the mythical idolatrous traditions of indigenous religion.

In the Christian European apparitionist tradition, the Virgin or the saints simply appeared as if prodigies in similar fashion to how Sánchez narrates the appearance of Guadalupe to Juan Diego. Another constant in the miraculous appearances is that they always manifest to the most humble people, such as the shepherds in the European tradition. In the case of Guadalupe, the miracle appears to a neophyte Indian, a most humble man who has begun catechism. And, as is usual in the Christian tradition, the meaning of the appearance of the Virgin is that she, through the building of her shrine, offers protection to her devotees, to those like the humble witness chosen to experience the miracle. That is, the poor Indians are those who will be the first to enjoy the protection of the Virgin. Other facts that tie the Virgin to the Indians are her dark skin and the flowers, the sign that the Virgin offers to Bishop Zumárraga, which in the indigenous tradition has always been an expression of the beautiful and pure. These characteristics of the appearance of Guadalupe

Figure 23. The Virgin of Guadalupe on the prickly-pear cactus, in Miguel Sánchez's interpretation.

along with the strong significance of the place where the miracle occurred, on the hill where the pre-Hispanic Tonantzin was adored, explain the rapid spread of the Guadalupan cult and its deep rooting in indigenous mentality. In cultural terms, it could be said that Guadalupe was the protective divinity of the uprooted universe of the Indians, the first divinity of the Christian religious pantheon that the indigenous made their own, and the first common symbol that identified the diverse social sectors that appeared from the Spanish Conquest.

Although the Creoles, as was seen in the case of Miguel Sánchez, continued in their task of appropriating Guadalupe for themselves, distancing her in turn from the Spaniards and the Indians, Guadalupe will no longer be separated from the Indians or the working-class sectors. To the contrary, her cult will extend throughout Mexico, particularly among indigenous peoples. Just one year after the publication of Sánchez's work in 1649, Luis Lasso de la Vega, another priest and close friend of Miguel Sánchez, published an account in Nahuatl of the appearance of Guadalupe, which he entitled *Huei Tlamahuizoltica omonextli tlatoca ihwapilli Sancta María*, which translated would be *The Great Event in Which Our Lady of Heaven, Saint Mary, Appeared*.[63] It has been argued whether this text is the mere translation of Miguel Sánchez's book or a plagiarism of a prior indigenous account written by the famous Indian sage, Antonio Valeriano, who was the most distinguished of the collaborators of Fray Bernardino de Sahagún. This controversy does not interest us here because no reliable proof exists about the dates and the authenticity of the indigenous texts that narrate the appearances of the Virgin, nor is there a basis to support the claim that these texts are prior to the first account published in Spanish about these appearances, which is that by Miguel Sánchez. The indigenous texts, all written in Nahuatl, are the so-called *Pregón del Atabal*, the *Relación primitiva de las apariciones*, and the *Nican mopohua*, or "History of the Appearances of Our Lady of Guadalupe," by the indigenous sage Antonio Valeriano. Independently of their date, what these texts prove is the diffusion in indigenous language of the account of the appearances of the Virgin of Guadalupe, an account that was certainly not invented by Miguel Sánchez, but rather, as he himself states, collected from preexisting tradition. What is certain is that the Nahuatl writing of Luis Lasso de la Vega, which contains the account of the appearances of the Virgin to Juan Diego and the descriptions of the first miracles performed by the Virgin, was added to the abundant group of oral, theatrical, and iconographic expressions that spread among the Indians the news of the miracle and the model of the appearances. The diffusion of these texts in the Nahuatl language, along with their oral transmission, made of the appearances of the Virgin of Guadalupe the most generalized model in the indigenous apparitionist tradition of virgins and saints, which, as in the case of the original model, will be apparitions bearing a demand for identity, claims for self-affirmation of isolated, forsaken, and uprooted indigenous populations of the Christian European tradition.

Following this model of the appearances and miracles of the Virgin of Guadalupe closely, the indigenous peoples of various parts of the country will invent other appearances of the Virgin in which they will place their desires for identity, assertiveness, and justice. As will be seen, this mechanism of appropriating of Christian symbols of the conqueror presents itself mixed with the revitalization of the deep indigenous religious impulses. It is impregnated with indigenous cults to nature, deities, wizards, and gods. It is joined to ancestral beliefs and myths and is wrapped in messianic, apocalyptic prophecies of Christian and indigenous origin.

Virgins, Saints, and Insurrections in Highland Chiapas, 1708–1712

The valleys, mountains, and jungles of Chiapas populated by indigenous groups of millennial antiquity and of diverse tongues (Zoques, Tzotziles, Tzeltales, Choles, Chiapas, Tojolabales, Lacandones) were the setting for the struggle that divided the Spanish settlers who invaded these lands where nature built spectacular formations. Fray Bartolomé de las Casas and the forty Dominican missionaries who arrived to evangelize the indigenous peoples of this region imagined building a society composed exclusively of friars and Indians and dedicated to making real the Christian ideals of the primitive church. From their arrival in these lands, they declared war on the encomenderos and the functionaries of the crown, engaged in and won battles against slavery and repartimientos of Indians, congregated the dispersed indigenous population into towns, and introduced into these towns a rudimentary system of ecclesiastical government and administration. In Ciudad Real, capital of the province, they founded the principal church and monastery of the Augustinian order and then built other churches in Copanaguastla, Chiapa, Comitán, Tecpatán, and Ocosingo. From these enclaves that they called doctrines or *cabeceras*, they evangelized the population in the surrounding areas and founded shrines and chapels where baptisms, marriage ceremonies, masses, and feasts of the patron saints of the towns were celebrated. In the majority of these towns, the friars introduced a type of religious organization that was greatly accepted among the Indians—the *cofradías* and the *mayordomías*. The *cofradías* (brotherhoods) were dedicated to a saint, and the brothers, who were generally the majority of the inhabitants of the town, participated in them with alms, personal work, and donations to maintain the devotion to the patron saint of the brotherhood. In this way, the Marian cult was introduced in Chiapas, with devotion to the Virgin Mary, Mother of God. The majority of the brotherhoods that the Dominicans founded in Chiapanecan territory were dedicated to the Virgin Mary and particularly to Our Lady of the Rosary. The monastery that they built in Copanaguastla was consecrated to the Virgin of the Rosary and the image of the Virgin that was

in the chapel was famous for having powers to cure the sick and aid the forsaken. A century and a half later, it was said that this image had performed no fewer than twenty-seven miracles.[64] The *mayordomos* (stewards) of the Marian worship in these towns were Indians initiated by the friars into the rudiments of Christian faith.

Nevertheless, by 1580, almost nothing was left in the fertile Chiapanecan territory of the Augustinian religious ideal. Uniting common interests, the encomenderos and royal functionaries had managed to destroy the power of the friars over the Indians and then they managed to establish direct relations with Indian caciques in the towns to impose tributes, remove workers for the haciendas, and control trade in the entire territory. Without the presence of mines and with the indigenous labor force reduced by epidemics, the Spanish settlers concentrated on controlling indigenous production, particularly of cacao, cotton, cochineal, grain, and maize, which were the products in greatest demand in the province and outside of it. They also had a monopoly on the sale of all imported products, which they forced the Indians to buy at extremely high prices. Around that time, the Augustinians also lost their evangelical fervor and devoted themselves to competing with the encomenderos and the functionaries in the acquisition of earthly goods and power. For their part, the Indians, the big losers in this process, saw a succession of great catastrophes that to them seemed to announce the end of the world.

Forced to live in the new towns where they were now exploited by all, the indigenous saw mass death arrive in inexplicable form through devastating epidemics that upset their weak communitary defenses. Between 1570 and 1610, great numbers of deaths, combined with droughts, plagues, and epidemics, decreased the indigenous population by more than one-half. The majority of the towns founded by the religious were abandoned. Many Indians fled to the jungle and to the mountains; those who stayed in the towns suffered greater pressure from the Spaniards. In this environment of catastrophe, unexplained death, and abandonment, several towns in the Highlands of Chiapas witnessed miracles and extraordinary apparitions.

The Virgin of Zinacantán, 1709–1710

So, where my account will begin is telling some things that happened shortly before, in the Indians' own tales, which in my opinion are related one to the other and above all I say: that the Indians are for the most part overly suspicious, very lacking in understanding, very inclined to idolatry and superstition, very averse to everything that is sacredly serious, for of the sacred

things according to their common inclination the only one to which they concur with pleasure in person and abundantly is the ceremonial, that which has representations of ceremony, that which brings with it many trumpets and sounds, rattles and dances, and will celebrate the saints who are on horses, such as Saint James and Saint Martin, and those that have animals, such as the evangelists and Saint Eustachia and other saints. Thus, as they are people of this ilk, some will judge them, as I do, that it was the devil [who moved] these poor things by means of malicious Indians [to see] several false miracles until the disorderly multitude was formed . . . they erupted in the barbarities that will be seen in this report. (Fray Francisco Ximénez, *Historia de la Provincia de San Vicente de Chiapas y Guatemala*, 1929)

In 1708, when the new bishop of Chiapas, Juan Bautista Alvarez de Toledo, was making his annual visit to the town of Chamula, he was informed by the Indians of the town of Zinacantán, located one-half league from Chamula, that "on the road to said town, within a log, was a God-fearing man who was preaching penance, and the image of Our Lady the Virgin could be seen inside that log, giving off rays of light." The "God-fearing man" was a hermit who stated that the Virgin had come down from heaven to favor the Indians. On hearing this news, the bishop sent Father Joseph Monroy, the parish priest of Chamula, to investigate the case. Monroy discovered the hermit wrapped in a blanket and inside a hollow oak he discovered the image of Saint Joseph, a notebook with many verses praising God written by the hermit himself, and many offerings of food and perfume braziers with balsam of liquid amber serving as incense for the cult, which was drawing a great "gathering of male and female Indians" to the place. Perturbed by this idolatrous cult, Father Monroy ordered the log destroyed, detained the hermit, and headed for Chamula, accompanied by the hermit, who was followed by many people who knelt before him "with such excess"—said Father Monroy—"that they even asked if there was to be tolling [of the bells] on entering Chamula." In Chamula the bishop and Father Monroy interrogated the hermit and then sent him to the monastery of San Francisco in Ciudad Real and finally freed him in May 1710.

The hermit returned to Zinacantán and immediately took up his old activities again, this time with more support from the people of Zinacantán. In May 1710, Father Monroy, in Chamula, again heard news of the hermit and of a new cult that was being celebrated in a shrine close to the town. Father Monroy gave the following description of that place: "Said shrine must have been eight paces, divided into dormitory and oratory, with an altar where there was a small image of the Virgin with

candles, cacao, eggs, tortillas, and other similar things that the Indians offered with all the perquisites. The shrine was highly decorated and lined with very clean straw mats. The hill on which the shrine stood was cleared, fenced, and planted with maize." What caught Father Monroy's attention was the wear that there seemed to be on the trail, even though the shrine had been erected only four days before. He was especially impressed by the great number of Indians who came to worship the image. Preoccupied by the rapid development of this cult, the father superior and Father Monroy decided to set fire to the shrine and once again take the hermit to Ciudad Real. There the Jesuits discovered that he had been possessed by the devil and put him in prison. He was subsequently transferred to New Spain, from where it was said he had come, but the latest news about this person indicates that he died on the road.[65]

As Victoria Reifler Bricker has indicated,[66] this event, so similar to many others repressed by the zeal of the friars, had repercussions in the appearances and insurrections that in 1711 and 1712 shook this region of the Chiapas Highlands. The characteristics observed in the appearance of the Virgin in Zinacantán will be repeated in the later appearances of the Virgin and miracles. It is certain that in the case of Zinacantán, the hermit who promoted and announced the appearance of the Virgin was a ladino , a mestizo who could read and write Spanish. But his message was directed to the indigenous population, which received it with great enthusiasm. In all other respects, the appearance of the Virgin in Zinacantán, which in general follows the model of the appearance of the Virgin of Guadalupe, created in this region a model that indigenous memory will faithfully reproduce in the following cases of appearances of the Virgin. The basic elements of this model are the following: (1) the Virgin descends from heaven; (2) she promises to help and aid the indigenous people; (3) she asks that a shrine be built for her; (4) the devotion to the Virgin takes on the traditional indigenous forms of worship: offerings of food and incense.

The Virgin of Santa Marta and the Miracle of Chenalhó, 1711–1712

The Virgin visited the region of the Chiapas Highlands for a second time in autumn 1711. This time she appeared to an Indian woman named Dominica López in the town of Santa Marta, located northeast of Chamula and Zinacantán. One afternoon in October 1711, Dominica and her husband, Juan López, were harvesting corn in their field when suddenly Dominica saw the Virgin, in human form, sitting on a log. The Virgin asked Dominica if she had parents, to which she replied that her mother had died and only her father was still living. The Virgin then told her "that she was a poor person named Mary, come from heaven to help

the Indians, and that she should go to tell [the] justice authorities so that on the edge of town a small shrine in which she could live would be built."[67]

Juan López at first did not believe his wife's account of the miraculous appearance of the Virgin. When he went to the place where supposedly the Virgin had appeared he did not find anything. Nevertheless, four days later he also saw the Virgin very close to where she had appeared to Dominica. The Virgin then indicated to Juan that he should talk to the authorities and tell them to build a house inside the town because she wanted to live in the town and not among sticks and stones on the hill. The authorities and principals of the town went to the cornfield to confirm the appearance of the Virgin. On the road, many people joined them, but when they arrived at the cornfield, the Virgin had disappeared. Nevertheless, the following day the Virgin reappeared and then the magistrates of the town were able to see her sitting on the same log as in prior appearances. The magistrates wrapped the Virgin in a blanket and led her to town, accompanied by a festive multitude that followed the Virgin with great unfurling of banners, candles, cornets, flutes, whistles, recitals of the rosary, and litanies. On reaching Santa Marta, the Virgin was placed on the main altar of the church, where she remained for three days, covered with the blanket that protected her. At the end of that time, when the magistrates removed the blanket, they discovered that the Virgin had been replaced by a wooden image.

These miraculous happenings created great popular expectation in Santa Marta and an exalted religious feeling that was communicated to the surrounding towns. Rapidly, the inhabitants, aided by the people of nearby towns, built a chapel to the Virgin. The authorities of Santa Marta named a standard bearer and two *mayordomos* who guarded the Virgin and her chapel. Domingo López, an Indian from Santa Marta, was chosen for the role of standard bearer. The witnesses of the first appearance of the Virgin, Dominica López and her husband, were named to serve as *mayordomos* of the Virgin. The standard bearer sang the mass and had in his charge the organization of the feast in honor of the Virgin. The two stewards were responsible for receiving offerings, which consisted of chickens, flowers, incense, candles, wood, and silver coins. Very soon, the town was invaded by a wave of intense religiosity, which increased with the arrival of continuous waves of pilgrims who came to worship the Virgin, coming from almost all Tzotzil-speaking towns in Highland Chiapas.

The chapel to the Virgin was built a certain distance from the church in town and was divided into two parts. The smaller was reserved for two images of the Virgin and patron saints of the neighboring towns of San Pablo Chalchihuitan, Santiago Huistan, and Santa María Magdalena.

The other part was made up of a corridor or gallery that the Indians used for their dances. This chapel was the setting for an important festival celebrated during Lent in 1712 to which Tzotzil-speaking indigenous peoples of the entire province came. Around this time, the Spanish authorities first learned about this cult and of its rapid spread in the region. In Totolapa, San Lucas, and other towns surrounding Santa Marta, the presence of the Indians at mass on Saturday had decreased at the same time as the pilgrimage of inhabitants of these towns had increased to Santa Marta. Alarmed by these facts, Father Bartholomé Ximénez, general preacher of the Augustinians, ordered the priest in Chamula, Joseph Monroy, to investigate what was happening in Santa Marta.

On the road to Santa Marta, Father Monroy passed through the town of San Andrés Iztacostoc, where the local authorities informed him of the miraculous appearances of the Virgin in Santa Marta. Taking advantage of his presence, the authorities and principal Indians requested permission to transfer the image of their patron saint to Santa Marta, as other towns had already done. Monroy refused their request.

Upon arriving in Santa Marta, Father Monroy went directly to the chapel, where he found Dominica López. When he interrogated her about the origins of the two images of the Virgin that Father Monroy had seen in the interior of the chapel, Dominica told him that the large image, which the priest identified as made by an Indian from the town of Santa Marta, was not the one that had appeared in the cornfield, but the other, smaller, one, which was wrapped in taffeta "that must have measured two quarters of a Spanish yard, just made by Indians" of Zinacantán as Father Monroy stated. To the question about when the event had occurred, Dominica replied, "In October 1711." Monroy reproached her because in the six months that had passed, she had said nothing about it to the parish priest, to which Dominica replied that the authorities of the town had asked her not to reveal the event.

In one of the documents that report on this appearance, it is said that the Virgin expressly prohibited the Indians of Santa Marta from communicating the miracle to the religious or to any Spaniard. According to this document, the Virgin said that she had come down from heaven only to help the Indians and that if her appearance was revealed, they would die. For the same reason, the Virgin was kept covered with a cloth the whole time. Also because of that, Dominica López had always remained close to her, because the Virgin could speak only to her and to no one else. The people in Santa Marta said that the Virgin had let it be known that all those who came in a pilgrimage to her and brought her offerings would go to heaven, even though they might have committed many sins, and that she would give them maize, beans, and many children.

During his stay in Santa Marta, successive groups of Indians approached Father Monroy and begged him to say mass in the new chapel of the Virgin, but he refused, adding that he needed to request the approval of the Preacher General of the order first. Father Monroy received instructions to expel the Virgin's *mayordomos* from the town immediately. In spite of strong resistance, he was so capable that in a short time he managed to get Dominica López and her husband and the principal servants of the Virgin out of the town, along with the image of the Virgin itself, taking them to Ciudad Real under the pretext that the Virgin would receive the honors she deserved there.

When Father Monroy managed to calm the people of Santa Marta, the image of the Virgin was placed in a box and taken first to the town of Chamula, where it arrived accompanied by of a multitude of Indians. In Chamula, the Indian crowd gathered around the church and spent the night scourging themselves and making offerings of eggs, chickens, candles, and money to the Virgin. The following day the image was taken to the church of the monastery of Santo Domingo in Ciudad Real, escorted by close to two thousand Indian women and men. In an atmosphere of great excitement, it was placed in the niche that was usually occupied by the Virgin of the Rosary, and all day long a great number of people of all classes came to contemplate the novelty. The next day the image was secretly removed from the church and hidden. Dominica López, her husband, and the man who had served as standard bearer of the cult to the Virgin were sent to jail. In the case that the religious brought against Dominica and Juan López, they tried to show, by various means, the idolatrous nature of the cult that the Indians had made to the image of the Virgin. Nevertheless, none of the witnesses and confessions obtained during the trial supported this accusation. To the contrary, these witnesses showed that the ceremonies and rites dedicated to the image of the Virgin were the same ones that the Indians normally held for the patron saints of their towns with the approval of the religious.

At the same time as the cult of the Virgin was developing in Santa Marta, news spread of new and surprising miracles occurring in the church of San Pedro Chenalhó, a town near Santa Marta, Chamula, and Zinacantán. Two days before the feast of Saint Sebastian, it was learned that the image of this saint had sweated two times. Shortly thereafter, news spread of the miracle that the image of Saint Peter, the patron saint of Chenalhó, had emitted rays of light on two successive Sundays. Moved by these happenings, the Indians decided to build a shrine to Saint Sebastian. The entire town became charged with religious fervor and in a climate of great expectation, its dwellers did "much penance and prayers because they said they were afraid that the town and the world were coming to an end, that what had happened must have been from their sins, which had offended God." According to Father Monroy, who again went to investigate these disturbing incidents, the instigator of these inventions was an Indian of humble origin called Sebastián Gómez, who, after spreading word of these miracles, became filled with pride and had himself called Don Sebastián Gómez de la Gloria. Father Monroy let some time pass so that the repression of this false miracle would not be connected with the events in Santa Marta and then burned the chapel, although this time he did not confiscate the images of the saints, as he had done in Zinacantán and Santa Marta. In this sense, as Victoria Reifler Bricker has stressed, the miracles of San Pedro Chenalhó were more successful than the cults of the Virgin in Santa Marta and Zinacantán. By appropriating the Christian images and cults, the Indians of San Pedro Chenalhó managed to create their own local cult, inspired by the traditions of the Christian church and, therefore, it could not be rejected by the Spanish religious authorities.[68] Nevertheless, they did not attain the principal objective that inspired these movements: to make the Spanish religious and civil authorities accept the miracles that sought to affirm the identity of the towns and underline the condition of the towns chosen by the divinity. Each time, in Zinacantán, Santa Marta, and San Pedro Chenalhó, the appearances of the Virgin and the miracles of the saints that the Indians thought they had witnessed were rejected and considered hoaxes by the religious authorities. In Zinacantán and Santa Marta, the images and the shrines of the new cults were destroyed and the witnesses of the miracles were declared possessed by the devil and jailed. Thus, to the extent that in these towns of the Chiapas Highlands the feeling of abandonment and greater need for spiritual relief for such desolation was stronger, the religious authorities showed themselves more orthodox and energetically rejected these "inventions" by the Indians.

The Ephemeral Kingdom of the Virgin of Cancuc, 1712–1713

In 1712, the Virgin made a new appearance in Chiapas, this time with transcendental consequences. In May of that year in a house on the outskirts of the town of Cancuc in the episcopal district of the province of the zendales, a young Indian woman called María de la Candelaria stated that the holy Virgin had appeared near her house. According to the account by María de la Candelaria, the Virgin asked that they build a chapel for her right there and that the news of her appearance be spread. The first devotees of the appearance were María de la Candelaria herself and her husband, Sebastián Sánchez, her parents, and another Indian woman, Magdalena Díaz, whom María de la Candelaria had first informed of the miracle.

Father Simón García de Lara, the parish priest of Cancuc, heard about these events on June 15, 1712, and the first thing he did was to destroy the cross that the Indians had erected on the site of the appearance and denounce María de la Candelaria's account as an invention of the devil. But as soon as Father García de Lara left town, the Indians built a chapel on the site of the appearance. The entire town participated in building this chapel. María de la Candelaria, together with Magdalena Díaz, entered it to deposit a bundle and placed it behind a mat. Then they announced to the town that the Virgin was already there in the chapel, and the whole town entered, prostrated themselves before the Virgin, and began to make offerings of candles and alms.

Pressured to obtain official approval for the new cult, the principal Indians of the town sent a delegation to the bishop of Chiapas to obtain permission to preserve the chapel and celebrate a mass in it. The delegation found the bishop in the town of Chamula but, on hearing this request, he ordered the group arrested and sent to jail in Ciudad Real, the capital of the province. Some Indians managed to escape and spread the news in Cancuc of the treatment that they had received. The authorities in Ciudad Real ordered the chapel demolished, but the people of Cancuc put up such resistance that the order could not be carried out.

About that time, Sebastián Gómez, an Indian from Chenalhó who gave a surprising turn to the events in Cancuc, came on the scene. In Chenalhó he had spread word of the miracles attributed to Saint Sebastian and Saint Peter. When he appeared in Cancuc he had an image of Saint Peter and a new idea to legitimize the appearance of the Virgin. He told the people of Cancuc that he was called Sebastián Gómez de la Gloria and that he had been in heaven, where he had spoken with the Holy Trinity, the Virgin Mary, Jesus Christ, and the apostle Saint Peter. In heaven Saint Peter had named him his vicar and lieutenant, and that was why he came down from heaven full of glory and wrapped in splendor. According to his account, Saint Peter had given him authority to name educated Indians to serve as priests in all of the towns of the province, and he had said that henceforth there would be no king, no tributes, no high mayor, or officials of Ciudad Real because he, Sebastián Gómez de la Gloria, had been sent to free the Indians of their heavy burdens. He also told the Indians of Cancuc that there would no longer be a bishop or priests and that that from then on the Indians would enjoy their former freedom and they would have vicars and priests they themselves chose to administer the sacraments.

Beginning with this radical subversion of the established order, the people of Cancuc and neighboring towns gave themselves to the surprising task of building, in an environment dominated by Spanish political power, Indian utopia: a society governed by religious and civil Indian authorities.

The chapel in which the Virgin was sheltered was converted into the religious and political center of the region. It was divided into two rooms separated by a straw curtain. In the interior room was the altar with the images of the Virgin of the Rosary, Saint Anthony, and other saints. The image of the Virgin was dressed in Indian clothing. In the other room there were two rows of chairs where the *mayordomos* of the Virgin sat. María de la Candelaria occupied the chair closest to the altar. She was the only person who had access to the altar when communication was required with the Virgin and she was the only one who spread such messages. The cult and the service to the Virgin adopted a model established by the religious *cofradías*. A group of about forty *mayordomos* alternated every two months to perform the religious services. María de la Candelaria was named *mayordoma mayor* (head steward).

Each of the towns participating in this religious movement sent their officers to Cancuc so that there they could be named vicars general or priests. The officials had traditionally been the Indian assistants of the Spanish priests in the parishes; that is, they knew how to read and write in Spanish and were familiar with the religious ritual. In the indigenous ceremony that was instituted to ordain the vicars of Saint Peter, the initiates spent forty-eight hours kneeling with a lighted candle in their hands. Then Sebastián Gómez de la Gloria sprinkled them with water and blessed them in front of the whole town. In this manner, they were ordained as priests or as vicars general.

This effort to create an indigenous priesthood of their own included the naming of a bishop, a position that was granted to an Indian from the town of Ocosingo. In general, the new indigenous clergy had the same tasks as the Spanish clergy had performed. Dressed in the clothing of the banned Spanish clergy, the Indian vicars celebrated mass, gave sermons that exalted the miracle of the appearance of the Virgin, administered the sacraments, and organized large processions. The most notable difference between the old and the new religious orders was the supremacy of the Virgin over God himself and the fact that heaven and the priesthood were now spaces reserved exclusively for Indians. Beginning with this new ethnic interpretation of the Christian religious tradition, the Indians became the chosen people of the Virgin and the Spaniards became "Jews," enemies and persecutors of the Virgin.

This transgression of the religious tradition was followed by an inversion of the political order. The Indians renamed Cancuc Ciudad Real and also called it New Spain, while Ciudad Real, the seat of Spanish civil and religious power, was named Jerusalem. Instead of the Real Audienca of Guatemala, they created an indigenous *audiencia* in the town of Huitiupa, which was renamed Guatemala. In Cancuc and the other Indian towns that joined the rebel movement, the elimination of tributes was announced along with that of *alcaldes mayores* and officials of Ciudad Real. A document prepared by the rebel Indians expressly ordered elimination of priests and religious and all Spaniards, mestizos, blacks, and mulattos so that only Indians lived in the land.

This total rejection of Spanish domination culminated in the formation of an Indian army, which adopted the Spanish military model. Three captains-general headed this army, one from the town of Cancuc, one from Bachajón, and the other from Huitiupa. Under them were other captains of lower rank, who in turn were heads of the different towns in revolt. Each of the soldiers in this army was considered a "soldier of the Virgin."

To strengthen the religious and political center of the movement, its leaders ordered the images and religious ornaments of the towns brought to Cancuc along with the books of the brotherhoods and the alms. In August 1712 they sent communiqués from Cancuc such as the following to the other towns of the region:

Jesus, Mary and Joseph. Honorable *alcaldes* of such and such a town. I the Virgin, who has descended to this sinful world, call you in the name of Our Lady of the Rosary and order you to come to this town of Cancuc and to bring with you all the silver from your churches, and the ornaments and bells, with all the coffers and drums and all the *cofradía* [religious brotherhood] books and funds because there is no longer God, nor King; and thus come at once because otherwise you will be punished if you do not respond to my summons and God's. Ciudad Real of Cancuc. The Blessed Virgin María de la Cruz.

Other versions of these communiqués announced the resurrection of the "emperor Moctezuma" who would join the soldiers of the Virgin to defeat the Spaniards. Around this time, Cancuc and particularly the chapel of the Virgin had been transformed into the heart of a great indigenous rebel movement in which some thirty Tzotzil and Tzeltal towns and some of the Chol ethnic group participated. The chapel of the Virgin was the religious center and the political and administrative nucleus. Every day mass was celebrated, the rosary was said, the Eucharist hymn was sung, and there was music in honor of the Virgin. From the alms and donations received, a special fund for the Virgin had been formed, which, besides covering the costs of the cult, served to pay the already-numerous "soldiers of the Virgin." To avoid fragmentation of this unity around the Virgin, other cults were forbidden: in Yajalón, a couple who claimed to have witnessed a new miracle of the Virgin were condemned to hanging. Also executed without delay was an Indian in Pila who wandered about with his arms as though on a cross and claimed he was Christ.

A number of traditional Indian beliefs in which supernatural powers, magical practices, eschatological prophecies, and old rituals dominated, mixed with Christian beliefs and practices flourished around the miracle of the Virgin of Cancuc and the messages she transmitted through María de la Candelaria (who had herself called María de la Cruz). This heightened presence of the magic and religious impregnated all acts that occurred in Cancuc. The people felt and believed that the Virgin communicated with María de la Candelaria and thought that, thanks to this miracle, Cancuc had become a privileged place, a town chosen by the divinity to have a unique destiny. Each of the soldiers of the Virgin thought he was a man touched by divine grace, privileged and unbeatable. The soldiers of the Virgin went into combat with the Spaniards convinced that they were protected by supernatural forces. They believed that the forces of nature combined in the form of hurricanes, floods, lightning, and storms would destroy the Spaniards. They believed that they had magical forces and divine powers on their side that made them invincible. Even when they died in combat, they would be resuscitated victorious.

The cult to the Virgin of Cancuc and the unusual religious movement that created a clergy of the Indians' own and a political organization that rebelled against Spanish domination were violently suppressed in the Chiapas Highlands when the Spaniards took the initiative and methodically vanquished the forces of the Army of the Virgin. In the investigations that the repressors themselves carried out to uncover the causes of the rebellion, what stood out were the excesses committed by Bishop Alvarez de Toledo on his visits to the towns of the region, the exorbitant economic burdens that the provincial governor and encomenderos imposed on the Indians, and other abuses. But no one paid attention to the undercurrent of animosity that had led these different towns to believe, based on their own religious tradition and Christian eschatology, that a providential messenger from heaven had arrived in their towns to redeem them and to terminate the domination that prevented them from having gods, saints, priests, and government of their own.[69]

The Canek Insurrection, 1761

Fifty years later, in the Yucatán peninsula, another indigenous movement exploded that combined the presence of traditional religious beliefs with a radical rejection of Spanish domination. According to the testimony of the Spaniards who put down the uprising, this rebellion began in a banal manner. On November 19, 1761, the Indians of the town of Quisteil, located six leagues from Sotuta, were gathered in a *conjunta*, or meeting, dedicated to planning the celebration of the upcoming feast in honor of the patron saint of the town, Our Lady of the Conception. As was common in the *conjunta*, a lot of liquor had been consumed and many of the participants were drunk. When the meeting was about to end, an Indian named Jacinto Canek proposed that the funds gathered for the next festivity be used to prolong the *conjunta* for another three days. The proposal was enthusiastically received and approved by the townspeople. In the drunken brawl that followed, a ladino merchant named Diego Pacheco was killed because he refused to sell the Indians the liquor they demanded.

The following day, Father Miguel Ruelas, the itinerant parish priest in charge of saying mass in Quisteil, was interrupted prior to finishing the service by a noisy, drunken multitude that threatened to kill him. And although other Indians pleaded for him to stay and offered him protection, Ruelas fled by horse toward Sotuta, where he spread an exaggerated account of what had happened in Quisteil. When Captain Tiburcio Cosgaya, military commander of Sotuta, heard this news, he immediately informed the governor of Mérida of the Indian uprising and he himself made the decision to go to suppress it, accompanied by fourteen men on horseback and one hundred on foot. Some sources report that, when Cosgaya reached Quisteil, he was attacked by the Indians, who, forewarned of his arrival, killed him and several of his men and took another named Juan Herrera prisoner. Other sources say that Cosgaya's men arrived in Quisteil drunk and that they entered the town slashing at the people who came to receive them, and in reply the multitude answered the attack with stones, sticks, and machetes. According to this version, to cover up a painful defeat and earn fame as a pacifier, the governor of Yucatán transformed this failed repression of a brawl into a general Indian insurrection and set in motion an ostentatious military plan to suppress it.

What is certain is that the riot in Quisteil took on the character of a menacing insurrection when the news was spread that in that town an Indian king had been crowned. According to one witness, when the celebration and preparations of the *conjunta* ended, Jacinto Canek gathered the population of Quisteil in the atrium of the church and said these words: "My very beloved children: I don't know what you are waiting for to shake off the heavy yoke and servitude imposed on you as subjects of the Spaniards; I have walked through the entire province and examined all the towns and considered with attention what utility or benefit this subjugation to Spain brings us . . . I find nothing other than a burdensome . . . servitude." Jacinto Canek spoke of the disregard that the religious had for the indigenous parishes, and he described the tyranny, punishments, and work that were imposed by the Spanish authorities.

On seeing that the people approved of his words, Jacinto Canek urged them to struggle against Spanish subjugation, assuring victory. "Do not fear," he said, "the valor of the Spaniards, for as we have set up camp in this town that was not conquered by them . . . we will take Yaxcabá by surprise . . . , without the strength of its fortress hampering our undertaking and let not the fire of the cannons strike terror in our souls, for among the many I have taught the art of witchcraft, I have fifteen very skilled ones who will enter the fortress with their art." He then put on an exhibition of his extraordinary powers, showing the gathered multitude a blank sheet of paper that, when it was delivered to one of those present, had everything that he had said written on it. "And having them completely charmed, he told them that he would touch the leaves of a tree, which would sound like trumpets with which a multitude of Maya soldiers and thousands of Englishmen would come to their aid." He finished by saying that, although many Indians might die in the battle, none need fear eternal death, for as long as they anointed themselves with an oil that he had and said God the Father, God the Son, and God the Holy Spirit," the gates of paradise would be open to them.

When Jacinto Canek gained the support of the people of Quisteil, he sent messages to the neighboring towns so that they would join in the struggle against the Spaniards. These missives transmitted messages like the following, which was intercepted by Spanish authorities: "Well, you may come without any fear, for we await you with open arms; have no misgivings, because we are many and the arms of the Spaniards are now powerless against us: bring your armed people, for with us is he who can do everything."

"He who can do everything" was none other than Jacinto Canek, who in the church at Quisteil and before the representatives of various towns of the region had been crowned king, "with the crown and blue cloak of Our Lady of the Conception, calling himself King Jacinto Uc Canek, Chichán Moctezuma, that is, King Jacinto Uc Lucero, Little Moctezuma." Apparently, the coronation of Jacinto Canek took place on November 19 or 20, although the sources are unclear on this point. The Spaniards themselves did not know who this Indian was who had been crowned king; the first definite news that they had of this happening was given to them by Juan Herrera, the Spaniard who had been held prisoner in Quisteil. He recounted that prior to escaping he was forced to kiss the feet of the Indian king. Herrera also spread the news that the revolt had been planned for more than a year and that all the Indian towns in the peninsula had been encouraged to support it.

Deformed, multiplied, and magnified, this and other news crossed all over the peninsula of Yucatán and created an environment of anxiety and anticipation of war. The Spaniards mobilized armed forces in Valladolid, Yaxcabá, Sotuta, Campeche, Sisentun, Tihosuco, Izamal, and Mérida to attack Quisteil. The towns closest to Quisteil were reinforced. At the news that the Indians were arming themselves, the governor prohibited by edict that they be sold gunpowder and imposed severe travel restrictions. In Mérida, waves of terror shook the white population, for it was said that the Indians who lived in the city were preparing an uprising. The rumor was rampant that the Indian *semaneros*, who were obligated to work without pay for the inhabitants of Mérida, would set fire to the city and kill its inhabitants. In this atmosphere of terror and suspicion, an Indian *fiscal* from the town of Uman was arrested because he was heard to say that the prophet Chilam Balam had predicted the destruction of the Spaniards.

Finally, on the morning of November 26, 500 Spanish soldiers marched against Quisteil. There they faced more than 1,500 well-equipped Indians who put up resistance. The battle was decided in favor of the better-armed, with a loss of 30 to 40 Spaniards and more than 600 Indians. A group of Indian leaders died in a house in which they had barricaded themselves when it was set on fire. Jacinto Canek was able to escape to the nearby woods with another 300 Indians and for a time took refuge in the hacienda Huntulchac, until on December 3 he was captured in Sibac, with 125 of his followers. On December 7, he entered Mérida on horseback with a crown of deerskin placed there in mockery by his escort. From that day on, he suffered unspeakable torture and his lips and his flesh were torn off with pincers until he was executed by a blow to the head on December 14. His body was ordered burned and his ashes were scattered into the wind so that there would be no trace of his human presence. Eight other Indian leaders were hanged and then quartered so that their dismembered bodies could be exhibited in various parts of the city and in the towns. The other prisoners suffered public floggings and all had one ear cut off to stigmatize their participation in the Canek uprising. In addition to these punishments as examples, laws were issued that under penalty of death prohibited Indians from using any type of weapon. They were also forbidden to practice their traditional feasts and to use their musical instruments. They were ordered "henceforth [only] to play Spanish instruments so that in this way all their wrongful ways can be dispelled." Finally, in 1762, the town of Quisteil was ordered razed so that no trace of it would be left on the face of the earth. Quisteil was never rebuilt and even today its precise location is unknown.[70]

The Millenarist Movement of Antonio Pérez, 1761

During the decade of 1760, around the time when the events headed by Jacinto Canek in Yucatán occurred, in the central region another Indian became the leader of a religious movement the outcome of which culminated in a radical rejection of Spanish domination. In this case, as in the religious movements of Cancuc and Quisteil, the Indians were mobilized by such powerful millenarist and apocalyptic ideas that they came to propose the destruction of the existing order and the creation of a new kingdom governed exclusively by Indians.

Notable recent research by Serge Gruzinski has uncovered some extraordinary collective events connected with Antonio Pérez and has illuminated several aspects of the complex personality of this Indian religious leader. The first known activity of Antonio Pérez was that of pastor in the town of Tlaxcoxcalco, near Ecatzingo, a region located between the spur of Popocatépetl and the valley of Cuernavaca. A large part of his life was spent in this countryside of high, snow-capped mountains and hot lands. From pastor he became a *curandero*, initiated by a Dominican friar who taught him several prescriptions and the use of herbs to cure the sick.

During those years, his knowledge of Spanish distinguished Antonio from the rest of other Indians and brought him closer to knowledge of European values and symbols. Antonio offered the sick whom he visited European prescriptions combined with Indian herbalism and magic. During his cures he recited the Credo and concluded his therapy by invoking the Christian Trinity: "In the name of the Holy Trinity, the Father, the Son, and Holy Spirit. Amen." He confessed that he regularly ate *pilpitzitzintles*, a hallucinatory plant that inebriated him, and in those hallucinatory raptures, the remedies that he was to use in his cures were revealed to him.

During the time when Antonio was practicing as a *curandero*, he acquired an old painting of an image of Christ, which he had cleaned carefully. He placed the image in his house and observed that, from that time, "many people came to offer flowers and candles" to the image. Thus, to his skills as a healer Antonio added the passion for the cult and adoration of religious images. The *curandero*'s house became a kind of local sanctuary that was visited both for Antonio's curing powers and for the image of Christ.

Nevertheless, this first attempt at handling religious images for personal purposes was punished by the priest of Atlatlahuacan with seizure of the painting and a visit by Antonio to the town jail. During this episode, Antonio tells of experiencing a rapture. He stated that when he was about to give the painting of Christ to the priest, suddenly he and the painting were transported through the air and then deposited in a cavern. He returned to the town in the same manner and then gave the painting to the priest.

A few days later, Antonio found a Diegan friar (a barefoot Franciscan) who asked him to accompany him to Puebla. They made the trip on a road that skirts the foothills of Popcatépetl, always keeping the impressive mass of the volcano in view. When Antonio expressed his sadness at the loss of the picture of Christ, the Diegan consoled him and told him he would give him another image. The friar gave him a head carved in rock crystal and told Antonio to complete the body with cypress wood. Later, with the help of a painter, Antonio finished the creation of this sculpture, which he baptized with the name of Christ of the Holy Burial. As in the case of the previous painting, Antonio placed the image of Christ in his house, and very soon he and other people began to say the Credo and the Eucharist hymn before the Christ of the Holy Burial and to give candles and offerings that were administered by Antonio.

On this hallucinating trip along the foothills of Popocatépetl, the Diegan revealed to Antonio a destiny that would change the course of his life and that of many Indians of the region. He told him that in the volcano he would find a cavern and under the cavern the Virgin, and immediately two springs of water would appear in the town of Chimalhuacán. According to Antonio, he forgot these revelations for a year and a half, but when he felt that he was going to give up the ghost, he decided to seek out Miguel Aparicio, Faustino, Antonio de la Cruz, and Pasqual de Santa María, so that they would accompany him to the cavern as witnesses. On arriving at the cavern, they discovered a woman covered with a resplendent mantle and saw that her body was like that of a dead person. Following the instructions that the Diegan had given to Antonio, they knelt before the body and said the Credo ten times before proceeding to make an image of the Virgin in *ayacahuite* wood. Once the image was made to resemble the Virgin of the Cavern, Antonio was to take it to the church of Yautepec and then again to the cavern, where he would find symbols of the Passion buried.

Perhaps because of the climate of repression in which they lived at that time, Antonio decided not to take the image of the Virgin to the church at Yautepec, but he did follow the other orders. Accompanied by "my son Matheo, his brother Felipe, María Theresa, Diego, and twenty-five other people from Izamatitlán, among whom was the *fiscal* Pedro, Pasqual de Santa María, and others," Antonio took the image of the Virgin to the cavern and there unearthed, as the Diegan had predicted, the symbols of the Passion, which were made of ceramic. Antonio took these symbols for himself and guarded them in his house. Pasqual de Santa María had the fortune of having the image of the Virgin in his house, and from then on, in this clandestine sanctuary, many followers of the Virgin gathered. They began to say the rosary, to sing the Eucharist hymn, to play music, and to dance in honor of the Virgin. Pasqual and Antonio became the receivers of the messages from the Virgin, and miracles occurred one after another.

From the time that Antonio and his companions returned from the cavern, the cult of the Virgin spread through the region of Yautepec and Chimalhuacán and became a collective phenomenon. Impelled by this mass movement that melded indigenous religious traditions with Christian religious symbols and ritual, Antonio Pérez took on the figure of a religious leader and became the bearer, before his fellow Indians, of a messianic message that announced an era of miracles and wonders for that abandoned population. Dressed in priestly garments of his own invention, he would administer baptism, marriage, confession, and even last rites to the followers of the Virgin. He appropriated the rites and sacraments of the Catholic clergy and mixed them with indigenous magical practices: in communion, he offered the communicants three kernels of maize and water, for he stated that "God was found in the kernels of maize as in the Host and that his blood was in the water." Antonio repeated to the followers of the Virgin: "My God is the ear of corn, and the three ears of corn, the Holy Trinity." To several people he said that he was a vicar, a priest, and that he would soon be an archbishop. *Curandero*, shaman, priest, archbishop, Antonio Pérez chooses for himself religious leadership. On the other hand, he assigned to Pasqual de Santa María, the custodian of the Virgin of the Volcano, political power: "Pasqual will be king of Mexico," he said.

This world of vision and wonders that the cult created around the Virgin, this intense religious sentiment that invaded the believers, plus the confusion of Indian religious traditions with the Christian ones, created in Antonio Pérez another transformation. He not only acted as priest and said he would be archbishop, he wanted to be God. One of the Indians who followed him stated: "He let himself be adored, incensed, his feet kissed . . . He told those who believed in him that they would lack nothing . . . Kneeling, he carried a cross on his back and said that he was doing penance for all the people of the world because he was like God . . . He had God in his body . . . Antonio had God in his chest." Another witness states that Antonio told them "that he was God and that's why we knelt before him and kissed his hand." To María Dolores, one of his most faithful adepts, he said: "I am God, and it is I who feeds the world." (*Translator's note*: See note 71 regarding all quotes in this section.)

At the same time as the actions of Antonio and his followers took control of Christian virgins, rites, and sacraments, there appeared from the depths of this movement a violent rejection of priests and the church. Antonio and Pasqual de Santa María, at the same time as they had the role of Spanish priests, directed fierce criticism toward the Christian church, worship, and priests. Some witnesses stated that "Antonio told them that they should not take off their hats when they pass in front of a church." Others stated that they had been advised "not to worship the holy images because they were human creations and only ours were good" . . . "Antonio wanted to burn the saints and insisted that we not worship Saint Catherine, the patron saint of Izamatitlán, because that is where the devils were" . . . "Pasqual said that they should not go to Chalma, Tepalcingo, or Totolapan because those sanctuaries were places of the devil."

The most virulent criticism attacked the corrupt practices of the church and denounced the priests' boundless greed: "The priests demand money from the Indians for any reason . . . The priests sell the world . . . They are not Christians, for they want nothing more than money . . . The priests are demons and impostors . . . In spite of all their books, they do not know anything and they are condemned from the start . . . The church is hell."

What is extraordinary and original about these religious movements is that, although they begin by attacking the church that denies them recognition of their Virgins, saints, and cults, this religious confrontation then becomes an ethnic antagonism, a frontal challenge by the dominated group to its dominator. Finally, it leads into a general criticism of the system of domination in a radical rebellion against the oppressing power. Beside the criticism of the church and of the priests, Antonio criticizes the colonial system as a whole: "The justices, he says, are not good . . . Tribute should not be paid to the king because that does nothing more than fatten the Spaniards . . . The archbishop 'represents Lucifer and it is useless to continue fattening him . . .'" The king, the archbishop, the tribute, and the justices or royal functionaries, the pillars that sustain the colonial system, are presented as examples of a boundless and insatiable appetite for money. This terrible and true image in the oppressed world of the Indians summarizes the irreducible antagonism that the Indians perceived between their situation and that of the whites. It is not surprising, therefore, that the most radical demand of this religious movement is expressed in ethnic terms and under the guise of an apocalyptic and messianic message: "Everything should be for the *natives*. Only they should remain, and the Spaniards and the *gente de razón* should be burned. All the riches should remain in the hands of the natives. The world is a pie that is to be divided among all." This new division of the world will take place when the end of time occurs, at the moment when the Holy Christ, who has lain buried for one thousand years is reborn and the Spaniards disappear. At that time, without evil or oppression, the Indians, the chosen of God, will be rewarded.

> Within two years and five months, the world will come to an end and Pasqual will be king . . . No more tribute should be paid to the king because that does nothing more than fatten the Spaniards, and that is why the world is close to its end . . . There will be an earthquake. The earth will begin to move. Within eight days, all of the converted towns should gather in the cavern and then the world will begin to shake . . . Antonio has announced that on the first day of September there will be a quaking of the earth and that in the month of May of 1762, there will be a great epidemic . . . Only we [the Indians] will survive while the Spaniards and the *gentes de razón* will be burned; this year the world will come to an end, but Antonio will be saved to create another one . . . All the *gachupines* and the *gentes de razón* will be burned. The archbishop will be chained so that the demons can take him away; all the riches will be consumed by the fire . . . [and the Indians] will be able to disinter the holy Christ, who was buried for one thousand years.

Nevertheless, the hoped-for millennium that Antonio Pérez and the hundreds of Indians who believed in his apocalyptic prophecies dreamed of would not take place. The cult of the followers of the Virgin of the Volcano was discovered and repressed by authorities in the summer of 1761. Around that time, the priest in Yautepec discovered in the barrio of Santiago 160 persons "idolizing" the Virgin of the Volcano in the home of Pasqual de Santa María. From that moment, the movement collapsed. Arrests were made one after another. The first confessions of the accused permitted more than 500 "idolaters" to be located in a dozen towns. In a few days, the movement was dismantled, its leaders jailed, and the Virgin and the saints confiscated.[71]

The New Savior of Tulancingo, 1769

In 1769, another important millennial movement shook the province of Tulancingo when several Indians united around a messiah who called himself the New Savior. This messiah was an old Indian who was accompanied by a woman who passed herself off as the Virgin of Guadalupe. Both were worshipers of an idol shaped like a cross and, driven by their relation with the sacred, disseminated in the regions of

Tulancingo, Tututepec, Meztitlán, and Tenango a millennial message that announced the death of the Spaniards, the creation of an Indian government, abolition of the Catholic hierarchy, its replacement by an Indian priesthood, and the end of tributes. The New Savior and the Virgin of Guadalupe said to their followers that the Catholic priests were demons who were not to be obeyed. According to their word, the only true God was theirs and he was dedicated to taking care of the maize and bean fields. Such sermons caused a deep religious shock among the Indian peasants of the province of Tulancingo and heightened the animosity between the Spanish landowners and the dispossessed Indians.[72]

Typologies, Organization, and Conception of Time and History in the Religious Movements

The Indian religious movements considered here, from the primitive cult to Tonantzin-Guadalupe to the insurrectionist movements of Jacinto Canek, Antonio Pérez, and the New Savior, are a small sample of the variety of religious movements that caused violent disturbances in the Indian towns during the viceroyalty. Each new study about these sectors discovers intense collective movements in the background of which throb social unconformity and political protest and outlines new charismatic characters who identify with these forces and become their leaders. In the pages that follow, I attempt to define some of the basic characteristics of these movements: the general conditions that produced them; their types and forms of organization; their dynamics; and the idea of time and historical development that is expressed in them. The particular situation of each Indian town and the general one of the Indian communities facing the challenges of the global society forced these groups to select from the past one part of their historical memory and to create survival mechanisms to resist the oppression of the present and to project hopes for improvement into the future. This interrelation between past, present, and future created an original discourse on the historical process, a specific vision of historical happening that distinguishes the Indian communities from other social sectors of the viceroyalty.

The Interrelationship between the Sacred and the Profane in the Indigenous Religious Movements

One characteristic distinguishes these movements: they are born and gain strength under the impulse of a sacred event that has occurred or is about to occur—the announcement of a miracle, the appearance of a

Virgin, the prophecy of an apocalyptic ending, the arrival of a savior who will wipe out injustice and establish an Indian millennium. In all these cases, the sacred event appears as an exceptional occurrence, as an extraordinary privilege reserved to the group that lives that event. This exceptional manifestation of the sacred is what makes the religious happening a hallucinating event, a miracle that electrifies the attention of the participants and sets off the multiplication of new marvels. Forged in heaven, wrapped in the aura of the sacred, the religious event always has an earthly and profane purpose: the apparitions, the miracles, and the prophecies announce an improvement in earthly life, particularly in the unjust condition in which the group that witnesses these extraordinary events lives. The Virgin of Guadalupe makes her appearance in Tepeyac to become the protector and "merciful mother" of the poor Indians; in Zinacantán and in Santa Marta, the Virgin comes down from heaven to relieve the forsaken condition of the Indians; in Cancuc, the appearance of the Virgin is interpreted by Sebastián Gómez de la Gloria as the end of tributes, authorities, priests, and the king of Spain and as an augury of an era in which the Indians will enjoy their ancient liberty; in Quisteil, the coronation of Jacinto Canek proclaims the disappearance of Spanish power and the creation of an Indian kingdom; the millennial movement that is headed by Antonio Pérez announces a new division of the riches of the world, the elimination of the Spaniards, and an era in which all wealth will be "in the hands of the natives."

In all these cases, the social convulsion takes on the forms of religious expression, but instead of postulating happiness or fortune in heaven, it proposes the transformation of the profane world, incites change in the existing political and social conditions of earthly life. The beliefs, values, and symbols that are manifested in these movements are religious, but the ends and aspirations that motivate them are profane. This sometimes-indistinguishable symbiosis between the sacred and the profane is a characteristic of the traditional campesino societies in which religion defines the social values, establishes the morals, watches for compliance with them, and is immersed in everything: it forms part of all institutions. Without "its presence no authority is legitimate, no initiative can be taken."[73] In cases like these, where the sacred invades the deepest niche of the social group, the social order can be changed only when it loses its sacred character or when that order is destroyed by an also-sacred mandate. As María Isaura Pereira says, "Political misfortune, economic misfortune, social misfortune will not be annulled by political, economic, or social measures; they will be annulled by religious measures and in general by a divine envoy who will come to put everything in order."[74] In these societies, religion operates as the only instrument capable of effecting a change in the existing conditions;

therefore, it is necessary for the transformation of the profane world to take on the form of a sacred action, of a divine mandate, of a religious movement. For that reason, in the Indian movements examined here, the divine announcement or eschatological message always plays an important part. Religious organization of the movement is essential, and the appearance of a charismatic leader endowed with extraordinary powers in constant communication with the sacred and resolved to transform the earthly world is necessary.

The Sociopolitical Background of the Religious Movements

Attempting a sociological explanation of the millennial movements, Max Weber discovered that in any nation having the characteristics that mark the Jewish people, messianic movements could occur. These characteristics were twofold: a persecuted and pursued people who finally loses its political independence and undergoes domination by another people; and the belief in a future kingdom in which the oppressed people would occupy a privileged place. The existence of a pariah community and belief in a messiah or divine envoy who would lead the unfortunate people into a millennium that compensates it for that people's misfortune were for Weber the basic conditions for millenarianism. To this notion of "pariah community," Weber added that of "pariah class"; that is, he indicated that in stratified societies certain social classes could be found in a situation of very accentuated inferiority in relation to the upper levels. In this case, in these abandoned classes, a messianic reaction would be manifested similar to that of the "pariah community," the purpose of which would be to invert the social relationship and place at the peak of the social hierarchy those who lived in a situation of inferiority.[75]

In this effort to find general sociological characteristics that, independent of the era or of the country, would explain the basic characteristics that make messianic movements appear, María Isaura Pereira discovered a third social situation that generates messianic movements: the anomie or social disintegration of traditional groups. "It is no longer a situation of political or social inferiority; it is only social disorder; the difficulties of daily existence in campesino societies multiplied suddenly by the decadence or the disappearance of certain social institutions due to the worsening of an economic crisis can disorient a community and the messiah is then the one who will establish the former balance."[76]

In the Indian religious movements that occurred during the viceroyalty, although few of them are in the category of messianic movements, we find similar political and social conditions present, acting as root causes of collective actions that seek to create common symbols of identity, to revitalize or to fortify the affected ethnic identity, or to create a new order where the oppressed have a privileged position.

The religious movement that concentrates around the Virgin of Guadalupe particularly starting with the interpretations of this miracle by the Creole Miguel Sánchez, is a typical case of creation of a sacred and patriotic symbol aimed at elevating the position of inferiority in which the original inhabitants of the country suffer. It expresses, in the condition of a pariah community invaded and dominated by a foreign country, the need to change that situation to one of a people privileged by the divinity, that is, by the highest recognized value of that society. In this classic colonial situation, in which the Creoles accept the legitimacy of the Spanish king and at the same time aspire to occupy the higher positions that are monopolized by the Spaniards, they are the ones who convert the Virgin of Guadalupe into Mother, Protector, Queen, Patron, Shield, Emblem, and Symbol of the Mexican homeland. In this fashion, the pariah community transformed the manifestation of the Mother of God in Tepeyac into irrefutable proof of the divine intention to favor the destiny of the Mexican land and created the hope that this Mother and Queen would lead her people to an exceptional future. In this sense, the Virgin of Guadalupe is a founding myth of the divine legitimacy of the Creole homeland. For the Creoles, as David Brading says, the appearance of the Virgin of Guadalupe "signifies essentially that the mother of God has chosen the people of Mexico for her special protection."[77] Beginning with the conversion of Mexico into a people chosen by God, all the stigmas that affirmed the inferiority of the pariah community are annulled and overcome: ancient idolatry, the charges of a degraded humanity consubstantial to the original inhabitants, the opprobrium of being condemned to live on the margins of the world, all this is denied and overcome by the appearance of the Mother of God in Tepeyac.

Nevertheless, by giving life to this founding myth of a divinity of their own and to this collective symbol that identifies those born in Mexico, the Creoles omitted the millennial and messianic sense that is characteristic of other religious movements of pariah communities. There is no announcement of the Second Coming of Christ the Redeemer here, nor the prophecy of a new kingdom, nor the hope of a final battle against the Antichrist. The appearance of Guadalupe indicates only that Providence has indicated Mexico among all the peoples of the world as its chosen people. Instead of the typical messiah, we are facing what we could call a Marian messianism: a conversion of the Virgin Mary into a divine envoy to announce a new era to the chosen people and to affirm before the powers that oppress that people the conditions of God's privileged people. Thus, without risking a frontal clash with Spanish power that subjugated them, the Creoles created a purifying myth, a divine symbol that granted those born in Mexico the quality of privileged people.

The movements born of "pariah classes" desirous of changing their situation and replacing the group that oppresses them were important in the viceroyalty, as can be seen in the movements that upset the indigenous populations. The colonial situation itself, by dividing the social levels in such a contrasting fashion into "castes" differentiated by the color of their skin, wealth, and social rank, created a battlefield where conflicts between one group and another were constantly breaking out. The deepest and most radical conflict was the one that opposed the white minority and the Indian peoples. The imposition of a Christian God, as well as the crushing pressures of tributes, royal functionaries, priests, hacendados, miners, and white merchants over the weak structures of the indigenous peoples, created an irreducible opposition between whites and Indians, making this relationship a permanent, festering, living conflict. Harassed by this continuous global pressure, the Indian peoples imagined all sorts of barriers to break this incessant offensive that threatened to destroy them. Under conditions of domination, they created a culture of resistance, a series of devices that permitted them to absorb the worst aggressions of the white world without ceasing to be Indians. They adapted their customs and traditions to the new values of the whites and by means of this symbiosis, constructed new community solidarity centered in the patron saints of the towns, the communal possession of the land, and ties of blood and parentage. But as they were defenses of minute, isolated communities, very frequently the towns' fragile balance would fail when pressure from outside erupted. Each new mineral or agricultural exploitation, each new transformation of the cities or of external demand, each new change originated in the political and cultural centers created new tensions that threatened the stability of the towns and put collective survival at risk. In all cases in which the integrity, stability, or cohesion of the towns was menaced by external forces, religious beliefs and symbols played a principal role: they served as a defense and as a rallying point for the threatened community.

The appearances of the Virgin and the miracles that occurred in Zinacantán, Santa Marta, and Chenalhó were strong expressions of the ethnic conflict in that zone. With the exception of the hermit of Zinacantán, who was a ladino, the other promoters of and actors in these events were Indians. Above all, the proposal to indigenize the Virgin and the miracles is deeply Indian. In each of these movements, the intention to create, in the face of the images of Virgins and saints imposed by the Spaniards, images and cults of indigenous spiritual manufacture is evident. Nevertheless, in all these cases, the objective of indigenizing

the Virgin and the miracles was frustrated by the intransigent intervention of the clergy and the Spanish religious. Thus, even when these
repressions suppressed the development of the indigenous religious
movement, they intensified the ethnic conflict.

It is also clear that the appearance of the Virgin or of the miracle is a
process aimed at raising the prestige, the authority, and the sacred rank
of the native people before the Spanish sanctuaries and before other
regional native cults. This is why the appearance of the miracle is
followed by the construction of a shrine and, immediately afterward, the
attraction to it of the natives of other towns and of the images of the
patron saints and relics of the neighboring towns. These actions wanted
to raise to a higher level the sacred condition of the town, to strengthen
cohesion and local pride, and to convert the chosen town into a regional
religious center, into a magnet, and a disseminator of the sacred.

In contrast to this type of movement are the religious movements that
occurred in Cancuc, Quisteil, the region of Chimalhuacán-Yautepec,
and Tulancingo. In these places, the unbridled antagonisms and ethnic
repressions exploded and nothing could contain the aspirations of
indigenizing the imposed divinities and establishing a native government and kingdom. Even when, at the start, these movements proposed
only to invert the religious order, they ended up by attempting an
inversion of the social and political order. In these cases, the ethnic
conflict between the Indian peoples and the white minority reached its
greatest radicalization: the pariah community demanded the destruction of the dominant class and the former's elevation to the privileged
place that it had occupied. In no other social upheaval, in no other ethnic
group was there present such an acute criticism of the multiple oppres-
sions that Spanish domination imposed on the native peoples as in these
native religious movements, nor was the reply that would put an end to
this heap of injustices so coherent: eradicate the foreign gods; create an
autochthonous cult and priesthood; suppress tributes and Spanish justice; establish a native government; organize an army endowed with
invincible weapons; finish off the white people and crown this extermi-
nating insurrection with the creation of an exclusively indigenous
millenary kingdom.

This native radicalism establishes a clear difference with the other
religious movements here reviewed. What marks the religious movements of Cancuc, Quisteil, Chimalhuacán-Yautepec, and Tulancingo is
the presence of a millennial message and the decisive participation of a
charismatic leader who propagates this message, organizes the population politically and militarily, and launches his followers into a radical
confrontation with the representatives of the power that subjugates
them. What is new here is the prediction of a better world, the mythical

belief that the abandoned, supported by magical forces, will upset the existing situation and be raised to a higher rank. Also central is the presence of a charismatic leader who mobilizes, organizes, and directs the action of the believers.

Both characteristics of this type of religious movement also have profoundly indigenous content. It is important to observe that the millennial ideas concerning the end of the world and the establishment of a new era, more than being inspired in the Christian apocalyptic tradition, come from the native mythic and eschatological tradition. In the Cancuc insurrection, the hopes for the triumph of the native movement are based on the miraculous resurrection of the Mexica *tlatoani* Motecuhzoma and the participation of supernatural forces: as in the pre-Hispanic myth of the destruction of the Suns, a succession of earthquakes, floods, lightning, and hurricanes would finish off the Spanish armies. These same forces, transformed into beneficial powers, would make the soldiers of the Virgin invincible and immortal warriors.

In the Quisteil insurrection, Jacinto Canek also turns to the mythic prestige of the emperor Motecuhzoma and has himself crowned with the name of Jacinto Uc Canek Chichán Moctezuma. In addition, the weapons that will defeat the Spaniards come from the native mythic arsenal: warlocks and wizards specializing in magic arts; soldiers immune to death; chiefs endowed with extraordinary powers; supernatural forces acting on behalf of the natives. This combination of magical powers and supernatural forces is also present in the movements headed by Antonio Pérez and the New Savior of Tulancingo.

Furthermore, the culmination of the movement adopts the form of a native millennium: between earthquakes, epidemics, and extraordinary happenings, the world will end; tribute, royal functionaries, the ecclesiastical hierarchy, and all the symbols of white power will disappear; the Spaniards will be exterminated and the Indians will take their place. In this new kingdom, "everything will be for the natives. Only they should remain and the Spaniards and the *gente de razón* should be burned. All riches will be in the hands of the natives." This disastrous ending of the world also signifies the destruction of the Spaniards. "Only we [the natives] will survive while the Spaniards and the *gentes de razón* will be burned."

In these native millenarianist movements, the earthly end that is sought is very clear: to destroy the existing order and to create a new order in which the indigenous people occupy the highest position. But whether it be movements that seek to create a collective patriotic symbol, movements aimed at strengthening internal cohesion and affirming the identity of a people, or movements aimed at destroying the prevailing order and founding a new kingdom, in all these cases, we are not facing pure religious movements, but rebel movements that utilize the religious beliefs, values, and practices to face concrete social and political problems. The origin of all these movements is dissatisfaction, discontent, or rejection of the existing circumstances. Thus, when unbearable social and political conditions exist, the religious movements become deliberate actions to transform that situation. In the traditional campesino societies, the religious movements operate as defensive instruments against the threats of social integration as a reforming means to reestablish the lost balance or as an offensive mechanism to end social inequality and political oppression. In all these cases, the religious movements are voluntary, concrete responses to the problems that the collectivity is facing.[78]

Organization and Leadership of the Religious Movements

Precisely because they are a typical expression of traditional campesino societies, religious movements are born and are organized based on the central axes of these societies: on the family unit, relationship bonds, and ethnic solidarity, in the territorial environment of the town or campesino community, and on the existing religious organization in the town. In traditional campesino societies, the relationships between the members of the community are direct, personal, and emotional and are determined by the presence of lineage or extended families that integrate the ethnic group. This is why it is common for the miracle or religious event that initiates the movement to be promoted by persons who are united by family ties; it then extends to other members of the community and sometimes goes beyond the environment of the town but without ever acquiring the dimension of a national collective event. Given the quality of these direct personal relationships and because of the limited size of the towns and ethnic communities, these movements were condemned to be local movements or, at most, regional ones.

Nourished by familial and ethnic solidarity, the religious movement grows and acquires cohesion when it rests on an already-existing religious organization. Whatever the type of religious movement, what is common to all of them is that, in order to reach their objectives, they use the already-established religious organizations: the brotherhoods and the stewardships (*mayordomías*), the cult of the patron saints of the town, the ritual and ceremonies created by the Catholic clergy. In all the religious movements described, the miracle or the new cult that attempts to develop rests on these organized ceremonial patterns. In the majority of these movements, the organization of the cult and the ceremonies are the same; what changes is the image that is the object of the cult, which is almost always of native manufacture. In the subversive religious movements, these patterns are also apparent, but those who preside over worship change. Instead of being Spanish priests, now they are natives. Also new is the appearance of practices and ceremonies from the indigenous tradition that are mixed with the Christian cult. In these cases, an indigenous priesthood is created. One or more native emissaries are in continuous contact with the divinity, and idolatrous mythical practices that come from the indigenous religious substratum are established. There is, then, a deliberate effort to indigenize religious organization and the cult. In Cancuc, Quisteil, and Chimalhuacán-Yautepec, the creation of an indigenous priesthood and of new forms of worship and ceremonies reaches extremes never before seen in the religious history of the viceroyalty.

These religious movements promoted even more radical changes for, by introducing the figure of the messiah and an armed body that was entrusted with the mission of destroying the Spanish enemy, the dynamic itself of the indigenous communities was modified. The messiah or charismatic savior is a figure absent in the majority of the religious movements considered here. But when it persists, as occurred in the insurrections in Cancuc, Quisteil, Chimalhuacán-Yautepec, and Tulancingo, the organization, the strategy, and the purposes of the religious movement undergo a deep change: the religious movement stops being a leveling action that reforms or restores social imbalances and becomes a revolutionary movement in an action aimed at subverting the social and political order. In the most radical insurrections, an offensive and defensive force is created that did not exist in the rebel tradition of the communities: an army formed by soldiers of the Virgin.

From Max Weber to the current scholars of the millennial and messianic movements, almost all authors have been interested in defining the characteristic traits that identify the messiah or savior. The typical traits of the Mexican messiahs essentially repeat that universal picture. According to Norman Cohn, the messiahs of the medieval period were, by their education, a kind of intelligentsia of the lower strata. The messiahs and the native religious leaders share this characteristic. They are individuals who possess knowledge superior to that of the other natives and who, like Sebastián Gómez de la Gloria, Jacinto Canek, or Antonio Pérez, lived for some time in direct contact with the Spaniards and their culture and particularly near the beliefs, symbols, and ceremonies of Christian religiosity. This knowledge of both cultures certainly broadened their understanding of the differences between them and also their hopes and the possibility of personal action. But, as has been reiterated, what is essential in the figure of the messiah does not reside in acquired qualities but in extraordinary personal qualities, in charisma as defined by Max Weber. The messiah can be destined to play this role from birth or receive this message at some other time in his life. In any case, this selection will be marked by extraordinary or supernatural events.

The messiah reveals himself to others by his extraordinary personality and his uncommon acts: he is in intimate contact with the sacred and has direct contact with the divinity through raptures, ecstatic moments, and trips that transport him to the beyond; he dominates supernatural forces, performs and foresees miracles, has divinatory powers and the power of prophecy. Because of these and other qualities, the messiah appears to the common person as an exceptional being, and his relationship with his followers is based on these extraordinary qualities. "His relations with the group that he leads depend strictly on his sacred qualities; his authority cannot be discussed because it is of divine origin. His orders are not judged either from the rational point of view or from the traditional point view, for he is a divine emissary, his orders are inviolable. Nor is his eminent position argued about; his supernatural powers are there to demonstrate that he has an indisputable right."[79] In this summary that describes the extraordinary qualities of the divine emissary, we can see reflected the personalities of Sebastián Gómez de la Gloria, Jacinto Canek, and Antonio Pérez.

The religious leader who possesses these qualities is also distinguished by his outstanding organizational capabilities, his knowledge and effective mastery of the multiple means that move the community in which he acts. In contrast with other religious or civil leaders, who manage to dominate only one part of the processes that they promote or in which they participate, the messianic leader is engaged in resolving the problems of everyday life, counsels and consoles his adepts, is attentive to outside events, and organizes his followers to create new hierarchies and commands. Finally, the objective of the messianic leader is to create a community governed by a new organization and new laws. Such is the case that Sebastián Gómez de la Gloria and Jacinto Canek exemplify as exceptional leaders who created a new religious, political, economic, and military organization, whose supreme authority rested on them or on a small group that included them. That is, they founded a new social hierarchy, organized a new "kingdom," a kind of charismatic theocracy with an economy, a social organization, a political structure, and an army dedicated to carrying out the most ambitious ideal that the native peoples proposed: to establish an autonomous and independent government run by the natives themselves.

The charismatic theocracies that Jacinto Canek in Quisteil, Sebastián Gómez de la Gloria in Cancuc, and, to a lesser degree, Antonio Pérez in the region of Chimalhuacán-Yautepec founded demonstrate the powerful presence of indigenous mythical beliefs linked to the decision to concentrate all the force of the population on the survival of the community; and also the inability to reach this objective through autochthonous political and social models of their own. If the engine that powers these movements is the native mythic tradition and the desire to continue being Indians, the means to reaching these ends are almost all of Spanish origin: the ecclesiastical organization, the forms of government, and the constitution and hierarchy of the army are taken from the Spanish model in use in New Spain. That is, if their mythical beliefs and their traditional religious practices are set aside, it can be seen that the model of political organization that the most radical indigenous insurrections propose is the kingdom imposed by the Spaniards, only inverted. Instead of the Spaniards at the head of that kingdom, the Indians will be the ones who occupy the ruling positions.

These theocratic kingdoms pursued the ideal of perpetuating the indigenous community through a clear link with the sacred, with the characteristic that the presence of the sacred, even when it was anchored in deeply indigenous content, adopted the organization and ceremony of the Christian church. This culmination of the dearest aspirations of the native peoples shows their extraordinary inventiveness in adapting the highest models of political and religious organization created by the Spaniards to their idealized plans of community: the kingdom of the Virgin of Cancuc, the millenarist utopia of Antonio Pérez, or the kingdom of Canek are projects that demonstrate the continuous capacity for adaptation of these peoples and an irrepressible intention of autonomy and freedom. But these religious utopias also demonstrate with terrible clarity the greatest weakness of the traditional campesino communities: unable to transform the earthly world by means of effective political and military action, these communities place their hopes in myths and sacred forces to make this transformation a reality. The result of this strategy was the total crushing of the indigenous religious movements.

The Mythic Conception of Time and History

Peoples without writing and therefore incapable of recovering and perpetuating their past, peoples without memory, without consciousness of their present, and without plans for the future, peoples without history—such are some of the qualifiers that the dominating classes used for the traditional campesino societies, and especially for the indigenous groups. Reiterated through time, these statements extended the conviction that the indigenous groups actually lacked memory of the past and a consciousness of historical events.

Today we know that these statements are false. As all human collectivities, in all times indigenous peoples invented or re-created different manners of gathering the past and developed a distinctive conception of historical events. Nevertheless, what is certain is that these indigenous forms of recovering the past and of thinking about historical development are not written in books in the western manner, nor are they expressed in the typical categories of western thought, nor do they narrate historical events, as western historiography does. Precisely because they are the product of traditional campesino societies, these forms of recovering the past and considering historical development are radically different from those of western thought. This fundamental difference between one concept of historical happening and another is what has prevented the recognition of the very characteristics of traditional societies' conception of time and history, first, because expansion of western culture negated and satanized the traditions of the autochthonous cultures and then because, in spite of the imposition of western values, the native communities continued to be traditional campesino communities, social groups joined by direct relations with like groups, with the earth, and with the sacred. The fundamental fact, as we have seen, is that these campesino societies never broke their strong link with the sacred, their relationship with the cosmos, nature, work, family, the community, the past, or the present; it was a relationship dominated by the sacred. What is essential is that that link, whether manifested in the cosmos, in nature, or in human life, was not explained by history, by the passage of events in time, but by myth. Myth is the peculiar form of "narrating" outstanding events that happen to a community. It is the means by which these societies perceive and live the sacred. What is distinctive about a mythical account is that it does not narrate a series in the time of happenings but that it reveals a creation. It puts on display a founding fact. As Mircea Eliade says, the myth counts how, thanks to the intervention of supernatural forces or the divinity, "a reality came into existence, be it the whole of reality, the cosmos, or only a fragment of reality—an island, a species of plant, a particular kind of human behavior, an institution. Myth, then, is always an account of a 'creation'; it relates how something was produced, began to *be*."[80]

In contrast to the western historical narration, whose assignment is to narrate the succession of human events that occurred in a place and at a specific time, the mythical account concentrates on sacred events, on the supernatural events, and particularly on the moment in which those events manifested themselves for the first time: in primordial time. What is important in the mythical account is not all the events but the founding events, creators of a new reality: the creation of the cosmos or of humanity, the establishment of the institutions, the founding of the town, the division of the land, the appearance of the Virgin. In this sense, "the myth is regarded as a sacred story, and hence a 'true history,' because it always deals with *realities*. The cosmogonic myth is 'true' because the existence of the World is there to prove it; the myth of the origin of death is equally true because man's mortality proves it, and so on."[81]

As we have seen in this essay, during the viceroyalty the mythic mentality is present in all the religious movements and in the center of the insurrections promoted by the indigenous communities. In the years that follow the Conquest, the myth of the return to the lost former age, which would be preceded by the expulsion and elimination of the Spaniards, drove the native insurrections that exploded in Yucatán and the region of the Mixtón. Later, when Spanish domination becomes stabilized, the awarding of communal lands to the towns and the erection of new Indian towns are reported in fantastic stories in which the presence of the mythic ancestors ratifies, along with imaginary Spanish authorities, the founding of the towns and the division of the land. In these cases, as in successive appearances of virgins and miracles, the myth mixes indigenous religious traditions with Christian traditions, but what is essential is that in these appearances of the sacred, the indigenous mythic conception prevails, the inseparable link of the sacred with the profane that is characteristic of traditional campesino societies. In all these cases, the myth legitimizes and consecrates a fundamental reality about the life of the campesino communities: it explains their origins, defines their basic relationships with the exterior, codifies beliefs, guarantees fulfillment of the rites, spreads the miraculous and supernatural events, decrees the ceremonies, and establishes practical rules and regulations for everyday use. As Malinowski observes, "These stories . . . are to the natives a statement of a primeval, greater, and more relevant reality, by which the present life, fates and activities of mankind are determined."[82]

This essential function of the myth is present in the religious movements that have been described here. All these movements are founded on sacred happenings that mythic thinking codifies and spreads through the population as evident realities; in turn, these new realities, by being accepted as such, unleash intense waves of religiosity and the aspiration of reaching determined goals. Under the guise of myth, there is spread in the community (generally in oral form but also through written information) the meaning of the sacred event. A new sacred reality makes itself known: the appearance of the Virgin, the presence of a divine envoy, the crowning of a native king, the end of the world. Once this fundamental revelation is established, the ceremonies, cult, and ritual that infinitely renew the sacred event follow, turning it into a living presence multiplied in the imagination of the believers. It is clear, then, that the myth is not concerned with narrating the story of the event or in telling its history and later developments; it simply reveals the original act, the first manifestation of the sacred.

In Mircea Eliade's classic definition, the mythic story is an eternal return to the origins, a concentrated search for the primordial moment of creation, when everything was new, strong, and full. This universal characteristic of the mythic account is also a constant of mythic thought that presides over the indigenous religious movements. The time that dominates the horizon of these movements is the founding time of the sacred creations and of the miraculous revelations. Neither the present nor the future has importance in the face of the primordial time in which the cosmos was created or the essential event for the community took place. The time that governs these communities is a past time, precise or undefined but belonging to the past in which founding events of the sacred reality occurred whose revitalization or new creation is considered indispensable for the survival of the community. In addition, the age or the kingdom that these religious movements propose to establish in the present or in the future is also a kingdom that once existed, in an idealized mythic past, in a golden age whose recovery becomes the highest aspiration of these movements. As we have seen here, the supreme ideal of the most radical religious movements is the return to the time in which the indigenous communities governed themselves without the presence of the Spaniards.

In this sense, it can be said that the majority of the indigenous religious movements are governed by the rejection of the oppressive conditions of the present and by the aspiration of restoring the lost past or of creating a perfect community inspired by the idealized memory of the past. The present is an ominous time that is rejected. Nor do they aspire to a new future, different from the past that is remembered and idealized. These movements yearn to reorganize or to reform the community so that the old traditions and values will prevail. They aspire to found theocratic kingdoms invested with the double prestige of the old and the autochthonous. They are movements dominated by protest against the present in the name of tradition; they are guided by the mythic idea of the return to a prior time in which the ideal bases of communal existence were established. Insofar as they reject the present and do not accept a future that is different from the mythic model, they are profoundly traditionalist movements turned toward the past.

In the beliefs in which the idea of returning to an ideal past age is manifest, the conception of cyclical time that returns time and again is implicit. We know that in the traditional native societies the idea of a cyclical coming into being based on the cyclical changes of the seasons and of human life was deeply rooted. Instead of a linear progressive time, these societies lived in a time that had a beginning, underwent an erosion, and reached its end, generally in a catastrophic fashion, in order to reinitiate the cyclical movement. For these peoples, life was composed of a succession of successive beginnings and ends, whose strength or erosion depended on the sacred and supernatural. The idea of an eternal return to the primordial time and the belief in a cyclical time are conceptions of life that reject the notion of a continuous historical happening, that deny the uniqueness of events in time, and that, in the last instance, seek to abolish time. This conception of time supposes that the passage of time erodes sacred creations and events, for life implies a weakening of the original forces that gave birth to the sacred foundations. To return to the origins is, then, to repeat the moment of original creation, when everything was new and replete with power. To repeat or regenerate time is equivalent to preventing the erosion of life, to suppressing the passage of time.

Another characteristic of the mythic conception of time is that of being a time occupied by the sacred; in the mythic account there is no place for human events as such. Mythical memory does not collect human events or actions, nor does it register profane human events. To the contrary, instead of individualizing or recognizing the particular and irreversible character of human action, myth ignores the historical individual and presents prototypes, archetypes, and models of action; it makes known exemplary behaviors converted into sacred prototypes. What is typical of the mythic story is to convert a real historical fact into a mythic prototype, into an archetype. In the myth, the individual happening is transfigured into a model or example, and the historical personage into archetype. It is true that the mythic memory gathers the outstanding act of the hero, it preserves the memory of the chief or the leader who performed notable deeds, and it also registers the historical happenings that affected the life of the community, but not as unique, unrepeatable historical facts. On the contrary, these events are remembered as exemplary sacred actions, stripped of their individual, concrete, historical data.

This generalized presence of the sacred in the life of native communities stressed its differences with global society and in particular with the white group. Throughout the eighteenth century, while in the native towns in the south, center, and north of the country miracles occur, new messiahs appear and more marvels are announced that seek to strengthen the cohesion of the community in the face of the disintegrative threats from outside, in the Spanish and Creole minority that rules the viceroyalty an opposite phenomenon is apparent: a strong reaction appears against superstition and tales of miracles, combined with a project of secularization of society, which, in imitation of what was already occurring in other parts of the world, proposed to diminish the presence of the sacred and to stress the profane world.

The encounter of these two opposing currents produced a new avalanche of pressures, breakdowns, and serious imbalances in the native communities. From the middle of the eighteenth century, the clash between the intense folk religiosity and the new desacralizing currents became a drama marked by successive confrontations. Under the combined impetus of the civil and ecclesiastical authorities, from 1750 the transfer of the Indian parishes that had been under the administration of the religious orders to the control of the secular clergy quickened. This process was resented by the Indian communities, for starting in those years, they had as spiritual leaders priests who did not share the missionary ideals of the friars who founded the original church of New Spain, or the "idolatrous and superstitious customs" that the natives practiced. In dozens of towns indoctrinated by these new priests, the natives protested and rebelled because they were forbidden cults or ceremonies that had been respected.

In the second half of the eighteenth century, a plan was put into action to accelerate the integration of the natives into the rest of society, through a program that sought to abolish the native languages and impose mandatory teaching of Spanish. Even though this plan to westernize the Indians met strong resistance in the majority of the towns, in some regions, such as in the archbishopric of Mexico, it had notable success and numerous schools were founded there, promoted by the magistrates

Around that same time, the Bourbon government violently attacked the foundation that supported the economy and solidarity of the native peoples: the community chests and the religious brotherhoods. The community chests, which were a kind of savings bank where the members of the town accumulated funds to cover collective costs and religious worship, were seized by viceregal authorities to satisfy the needs of the Spanish government. A similar plundering affected the savings and property handled by the brotherhoods. In New Spain the *cofradía* (brotherhood) was a uniting factor because it congregated the population around the cult to the patron saint of the town, and it was an instrument of social protection because the collective work and savings of the community had been turned over to it. In this fashion, the cofradías of the towns became organizations that owned lands, cornfields, orchards, cattle, and other property donated by the members, who also provided free labor. Traditionally, the administration of these properties had been in the hands of the natives themselves, who assigned part of their production to the expenses of the cult and to the feasts of the patron saint; another part was dedicated to strengthening the economic base of the cofradía, which in this manner became the greatest defense of the town to face the difficult years of droughts, famines, and epidemics. Nevertheless, these productive enterprises that the Indians had managed to consolidate were drastically affected by the government's and the secular church's new ideas: in the 1770s and the 1780s, the suppression of thousands of cofradías throughout the territory, the seizure and sale of their property, and the church's direct intervention in the administration of the provisions was ordered, with the justification that this would avoid the natives' squandering their property on drunken binges, idolatrous feasts, and other excessive expenditures.

This brutal and unexpected attack by the Bourbon government affected the economic and social base that sustained the towns and put their survival at risk. To this series of aggressions were added the new activities that the high secular clergy and the civil authorities manifested against the native peoples' form of worship, devotions, and religiosity and that of the urban folk groups. In almost all of the regions of the country and at all levels of the secular church, the uses and customs of indigenous religiosity were condemned and violent criticism appeared against the miracles, idolatry, forms of worship, processions, feasts, and superstitious mentality of the Indians.

Successive edicts, provisions, accords, and sermons concentrated their criticism on the "excesses" of the feasts of Holy Week and Corpus Christi, on the "nonsense" of the dances and feasts of the *santiaguitos*, on the "indecency" seen in the processions, on the "profane uses," "the scandal," "the unseemly women [*las indecentes*]," and other popular manifestations that before seemed normal and now were looked on as scandalous deformations of poorly assimilated religiosity, as clear examples of the superstition and ignorance that predominated in the lower groups. For the new priests and the new mentality, the traditional religious practices of the indigenous people became "demonic feasts," "hoaxes," "supposed marvels," "undue and pernicious cult," and serious transgressions against the true faith. One after another, the traditional expressions of indigenous religiosity, theatrical presentations, dances, and popular participation in processions were condemned by the new enlightened mentality. As has been seen here, it was this new mentality that was charged with denying the announcements of miracles and appearances of virgins that the Indians spread so lavishly throughout the eighteenth century.[83]

At the same time as the native peoples generated intense religious movements aimed at strengthening their ethnic integrity and their communal solidarity threatened by external changes, in the dominant group a violent reaction manifested itself against this type of expression by the peasant and folk mentalities. In the second half of the eighteenth century, the encounter between these two mentalities divided the relationship between the Indian peoples and the Spanish and Creole minority. The new enlightened mentality clashed head-on with the indigenous and folk mentality because one of the objectives of its modernizing plan was to limit religious expressions to their own ambit and to prevent them from invading the profane world. And, in addition, the enlightened mentality was resolutely against tales of miracles, fanaticism, and superstition, dark presences that it identified with indigenous and folk religiosity. Thus, precisely when the ruling minorities of the country opened themselves to the outside and adopted foreign ideas, institutions, and customs, the indigenous communities turned inward—in complex and poorly understood religious movements that attempted to strengthen their identity and "indigenize" the religion imposed on them. The radical separation between the indigenous majorities and the ruling minority was produced precisely by the invasion of new, modern, and enlightened ideas, and their political corollary: the adoption of a model of society foreign to the country and the certainty that in order to reach this goal society had to be modernized through a process directed by the state, by the secular power, not by the church.

This political and mental change of direction, induced from outside and from the heights of power, produced a radical bifurcation between the supporters of the project, who were a minority, and the rest of the population, who were the majority. Starting then, the project to modernize society provoked a conservative reaction from the majority, which was expressed as a rejection of the new impositions coming from abroad and in the determination to maintain and revitalize what was distinctively theirs, what was considered constitutive, traditional, and inherited. The native religious movements cited here give eloquent testimony about this very deep division between conservation and change, between tradition and modernity: the most radical are at once a rejection of the oppressive present imposed by the white minority and a complete turn toward the past. They express a violent rejection of the present, they fear the future, and their principal yearning is to return to a lost ideal age. Their perception of time and of historical development is diametrically opposed to the historical plan of their dominators, which goes against tradition and the past and is entirely directed toward the future. Contrary to the indigenous historical project, which has as a model an ideal past age, the modernizing plan is a bet on a society or a country that does not have roots in the past, that has not existed before, and that can become concrete only in the future.

5.

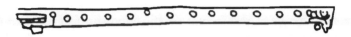

Creole Patriotism, Independence, and the Appearance of a National History

There is a notable difference between the historical discourse of the pre-Hispanic age and that of the viceroyalty. Whereas in ancient Mexico the ruler defined what to recover of the past and maintained almost absolute control over its interpretation and means of dissemination, in the viceroyalty there is a multiplicity of means of collecting, interpreting, and disseminating the past, with the peculiarity that each of these discourses differs from and even opposes the others. In contrast to the single discourse of the past that the ruler of ancient Mexico produced, in the viceroyalty there is a fragmentation of the historical memory and a varied and conflicting interpretation of the past.

The dominion that the rulers exercised over the production and dissemination of the past and the existence of a single protagonist in the historical narration determined the unity of historical discourse in the pre-Hispanic era. The protagonist was a people or ethnic group united by one language, one origin, and one territory. This is the unity that the Conquest broke. Spanish domination sought to create larger integrated political units (the viceroyalty or kingdom of New Spain), but in fact, it shattered the unity of the aboriginal groups by dividing them into hundred of towns without any connection between them. In addition, by gathering in one territory peoples of different languages and cultures and introducing ethnic groups that were foreign to the original population, Spanish colonization fragmented the old social unity. In fact, the viceroyalty came to be a disintegrated mosaic of contrasting peoples, ethnic groups, languages, and cultures, disseminated in an extensive territory with poor communication.

This primordial disintegration was deepened even more by the shock of contradictory historical memories that the Spanish domination brought on. To the initial confrontation between the Christian conception of historical happening and the indigenous groups' mythic conception of time were added the new and divergent interpretations of history produced by distinct social groups that sprang out of colonization. As was seen previously, next to the providential and imperialist discourse disseminated by the chroniclers of the Spanish Crown, there appeared the mystical and apocalyptic discourse of the Franciscans and a historical project that, instead of exploiting the Indians and the silver mines, contemplated the creation of a monastic community dedicated to the praise of God and the founding of a church similar to that of the primitive Christians. A little later, specific and exclusive discourses were developed by each of the religious orders, by the official chroniclers of the empire, by the chroniclers of the viceroyalty, by the chroniclers of the cities. The specific discourses of the Indian towns were also present, which, beginning with their slight individuality, sought to reconstruct their blurry memory of the past and to establish solidarity that would reconcile their destroyed past with their continually menaced and difficult present.

The presence of different conceptions of time and historical development and the continual collision between opposing historical memories favored the development of hybrid discourses, likewise particular to the new social groups. The incomprehension that has prevented recognizing the characteristics of the historical discourse of the descendants of the old Indian nobility or the historical memory of the new Indian towns or the discourse of the Creole group is perhaps explained because they are discourses that come from hybrid social realities, from a mix of different cultural traditions, and because they are discourses that reveal their own historical projects, different from the ethnic and cultural roots that originated them. The discourse of the descendants of the old Indian nobility is based on original indigenous texts, but it is expressed in European narrative forms; it adopts as an explanatory line the Christian conception of history; it is directed to readers who know Spanish; and it seeks to serve the particular interests of the Indians who collaborated with the Spaniards in the domination of the Indians themselves. This mixture of ambivalent and contradictory interests is observed in the processes of recovering historical memory of the Indian towns reestablished or created during the viceroyalty. In this case, apparently the towns had accepted the Conquest, the Christian religion, and political and social domination to the extent that their memory and daily practices struggled to incorporate European values into their most deeply rooted tradition, converting these values into Indian presences, or into values that made indigenous life and traditions legitimate. Nevertheless, when these attempts at indigenizing the foreign were rejected by the Spanish authorities, the rebirth is immediately seen of the indigenous mythic consciousness, the explosion of primitive religiosity, and a mobilization of all of the forces of the community to reach its objectives, to the point that the refusal to accept the miracles declared by the Indians leads to a radical subversion of the previously accepted religious and political order and, finally, to the definition of their own totally indigenous historical project.

What characterizes these discourses is that they are memories of the past and particular conceptions of history that, in addition to being founded on what is unique and distinctive about the group, reject or are unaware of the historical presence and the memory of the past of other groups. In the viceroyalty not only is there no single conception of the historical process that dominates or integrates others, but all those that are put forth by the different groups conflict with and negate each other. In this sense, these contradictory discourses faithfully express the social disintegration and deep division that separated the settlers of New Spain into antagonistic classes, groups, and ethnic enclaves. Politically and culturally, this presence of multiple memories of the past and of opposing interpretations of historical development was the principal obstacle to integration into one nation with a common memory, to creating a nation unified by a shared past.

In this battle among different memories of the past, only the Creole group attempted to create a common memory of the land it shared with other ethnic groups; it was also the only one that proposed to make the memories and historical traditions of the other ethnic groups its own.

The Formation of Creole Patriotism

The first Creoles, because their position and prestige were based on the deeds performed by their forebears, were proud of their Hispanic ancestors. Their social and economic situation rested on the prestige of being Spanish and the descendants of conquerors. This original support of being Creole fell into crisis when the crown attacked the basis of their economic and social position (the *encomiendas*) and set up in the viceroyalty a bureaucracy of Spanish functionaries that excluded the Creoles from positions of leadership. At the end of the sixteenth century, Creole resentment of the continued deterioration of their social position was expressed in a bitter animosity toward the *gachupines*, the Spaniards who came to build America, remained a few years, and returned to Spain rich.

To this frustration created by the contradiction between the aspirations of the Creoles and the realities of their era was added the problem of identity. The Creoles were Americans by birth and from the second generation they were so by destiny: their lives and aspirations could be fulfilled only in the land where they had been born. To be Creole became a problem of identity when the Creoles had to present evidence that the land they claimed as a right of inheritance was truly theirs. The Creole consciousness had its first moment of instinctive affirmation in the act of rejecting the *gachupín*, but the consciousness of creating a specific social group, with a common identity and aspirations, was formed through a more complex process of progressive physical, social, and cultural appropriation of the strange land that had been imposed on them as their destiny.

To conquer and to populate, not just to administer, was the motto of Cortés's men and of the successive waves of Spanish colonists. Also, the size of the territory, its ecological diversity and very rich human variety forced a few thousand Spaniards to spread out throughout the land and to establish mines, haciendas, workshops, artisans' shops, monasteries, ports, settlements, and cities that radically transformed these spaces. This characteristic of Spanish settlement turned even the first generation of Creoles into an Indianized generation of Spanish ancestry, but strongly influenced by Indians and mestizo foods, customs, and way of life. In contrast to the other European colonists who settled in America, the first groups of Spanish colonists felt they owned the land they populated, both materially and culturally, for no one else had created that new economic and social reality that they called New Spain.

This appropriation of the land by works and deeds was completed by an appropriation carried out through the conscience. At the same time as the Spanish language became the principal communication vehicle of the inhabitants of the viceroyalty, the Creoles subjected it to a constant process of Americanization. The first chroniclers stressed the contrast between the harsh speech of the peninsular Spanish and the more florid, delicate, and high-sounding language of the Creoles, as well as the notable differences of tone and accent of the Spanish spoken in New Spain. In a fashion parallel to the creation of distinctions of what was properly Spanish, in the Creoles there was an emphasis on the inverse process of approximation to the ground, geography, and traditions of American lands.

At the end of the seventeenth century, the Creoles found in the pre-Hispanic past and the exuberant American nature two distinctive elements that separated them from the Spaniards and affirmed their identity with the land that protected them. In this century, the chroniclers, particularly Juan de Torquemada, Carlos de Sigüenza, and Agustín de Vetancurt, praised Indian antiquity and offered an exalted presentation of the natural riches of American lands. In the *Monarquía indiana* by the Franciscan Juan de Torquemada, the pre-Hispanic past is raised to the level of classical antiquity, even when Torquemada considers the Indian religion, as do Sahagún and Gerónimo de Mendieta, as a perverse product of the devil. But for Torquemada, the pagan essence of the Indian was redeemed by evangelization: "the [Indians'] things lasted until the trumpet of the divine voice sounded, which was for the Christians to come, with evangelical law and our people's conquest of these peoples, because God wished that they be divided so that those who were to conquer them might better come in." Torquemada compares Cortés to Moses, who freed the children of Israel from paganism, and presents the missionaries as the providential redeemers of a humanity that had fallen into the hands of the devil. According to this interpretation, the true founders of New Spain were then the friars who started their missionary task in 1524, not the conquerors.

In turn, Agustín de Vetancurt reached the conclusion that the New World was superior to the Old in natural resources and beauty. For his part, Carlos de Sigüenza y Góngora repeatedly confessed "great love, which I have owed to my homeland," and with that patriotic spirit for his place of origin, he gathered codices, collected archaeological pieces, and defended the kings and cultures that flowered in Indian antiquity. He added a new argument to the impulse to separate New Spain from its familial link to the conquerors: he identified the Indian god-hero Quetzalcóatl with the apostle Saint Thomas, to support the idea that the gospel had been preached in America many years before the Conquest. Furthermore, following Torquemada, Sigüenza y Góngora saw in the laws and ancient Mexicans' ways of governing political virtues like those of the kings of classical antiquity. So convinced was he of this that on the occasion of the arrival of a new viceroy, he had the audacity to build a triumphal arch decorated with the figures of Indian kings and sages. He later reiterated this message in his *Teatro de virtudes políticas que constituyen a un príncipe: advertidas en los monarcas antiguos del mexicano imperio, con cuyas efigies se hermoseó el arco triunfal. . . .* [1]

In addition, toward the end of that century and during the first half of the eighteenth, the Guadalupan devotion became a generalized patriotic cult. In 1757 Pope Benedict XIV declared the "universal sponsorship" of the Virgin of Guadalupe over New Spain, and around that time the new collegiate church building of Guadalupe was constructed. Already converted into official patron of the Mexicans, Guadalupe will enjoy in this century a generalized cult and fervor, to such an extent that the "devotion to Guadalupe eclipsed the devotion to Jesus."[2] The majority of the sermons, the most emotional acts of faith, the new sanctuaries, and many other religious actions were aimed at exalting the image of Guadalupe as patron and protective goddess of a patriotic religion and to consider her shrine in Tepeyac as the seat of the Universal Church, "because it is in the sanctuary of Guadalupe where the throne of Saint Peter will come to find refuge at the end of time."[3] For these Creoles, obsessed with exalting the values of their homeland, the sponsorship of Guadalupe converted Mexico into a new Rome.

Principal devotion of the Jesuits, of a good part of the mendicant orders, and particularly of the high and low Creole clergy, the Virgin of Guadalupe was also the center of the popular mass cult. Periodic visits and processions to Tepeyac, theatrical representations of the appearance of the Virgin to Juan Diego, and folk imagery elevated the Guadalupe cult to the highest seat of honor of Mexican religiosity and reproduced the name of the Virgin in hundreds of new altars, sanctuaries, shrines, brotherhoods, toponyms, and names of persons.

It is not, then, by chance that indigenous antiquity and the Guadalupe cult were the attractions that captured the imagination of Lorenzo Boturini Benaduci, an Italian gentleman who visited Mexico between 1736 and 1743 and for the rest of his life was tied to these two axes of Creole patriotism. Boturini's stay produced three important results. First, obsessed with knowing and explaining the history of the ancient indigenous cultures, he undertook a laborious search for codices and written testimony that in seven years made him the possessor of the greatest documentary collection on ancient Mexico that had been gathered in New Spain. Second, Boturini was one of the first enthusiastic admirers of *La scienza nuova* (1725), the work by Gianbattista Vico that set forth a revolutionary interpretation of the development of human history, taking as example the ancient history of the west. Influenced by this new interpretation of the historical process that Vico divided into three ages (that of the gods, that of the heroes, and that of human beings), Boturini decided to apply Vico's conception to the Indians' ancient history in Mexico. With this purpose, he wrote his *Idea de una nueva historia general de la América septentrional* and planned to write a *Historia general de la América septentrional*, which he did not finish. In Boturini's *Idea*, the methods of new European philosophy are applied to discover the origin and development of Mexico's ancient culture.

Third, in addition to his scientific obsessions, Boturini was attracted, without a doubt, by his relationship with the Creoles, by "a superior impulse" to investigate "the prodigious miracle of the appearance of our patron Guadalupe." To that end, he gathered a great number of documents on that topic. Converted to a devotee of Guadalupe, he promoted in Rome nothing less than the coronation of the Virgin, an enterprise that, since it did not take into account the patriotic and religious zeal of the inhabitants of New Spain, led him to exile and the loss of his extremely valuable collection of historical and religious documents.[4]

At mid-eighteenth century, the Creole attempts to recover the indigenous past and other intense forms of religiosity were the center of a devastating attack by some of the most influential authors of the European Enlightenment. Between 1749 and 1780, the Count of Buffon, Abbot Raynal, Cornelius de Pauw, and the distinguished Scottish historian William Robertson proclaimed a peculiar degeneration of American nature, discovered a natural inferiority in native American creation of works of culture, and attacked the religious fanaticism of the Spaniards.[5] Robertson states in *The History of America* (1777) that the Aztecs had barely reached the state of barbarism without reaching the heights of true civilization. With Protestant severity, he criticized the influence of the Catholic religion in the administration of the Spanish colonies and issued multiple judgments against the obscurantism, superstition, and administrative inefficiency of the Hapsburg dynasty, whose monarchs he blamed for the decadence that struck down Spain beginning in the seventeenth century.[6]

When this critical wave reached New Spain, it raised unanimous indignation in the religious and the educated Creoles, who were the group that had done the most to build a positive image of American nature, to create a new and favorable interpretation of the pre-Hispanic past, and to support the creative virtues of those born in America. To the derogatory statement that New Spain was an "intellectual desert," Juan José Eguiara y Eguren replied with the first monumental *Bibliotheca mexicana* (1755), a work dedicated to demonstrating the scientific and literary production of the Mexicans from most ancient times to the first decades of the eighteenth century.[7] But the most consistent reply of the Americans to the European criticism was produced from his remote Italian exile by the Jesuit Francisco Javier Clavijero, who wrote his *Storia antica del Messico* (1780), without a doubt the most outstanding American contribution to the dispute about the New World and a key work in the affirmation of Creole historical consciousness.

Handling the theses of enlightened thought with confidence and imbued with profound patriotism, Clavijero destroyed the prejudiced statements of the European critics and in their place presented a glowing portrait of Mexico's ancient history, which, by placing this history within the perspective of the development of classical civilizations of Europe, shows it to be an original history deserving of admiration. By proposing the uniformity of human nature as an analytical principle, Clavijero destroyed, on the one hand, the thesis of "natural inferiority" that Enlightenment critics argued and, on the other, disqualified the interpretations about the intervention of the devil that had been made by Spanish friars to denigrate the paganism and idolatry of the indigenous people.

Clavijero's response to the European critics had an immense and definitive effect in his own country, in the first place, because his history came to be the first coherent, systematic, and modern integration of the Mexican past into a single book, the first successful image of a blurred and until then incomprehensible past. In the second place, by taking up the defense of this fragmented and demonized past, Clavijero took the hardest step in the complex process that had perturbed the Creoles for more than two centuries in order to found their identity: he accepted that past as his own, as the root and substantial part of his homeland. Beginning with this conversion of the foreign into his own, Clavijero was able to offer a reconstruction of the indigenous past as a proud inheritance of the Creoles without connecting this illustrious past with the degraded situation of the surviving natives.

In contrast with the Creole elites of the viceroyalties of Peru or New Granada, which for various reasons distanced themselves from the pre-Hispanic past and from their indigenous descendants, the Creoles of New Spain had the inspired notion of appropriating the indigenous past to give historical legitimacy to their own claims and separated that past from its true historical descendants. This expropriation of the indigenous past, which was carried out by the Creole intelligentsia, marks the essential difference between the Creoles of New Spain and those of the other viceroyalties of the continent, it explains the basis the Creoles of New Spain used in taking up the political leadership of their own country and demanding from the peninsular Spaniards the right to rule and govern the destiny of their homeland.

The *Historia antigua de México* culminates the long process that was initiated by the missionaries and the Creoles to recover the pre-Hispanic past and take it up as their own past. From the dedication, Clavijero states that his book is "a history of Mexico written by a Mexican," which he delivers "as a testimony of my very sincere love for my homeland," and whose principal aim is the "utility of my compatriots." Clavijero is the first historian to present a new and integrated image of the indigenous past and the first writer to reject European ethnocentrism and support the cultural independence of the Mexican Creoles from the Europeans. Another contribution was to open a broad historical horizon to the development of the notion of homeland, which, at that time, by including pre-Columbian historical background, takes on the prestige of the past and projects an extraordinary political dimension to the future.[8]

Clavijero's homeland is the complex of values that the Creoles identify as their own. It is a homeland that is not given, but constructed and declared beginning with the recognition of communal values. First was a homeland identified by the originality of its geography, recognized by its qualities as a prodigious land, exuberant and good until it became the belief of many that Mexico was an earthly paradise, a gift of God. Later, this geographic notion was enriched by the incorporation of intimate cultural values and traditions, by the unity of sentiments, beliefs, and practices that the Catholic religion spread, by the presence of the unrestrained baroque style and the proliferation of various forms of painting, music, handicrafts, foods, customs, and manners of expression, created in the country itself and produced especially to satisfy the tastes of its people. Finally, this community of values and practices was expressed in symbols whose purpose was to denote a shared identity, affirm a unity located beyond the divisions created by race and abysmal economic and social differences. The Virgin of Guadalupe was the most successful unifying symbol of this unevenly divided society. She united Catholics and Indians in one nationally celebrated cult. To this group of integrated values and symbols, the Creoles of the eighteenth century added the idea that that homeland had a remote past, a past that, by being accepted by them, stopped being only Indian to become Creole and Mexican. Thus, by integrating indigenous antiquity into the notion of homeland, the Creoles expropriated their own past from the Indians and made of this past a legitimate and prestigious history of the Creole homeland. The Creole homeland now had a remote and noble past and a present unified by shared cultural values and religious symbols, and it could therefore legitimately demand the right of governing its future. No other group or class created integrated symbols endowed with that force, nor did any other group have the ability to introduce and extend those symbols to the rest of the population.

Clavijero's work, by being so decisive in the creation of a new dimension of the historical consciousness of the Creoles, was one of several that were published between 1750 and 1810 that changed the conception of the past. The deepest root of this past, ancient Mexico, was seen in a new light by the Creoles who were educated under the influence of the modern ideas and the Enlightenment. In the same years during which Clavijero was writing his *Historia*, Mariano Veytia, a Creole educated in Spain and influenced by Boturini, finished his *Historia antigua de México*, which was published many years later, in 1836.[9] The proverbial curiosity of José Antonio Alzate, the famous editor of the *Gazetas de literatura*, got him interested in ancient monuments, for he said that a "building manifests the character and culture of the people." He thought that the buildings were a valuable witness for "finding out" the "origin of the Indians." Driven by those interests, in 1788 he published a text in which for the first time he described the archaeological monuments of Tajín and later came out with a work entitled *Antigüedades de Xochicalco* (1791), which is the first publication illustrated with prints that provides information about an ancient city.[10]

To another Creole, Antonio de León y Gama, is owed, according to José Fernando Ramírez, "the first and only rigorously archaeological research that Mexico can claim." Educated in astronomy and physics, León y Gama published in 1792 his *Descripción histórica y cronológica de las dos piedras*, which he dedicated to the analysis of the Coatlicue and the Sun Stone, two monoliths discovered accidentally in 1790. As a sign of the change that had taken place in the viceroyalty, instead of the monuments' being destroyed, as had been common, the viceroy himself, Revillagigedo, ordered them preserved. Another indication of the changing times was that the study that León y Gama dedicated to the Sun Stone left its mark on archaeological investigations. León y Gama, for the first time, took an archaeological monument as a primary source for explaining an entire system of ideas and he undertook this enterprise with unusual intellectual skills: to his knowledge of astronomy and mathematics he added that of Nahuatl and consultation of most of the codices and Indian texts known at that time; against the current of his time, he made it clear that the indigenous calendar was governed by its own concepts and could not be studied using the categories of the European calendar. He demolished the prior errors of interpretation and shed new light on the system of computing time and the indigenous chronology.[11]

Pedro José Márquez, another Jesuit exiled in Italy, published in 1804 *Due antichi monumenti di architettura messicana*, a popular work based on Alzate's publications on El Tajín and Xochicalco. Along with these new works about ancient Mexico, the exploration of a historical world at that time unknown was started: the exploration of the ancient cities and archaeological monuments. This new look at a very old and until then almost hidden presence can be said to have had its origins in 1790 in Palenque, when Father Antonio de Solís was named pastor of that place. Very soon he and his family began to make known the existence of the archaeological monuments. In 1773, Father Ramón Ordóñez, who as a child had discovered Palenque through the family of Father Solís, organized the first expedition to visit the archaeological ruins. He also informed the governor of Guatemala, José Estachería, of the existence of Palenque, and the governor, in turn, ordered José Antonio Calderón to prepare a report on the place. The text and the drawings of Palenque that Calderón prepared in 1784 can be considered the first archaeological report about an area of ancient monuments, although Calderón, impressed by the grandeur of the constructions he saw in the jungle, thought that the authors of these buildings must have been "Romans." One year later, the governor of Guatemala ordered another exploration of the site. The reports of these visits were sent in 1786 to the emperor of Spain himself, Charles III, who approved them and ordered new explorations carried out.

The enlightened mentality of the Spanish rulers of the second half of the eighteenth century, then, canceled the prohibitions of the authorities and the church at the end of the sixteenth century on the study of Indian antiquities. Beginning then, expeditions especially dedicated to examining the archaeological monuments began to spread rich information about them. Juan Bautista Muñoz, chief chronicler of the Indies, became acquainted in Madrid with the reports on Palenque and in 1786 recommended a detailed investigation of the site and the necessary excavation to learn about the system of construction and the characteristics of the city and its monuments. Captain Antonio del Río, who was designated to carry out this mission, spent a long time in Palenque, made numerous excavations, drew up plans and drawings of the zone, and much later (1822) published, in English, the results of his expedition.

Charles IV continued this policy and ordered a broader scientific expedition, dedicated to discovering monuments, recovering collections, and preparing the corresponding studies. Guillermo Dupaix, an Austrian military man who had studied in Italy, and the Mexican artist Luciano Castañeda, headed this expedition. Between 1805 and 1807, Dupaix and Castañeda made three visits to the center and southeast of the viceroyalty. Their first tour encompassed part of the states of Puebla, Veracruz, and Morelos. On the second trip, they concentrated on the outskirts of the Valley of Mexico. They visited Oaxaca, where Dupaix was astounded by Monte Albán, and produced the first literary description of this archaeological zone. On the third trip, they covered various parts of Puebla, Oaxaca, and Chiapas and stopped for some time in Palenque. This expedition confirmed the existence of new and grand archaeological zones, permitted the gathering of one of the first collections about monuments, and redoubled the scientific interest in the antiquities.[12]

The work that most successfully spread news of the antiquities and spectacular geography of Mexico was, however, *Vue des cordillères et monuments des peuples indigènes de l'Amérique,* by Baron Alexander von Humboldt, published in Paris in 1810. This large album contains sixty-nine plates with corresponding explanations, of which thirty-two refer to Mexico. Five reproduce archaeological monuments (Cholula, El Tajín, Xochicalco, and Mitla), seven others reproduce recently discovered monoliths, including the Coatlicue and the Sun Stone, and the rest illustrate pages or details from pictographic codices. Of these the famous Borgia Codex stands out.[13]

The importance of these reports is that, for the first time, their authors provide surveys, plans, and technical drawings of cities and ancient monuments. They ask about the origin of the peoples who created these works and discuss the degree of cultural development, comparing this with that of the classical civilizations of Europe. It is also common in these authors to submit the American artistic works to a comparison of archetypes of the beauty of classical antiquity. No one followed the path away from mental subordination that Antonio de León y Gama started by rejecting the categories of the European calendar in order to investigate the indigenous chronology and calendar. Nor did anyone follow the path Clavijero opened. On the contrary, the authors of these reports refuse to accept that the ancestors of the Indians, who accompany them as guides and bearers, might have been the builders of these architectural marvels that they are contemplating. This is why they attribute the creation of these fantastic cities to Greeks, Romans, Phoenicians, and Egyptians, and even to the inhabitants of Atlantis. Only Humboldt states that in recent years, "a happy revolution has taken place in the manner of examining the civilization of these peoples," and this is why he says of his investigations about America, "they appear in an age in which that is not considered unworthy of attention which is distant in style from that which the Greeks have given us as inimitable models."[14] Nevertheless, although this attitude did not take effect until a century later, what is certain is that these first plans and drawings of strange cities and the reproductions of buildings, sculptures, and magnificent monoliths spread a new image of American antiquity.

The discovery of the monumental richness of ancient Mexico coincided with the appearance of new studies about the recent history of the viceroyalty. Another Jesuit living in Italy, Francisco Javier Alegre, concluded in the decade of 1760 the *Historia de la provincia de la Compañía de Jesús en Nueva España*, which became the first general history of the order from its establishment until 1767. Around this time, Father Andrés Cavo, also a Jesuit, wrote in Rome what could be called a general history of the viceroyalty between 1521 and 1766; it later was published with the title *Historia de México*.[15] In this work, in addition to treating the mandatory theme of the Conquest, Cavo collected, in the form of annals, the principal events that occurred during the viceroyalty. Considered individually or as a group, these works, which recover large portions of an until-then forgotten past and present new methods and interpretations, are a product of the mental change introduced by the ideas of the Enlightenment.

In the mid-eighteenth century, a distinguished group of religious overcame the resistance of scholastic tradition to modern philosophy and the new experimental science. But the great revolution that precipitated the separation between religion and education, between theology and science, and between religious state and profane society had as its backdrop the years 1770 to 1810, when the Spanish monarch himself decided to govern his possessions under the principles of the Enlightenment, and new political projects and new institutions were born that transformed the life of the viceroyalty.

The principal change that the enlightened policies of the Bourbons introduced was the substitution of the project of creating a church-state with a modern lay society no longer directed by the religious and moral values but by the principles of enlightened modernity. The new state that the Bourbons proposed was not only a state distanced from the church but one that pursued earthly ends and whose goals were industrial, technical, scientific, and educational progress, not eternal salvation or religious values. The conviction that these goals should be promoted by the government and by enlightened rulers was the decision that most affected the established order. Starting then, direct state intervention in the economy, society, and cultural institutions wrested powers and privileges from the church, the merchants, the hacendados, and the Creole bureaucracy. This time, the interests and plans of the government were opposed in a radical fashion to the interests of the colonial oligarchy.[16]

The ambitious Bourbon project of modernizing society took shape within these contradictions and had on its side the active participation of the Creoles, who played a major role as transmitters and executors of the ideas of the Enlightenment. Further, by carrying out this project of renewal, the Creoles successively occupied the new intellectual and scientific centers that the Enlightenment created. In a few years, the proposal to establish the ideals of the Enlightenment and to found new institutions changed traditions forged over two centuries. In 1768, the Royal School of Surgery was created, which, contrary to the university tradition, replaced Latin with Spanish for teaching and, instead of the predominance of theory, put an emphasis on medical practice. The founding in 1792 of the Royal Seminary or College of Mining produced even more decisive changes, for it came to be the door through which entered a group of distinguished Spanish mineralogists, technical and scientific teaching applied to mining production, new classes and knowledge, and the most modern physics, mineralogy, and chemistry laboratories. This new institution educated a brilliant generation of technical and scientific Creoles. It became the center of scientific activity of the viceroyalty and was the point of contact with European science.[17]

Another radical change, but in the field of the arts, was introduced by the founding in 1781 of the Royal Academy of the Noble Arts of San Carlos. The opening of this royal institution brought about the transfer to New Spain of an important group of Spanish artists and the sudden introduction of the neoclassical style, which had been established in the Spanish court. From the beginning of its activities, the academy broke the monopoly that until then had been enjoyed by the teaching guilds, production and sale of artistic and artisanal works, and ceded this monopoly to its own teachers and graduates. In addition, it became the institution that granted construction permits for public works and was the only one that granted titles and prizes in fine arts (architecture, painting, sculpture, and engraving). Its members acted as the principal arbiters of public taste. Further, the academy was responsible for the introduction into the viceroyalty of lay and state art, which instantly came into conflict with religious art and with the traditional conception of the beautiful, which was also very marked by the religious spirit of the era.[18]

Thus, with the strength of academic rules and monopoly of action, the teachers and graduates of the academy began to change the baroque face of New Spain; everywhere, formerly praised *retablos* and baroque porticoes gave way to sober neoclassical models. Public works in the cities as well as new religious construction were completely dominated by the new style. In this manner, the state, not the church, came to be the arbiter of urban design, architectural style, and aesthetic taste and the new Maecenas of artists and artisans. In sum, the seal that during those years distinguishes the new architecture and the "noble arts" is its lay and state character, it being an art that, in addition to having classical antiquity as its model, turns toward public life and celebrates the rulers and their symbols.

Along with these new scientific and cultural institutions, there developed a form of communication that revolutionized the flow and spread of ideas. With an intellectual fervor similar to that which in France drove the appearance of the *Encyclopedia* or in Spain the extraordinary popular work of Benito Jerónimo Feijoo, the Creoles gave themselves to spreading in their country the transformative potential of science and the new economic, social, and educational ideas that they thought would convert New Spain into a modern country equal to the most advanced ones. In 1772, José Ignacio Bartolache began to publish his famous *Mercurio Volante*, which was the first medical magazine published in the Americas and the medium for popularizing the new scientific methods.

Perhaps the most representative spirit of the enlightened mentality of New Spain was embodied in José Antonio Alzate. A priest, like the majority of the intellectuals of the time, Alzate personified the principal characteristics of the enlightened temperament: a follower of the new philosophy and enthusiastic promoter of experimental science, he was, above all, a believer in the transformative power of reason, an ideologue of mental and social change, and a man of encyclopedic curiosity. In addition to these qualities, he developed another typical of the enlightened spirit: the problems that awakened his curiosity became public topics in his famous *Gazetas de literatura*, the magazine that, between 1778 and 1795, disseminated and promoted the discussion of these topics in New Spain. In addition, between 1784 and 1817, the *Gazeta de México* was published, which, along with news of public celebrations, earthquakes, processions, droughts, crimes, and other local events, made known European political events, scientific advances, and the latest news in machines and technical inventions.

Prompted by this propitious, enlightened environment, a group of Creoles connected to the Ayuntamiento of Mexico City promoted the publication of the first *Diario de México* (1805–1812), which opened its pages to critical reflections on social and political matters that proclaimed the inclinations of the most politicized Creole group. In light of the participation of persons such as Carlos María de Bustamante, Francisco Primo de Verdad, and Jacobo de Villaurrutia (the three implicated in the later independence movement), and the topics on its pages, the *Diario de México* can be considered the first case in which a social group attempted to use a modern communications medium as an ideological instrument.[19] Triple novelty: in the *Diario de México*, the establishment of the first newspaper, the training of a group of Creoles in handling a modern communications medium, and a marginalized social group's transformation of this medium into ideological warfare all converge.

Almost everything that is created in New Spain at the end of the eighteenth century reflects the change brought about by the introduction of modern, enlightened ideas. Everywhere we see the presence of a sensitivity preoccupied with the things of this world and of a mentality that questions, classifies, and interprets natural and social reality using new analytical instruments. Mining, for example, was subjected to minute scrutiny by a distinguished group of Creole and Spanish specialists; said scrutiny clarified its history, its legislation, and its systems of production and brought about the creation of a new legal framework, new financial policies, and new institutions dedicated to its development.[20]

This tendency to consider the aspects of the material or social reality using new analytical instruments and arguments supported by rigorous technical expositions is common in the majority of discussions and proposals of this period. The same can be seen in the polemics caused by the introduction of vaccination or the establishment of the *intendencia* system, as in the discussion of the laws about free trade or in the analysis of agricultural, mining, or ecclesiastical problems. What is new is that, instead of having recourse to the argument of authority or presenting dogma as an unquestionable proof, in this era there is an extraordinary development of the inventory and the catalog as elements on which to base arguments, explanations, or judgment. During these years, a veritable rage for investigating, measuring, cataloguing, and inventorying the natural and social world develops. In 1769, beginning with Miguel Costanzó, Juan Crespi, and Junípero Serra, the scientific expeditions dedicated to maritime, geographic, and astronomical exploration and to collecting samples of the flora and fauna of the viceroyalty begin. This was followed by other expeditions, among them the one headed by Alejandro Malaspina and the very famous one that Charles III sent in 1786, which produced the first scientific herbarium in Mexico, the founding of the Botanical Garden, the creation of a chair of botany, and the first natural history laboratory. These and other expeditions traveled over a great part of the territory and contributed to determining latitudes, carrying out astronomical observations, drawing maps and charts, applying new scientific knowledge to these tasks. Thus, in a few years, this curiosity, guided by systematization, produced a new image of the resources and geography of the viceroyalty. To this scientific analysis of the natural environment were added the first population censuses and the reports of the *intendentes*, bishops, priests, merchants, miners, and farmers about the economic and social situation of each province, and quantified information about the principal economic activities of the viceroyalty. On the basis of this very abundant information, organized under the rational patterns of the Enlightenment, works and observations were drawn up that it would not have been possible to imagine years before. An example of the qualitative leap that occurred then in the organization and management of information is the *Historia general de la Real Hacienda* (1791), a compilation that, for the first time, organized the chaotic accumulation of data about the income and expenditures of the viceroyalty, explained the origins of each item, and transformed the disorder into a modern accounting system that was in use until late in the nineteenth century.

Another case that shows how the new systematization of information led to qualitative changes in analysis and to the capture of previously unencompassable aggregates is the *Memoria de estatuto o idea de la riqueza que daban a la masa circulante de Nueva España, sus naturales producciones* (1877).[21] This work by José María Quirós is the first attempt to do what we would today call a calculation of national income, or, as Quirós himself said, to create "as correct an idea as possible of the territorial and industrial production of this New Spain." Without the accumulation of sectoral, regional, and general information, without the purifying ordering of these complex data, and without the new theoretical instruments brought by the Enlightenment, this high moment in the analysis of economic reality would not have been reached.

The introduction of the reasoned discourse of the Enlightenment and of experimental science methods brought about, then, a quantitative and qualitative change in the systems of collecting information, for these were now able to capture a broader universe and had at their disposal sharper instruments for collecting and refining the information. This important change was followed by a fundamental change in the processes of analyzing, interpreting, and explaining accumulated information. The most representative works of this era—the *Historia antigua de México* by Clavijero, the *Descripción histórica y cronológica de las dos piedras* by León y Gama, many pages of the *Gazetas de literatura* by Alzate, the *Comentarios de las ordenanzas de minas* by Francisco Javier Gamboa, the *Memoria sobre el influjo de la minería en la agricultura, industria, población y civilización de la Nueva España* by Fausto de Elhúyar, the *Historia general de Real Hacienda* by Fabián de Fonseca and Charles de Urrutia, or the *Memoria de estatuto* by José María Quirós—are the systematized sum of known information and an exposition governed by the logical demonstration of the facts, the internal coherence of the arguments, and reasoned and convincing explanation. There is in these works a new language that translates a new way of seeing reality, of analyzing and explaining it.

Another outstanding example of the depth that the analysis of reality had reached can be seen in the works of the bishop-elect of Michoacán, Manuel Abad y Queipo. In the *Representación sobre la inmunidad personal del clero . . .* (1799), and in other writings about the economic, social, and political situation of the viceroyalty, Abad y Queipo demonstrates extraordinary dominion of the information (he always has at hand the most significant and current data) and masterful managing of the arguments and of reasoned explanation. By devoting himself to the most unjust economic and social aspects of the viceroyalty, he took a step forward in the development of analysis and showed himself to be a coherent, enlightened man. He discussed the most advanced social reforms of this time. In a letter addressed to the king and signed by Bishop Antonio de San Miguel, he proposed radical measures to overcome the terrible situation the castes and the Indians were in: abolition of tributes; suppression of legislation that degraded the caste groups; division of the lands that belonged to the state among the Indians and the dispossessed castes; an agrarian law that permitted working on uncultivated lands of the large landholders; and the division of community lands as private property among the Indians of the towns.[22]

Abad y Queipo's proposals and the works of his contemporaries confirm that, at the end of the eighteenth century, the new analytical methods and the new forms of recording, inventorying, and explaining reality were concentrated in the profane world: in the transformation of the economy, society, and forms of government. This secularization of analytical thought is one of the most notable manifestations of the great change occurring in the mentality of the ruling groups of the viceroyalty.

The secularization of government that the Bourbons began by separating the interests of the state from those of the church was taken to its ultimate consequences by Enlightenment ideology. At the end of the eighteenth century, there is a progressive secularization of the social and political order, of education, sciences, arts, and customs. If in the first half of this century the officials of the Holy Inquisition were exclusively occupied with persecuting heretical philosophical ideas or those contrary to religious orthodoxy, in the last twenty years of the century, they faced a surprising secularization and politicization of the attitudes of the people of New Spain. In these years, the books that the alarmed Inquisition confiscated were the works of Rousseau, Diderot, Voltaire, Montesquieu, and D'Alembert and of other popularizers of the libertarian principles of the French Revolution.

This change in readings was followed by a change in the readers. These are no longer only ecclesiastics and learned Creoles, but minor and middle-level officials, higher and lower clergy, members of the army, and a growing number of individuals from the middle sector of the urban population.[23] All of them, say the inquisitors in consternation, are permeated by "purportedly strong spirits, which under the name of modern philosophers and with the reality of Atheists, Deists, Materialists, the Impious, [and] Libertines, attack religion and the state in our century." What disturbs the spirit of the inquisitors is the violent propagation of seditious ideas, the unexpected "passion for French books that have precipitated so many into the abyss of corruption," and the unrestrainable spread of a subversive political philosophy that invades the most traditional redoubts. This is why the inquisitors lament "this ill-fated era in which the intemperate echoes of liberty have reached the" most remote provinces. This invasion of revolutionary political ideas ended by destroying the ideological monopoly of the church and heightened the conflict with traditional values.[24]

The secularization of thought and the invasion of the profane in environments previously dominated by religious values was manifested also in the popular sectors of the cities and the country. In these years, an infinite variety of dances, songs, and profane distractions multiplied. What is new about these forms of profane distraction is no longer their growing and multiplying number or lascivious, sensual, scandalous, obscene, or lewd character, but their ever more irreverent, antireligious, and subversive tone. What now worries the inquisitors who pursue these dances and songs is not just their unrestrained impetus but their conversion into instruments that mock traditional values.

A century earlier, what was exceptional and punished was a mixture of the religious with the profane; at the end of the eighteenth century, what alarms the inquisitors is the spread of the profane over the religious, the relaxation of customs and traditions, insolent play with previously untouchable religious symbols, the irreverence toward holy things, and the mocking of the most sacred Christian values. In this process, a new fact is the transformation of the profane spirit into criticism of traditional values. Dance, song, anonymous satire become the weapons of criticism. Little by little, derision and mocking leave by the wayside the individual, the circumstance, or the anecdotal to become mocking of institutions, authorities, and governments. Imperceptibly, from the mocking of priests, it passes to the mocking of the church or religion, from the mocking of an official to the mocking of government, from the mocking of the greedy Spanish carpetbaggers to criticism of Spanish domination. Festive satire becomes political satire, and both become confused and spread by means of anonymous writings that multiply through the effective channels of rumor.[25]

The division that the ideas and practices of the Enlightenment established between the profane and the religious accentuated the criticism of obscurantism, fanaticism, and miracles that predominated in the religious world. This division, previously nonexistent, was what was imposed in the last quarter of the century in painting, architecture, sculpture, theater, and the so-called noble arts for, in addition to spreading Enlightenment styles and models, these activities stamped a worldly content on their creations. Music was opened to new European airs, and poetry and literature were peopled by Olympus, Hades, nymphs, heroes, and Greco-Roman myths. This new literature also becomes a critical and contradictory literature, as can be seen in the first and most important novel of the era: *El periquillo sarniento*, by Joaquín Fernández de Lizardi. It criticizes the morals, customs, and traditional forms of life. In this way, the artistic and cultural world dominated before by Christian values, religious sentiment, and edifying example, became a medium that created profane objects guided by worldly values and stimulated by nonecclesiastical sponsors.

There is, then, a correlation between the progressive secularization of social reality and the scientific, artistic, and cultural products and the creation of new spaces that permit the expression of this new mentality without the constraints that the religious medium previously imposed. The new scientific and cultural institutions, the new centers created by the government to spread the ideals and fashions of enlightened thought, the new subject areas, and journalism are secular institutions and spaces, not religious ones. In these environments opened by Bourbon and Enlightenment policy, the Creoles completed their ideological and political training. With the exception of the highest posts of government, the Creoles dominated these new seats of knowledge, analysis, criticism, and diffusion. The Creoles were the students, the teachers, the popularizers, and the directors of this new knowledge and the forces and direct beneficiaries of the conversion of analytical thought into a critical instrument of social reality. In the new scientific and cultural institutions, in the new subject areas, and in journalism, which then developed with great force, the Creoles came into contact with philosophy, sciences, and techniques that were introduced by the Enlightenment and became experts in the new areas of knowledge and specialists in the handling of the new medium of diffusion of modern society: journalism and books. It is not by chance that, beginning then, the most advanced ideas are spread through journalism, pamphlets, fliers, anonymous papers, and books.

It was precisely a book that came to integrate the new knowledge created by the Creole intelligence and to reaffirm the historical conscience and images of identity that the Creoles had forged of their homeland: the *Ensayo político sobre el reino de la Nueva España*, by Baron Alexander von Humboldt. Humboldt personified the qualities required to write the first globalizing, systematic book on New Spain. His ambition was to join scientific knowledge with humanistic. He had an exceptional encyclopedic education and "an astonishing capacity for work, an immense power of assimilation, and an extraordinary ability to synthesize data and information."[26] With this basis, during his travel through America he conceived the idea of presenting to the European public the most complete portrait of geography, geology, botany, ancient history, and the economic and political situation of the Spanish possessions in America. This encyclopedic ambition was combined with a practical, utilitarian disposition: Humboldt knew that in Europe and the United States there was a lively interest in knowing precisely the real potential, the condition of the military force, and the mineral riches of Spanish possessions in America and particularly of New Spain, the greatest and richest of all. This is why he thought first of preparing *Tablas geográficas políticas del reino de Nueva España*,[27] which he completed in 1803, and then thought about an *Estadística de México*, which kept growing in size and complexity until it took the final form of his famous *Ensayo político*, published in Paris between 1808 and 1811.

But if the conception and structure of these works are properly part of Humboldt's genius, the rich information that nourishes them is the result of the accumulation of knowledge that the enlightened spirit promoted in the last decades of the viceroyalty. In the gathering of data that support the *Tablas* and the *Ensayo*, Humboldt had in his favor felicitous circumstances that smoothed his path. In the first place, he found already elaborated the quantitative and qualitative information on the physical and natural environment, the population, the treasury, agriculture, industry, mining, and trade that had been gathered by the officials and learned persons of New Spain. In the second place, he had as principal informants the most illustrious Creoles and the most open and critical minds of the viceroyalty. The best-informed men of New Spain, desiring to display their knowledge, wanting the approval and advice of the German scholar, and deeply interested in showing him the potential of their homeland, generously furnished the data he solicited and everything that they could imagine would serve the purpose of making known to the world through such an illustrious agent the grand image that they had formed of their country.

As Ortega y Medina says so well, the generation of enlightened Creoles who, for years, had been constructing a new idea of themselves and of their country, on meeting with "Humboldt, idealize him and see themselves reflected in him." The ideas that the Creoles had formed of the greatness of their country, the knowledge that they had gathered about its history and its current situation, their criticism of the government and the power that marginalized them, their exalted evaluation of scientific and artistic advances, their resentment, and the boundless optimism that they had conceived concerning the resources of their country, all these Creole ideas and sentiments are present in the *Ensayo político sobre el reino de la Nueva España*. In this sense, Humboldt came to sanction the Creole image of a great and vigorous Mexico.[28]

The powerful impact that this work had on the people of New Spain and on the Creoles in particular is explained by the unitary focus that embraces the entity of the viceroyalty and by the sectoral treatment of topics. For the first time, this approach offered those born in New Spain a precise idea of the territory they inhabited, of the number of inhabitants and their distribution in the *intendencias* or administrative jurisdictions into which the kingdom had been divided, of the agricultural richness and its famous mineral potential; of the increase in manufacturing and trade; of the military defenses and the vast income that this varied production furnished the Spanish crown. By uniting in his analysis all these parts, Humboldt composed a global image of an immense country that, until then, had lacked an eloquent portrait that displayed its true dimension. It should be added that this first modern vision of the whole of New Spain appeared precisely at the moment when the independence movement began. Through this sum of intrinsic qualities and historical juncture, the *Ensayo* became the most read, influential, and quoted book of many written in the nineteenth century about Mexico. Thus, through one book, one work peopled by scriptural images and the new scientific arguments of the Enlightenment, those born in Mexico stated and confronted the ideas that they had formed of their homeland. Justly, Lucas Alamán was able to say that Humboldt's work "came, to say it in this way, to discover the New World for the second time."[29] And for the Creoles, it can be said that this book was the mirror in which for the first time they saw reflected the opulent image

of New Spain that they had dreamed: an extensive geography; a cornu-
copia of agriculture, cattle, and mining; a vigorous country that to reach
the level of the most prosperous nations of the world lacked only the
development of its trade and industry and improvement in its government, from which the Creoles were excluded.

It is clear that in the last decades of the viceroyalty the historical
consciousness of the Creoles underwent changes that strengthened their
own interpretation of historical development and extended their capacity to recognize and absorb other memories of the past. Their specialized
education (philosophy, theology, sciences, arts, and letters) led them to
create an open relationship with Enlightenment ideas, and their intellectual and political compulsion persuaded them to convert those ideas into
their own habits of reflection and to promote their spread in other social
sectors. Through these channels, Gianbattista Vico's theories of human
development were known in New Spain. Through William Robertson's
innovative conception, which considered social development as a succession of progressive stages (savagery, barbarism, civilization), filtered
the first enlightened ideas that conceived of historical development as a
continuous march for progress. Also arriving with them was a group of
new techniques for managing, criticizing, and refining historical information. In this way, for many Creoles, historical development ceased to
be a process guided by the Christian teleology of eternal salvation and the
fulfillment of God's plans and became an earthly, profane process
determined by its own internal causes, which were susceptible to being
clarified through observation and analysis of the historical reality itself.
In the countries where the Enlightenment flowered, this descent from
heaven to earth expelled Providence from historical discourse, began an
earthly search for meaning that could be attributed to historical events,
and borrowed from the experimental sciences several methods that
allowed the confrontation of hypotheses and theories with empirical
research results. In this way, the explanation of the historical facts and
the interpretation of historical development became a critical exercise
in a persistent search for the credible and confirmable. This was the
legacy that the spirit of the Enlightenment left scholars of historical
events and that in New Spain became embodied in such works as *Historia antigua de México* by Clavijero, *Descripción histórica y cronológica
de las dos piedras* by León y Gama, or *Ensayo político* by Humboldt.

Mythic Discourse in the Insurgency

At the end of the eighteenth century, the memory of the past and the
conception of historical development that the Creoles created dominated the sphere where historical discourse was expressed in the form of

books, as a written message. But this was not the only discourse, nor was it the most generalized among the population. Alongside it was manifest the multiple presence of the mythic, indigenous, popular discourse, charged with polyvalent, strange, and disturbing symbols, meanings, and messages. It was a discourse all the more perturbing and difficult to grasp, for only in recent years have researchers become aware of its presence, generally expressed in oral form. In addition, it should be reiterated that this presence comes to us through the distorted record that the repressors made of that discourse. Nevertheless, as in the previous chapter, examples are presented of this multiple, exalted discourse. In this part, room is left for mythic imagination, which before and during the course of the insurgent movement, anticipated new millennia, crownings of kings, divine envoys, and miraculous salvations.

The Deranged Messiah of Durango, 1799–1801

On January 25, 1801, Francisco Antonio de la Bástida y Araziel, principal authority of the village of San Juan Bautista del Río, a town located to the north of Durango, had an interview with an Indian who appeared under the name of "Capitán Cuerno Verde," who later claimed that his name was José Silvestre Sariñana, and finally ended up being José Bernardo Herrada. In his interview with Bástida, Herrada requested permission to remain a few days in San Juan Bautista del Río to participate as "toreador" on foot in the upcoming festivities of the town. Nevertheless, a few days later, the indigenous governor of the town informed Bástida that "Cuerno Verde" was stirring up the population with seditious expressions. Bástida himself received a paper from Herrada in which he noticed messages that could upset the Indians and ordered him jailed. Subsequently, José Bernardo Herrada underwent an intense interrogation that threw some light on his "seditious ideas," but did not get to the bottom of his complex and disturbed mind.

Herrada drew the attention of the indigenous governor of San Juan Bautista del Río when he assured him that he could make it rain fire from the sky during the town's festivities. He told the Indians that in Durango he had been jailed for presenting himself as a mysteriously masked man and stated that he had come to win them over by fire and blood. He told the principal Indians that it was his duty to defend them from the Spanish authorities and announced extraordinary events in the days to come. Subjected to questioning, he caused a disturbance among the Spanish authorities when he confessed to having traveled through dozens of places in the north of the viceroyalty to gather signatures in favor of the crowning of an indigenous king, his own father, who was to be coronated on March 29, 1801, presumably in Tlaxcala. He stated that he had been born in the Analco ward in the city of Tlaxcala, where he had been "captain" of 133 towns in his district. He then gave an imaginative account of his travels through the north of Mexico. According to his testimony, on September 3, 1799, he left Tlaxcala and the following day (?) reached the capital of the viceroyalty, accompanied by several relatives and fourteen Indians from the various towns around Mexico City, his father, the governor of Tlaxcala, had provided to accompany him on his tour. Under the guidance of Herrada, this group traveled together for several days, and when it reached Río Verde, a town near San Luis Potosí, each of its members followed his own itinerary indicated in a royal warrant given to Herrada by the former viceroy, Miguel José de Azanza. According to this document, which was never presented as evidence in the interrogation, Herrada's mission was to collect alms and military deserters for unspecified purposes. Nevertheless, in another part of his statement, Herrada said that his mission was to collect the "signatures" of 40,000 Indians and especially of the authorities of the towns, with the goal of having the signers support his father's government and be present at the coronation, to take place on March 29, 1801. He also said that the collection of signatures was a pretext for finding out the number of Spaniards in each town and rural area. This information was to be gathered because, according to Herrada, the Spaniards "had oppressed and enslaved the Indians, and his father had the crown and power necessary to expel them all [the Spaniards], as had been done with the Jesuits." In reply to a question from his inquisitors, Herrada said that his father's right to the throne was based on a royal warrant of 1786, issued by King Charles IV of Spain, in which it was recorded that his father "should be crowned with absolute powers to command, perform, and execute." He caused even greater alarm when he assured them that his father's plans were supported by a force of 500 English and 300 French soldiers posted at an unidentified point on the coast and with whom his father was in constant contact. This news, together with the rumors of probable English attacks, reports of indigenous uprisings, and conspiracy rumors, forced the authorities of New Vizcaya to take Herrada's statements seriously and to clarify his link with another indigenous leader who around that time was promoting an uprising in the region of Tepic.

The interrogations that Herrada underwent were unable to establish a definite link between him and Mariano, the indigenous messiah of Tepic, and even less with English forces, but they did demonstrate the fantasy, contradictions, and madness that inhabited Herrada's mind. The supposed father and indigenous governor of Tlaxcala was a product of his disturbed imagination, for Herrada had lost his father as a child. Nor does it appear certain that Herrada had visited the towns he claimed to have toured, for many of them were creations of his fantasies, as were the names of the persons he said had signed the communiqués favoring his father's coronation. Also imaginary were the credentials, the royal warrants, and other official Spanish documents with which Herrada intended to lend credibility to his actions. But what was very certain was the seditious character of his program: among fantasies, deliriums, and contradictions, Herrada clearly preached the advent of a kind of indigenous millennium in which the government would pass from the hands of the Spaniards into those of the Indians through the person of an indigenous king. As soon as the government was in the Indians' hands, the Spaniards were to be expelled from Mexican lands. Nevertheless, this clearness of the principal purpose of Herrada's plan is decreased by the lack of response from his indigenous audiences. Herrada is a frustrated messiah because he does not have followers: he announces a program of liberation but lacks the capacity to mobilize around him the indigenous population he leads. This is perhaps why his message is confused and contradictory. The most contradictory trait of Herrada's plan is his reiterated call to the highest Spanish authorities to legitimize his subversive action, which intended to bring down Spanish power. He says, for example, that the itinerary that he pursued on his trip through the north of New Spain and the mission that he followed were authorized by the viceroy, Miguel José de Azanza. It appears even more absurd that Herrada supported his father's claim to be "crowned with absolute power to command, perform, and execute" by producing a royal warrant from Charles IV!

For several days in February 1801, Herrada replied with these and other statements to the interrogation that the Spanish authorities conducted, until his testimony made up a thick file of 235 folio pages. During the first days of February 1801, he related everything we know of him and his plan. Then he fell silent. He was jailed in Durango in 1801, and in 1805 he was sent under guard to Guadalajara, to be taken to Veracruz and finally to Havana, where he was to serve out a sentence of six years. On the night of December 14, 1805, however, he escaped from the Hacienda de Tlacotes near Zacatecas, and nothing more was heard of him.[30]

The Phantom of Mariano in Tepic, 1801

At the beginning of the nineteenth century, the consuming war that Spain waged against England and the ever more disturbing fear that the power of the United States awakened increased the susceptibility of the viceregal authorities to external conspiracy rumors combined with internal rebellions. Within this climate of suspicion and fear, there reached the hands of the authorities of the port of San Blas and of the subdelegations of Compostela and Aguacatlán in New Galicia copies of seditious papers that called for a general insurrection of the Indians in the region of Tepic. Thus, beginning with rumors whose origin was difficult to verify, the mysterious phantom image of Mariano, the supposed leader inspiring this uprising, was formed. According to imprecise and legendary information, Mariano was the son of the indigenous governor of a town named Tlaxcala in New Galicia.

According to these reports of unknown origin, Mariano had decided to send notices to an undetermined number of Indian communities to hold a general meeting in Tepic. Subsequently, speculation and rumor about Mariano and his seditious strategies increased. There was talk, then, of an indigenous king or of the election of a leader endowed with very broad powers and of the formation of an army of thirty thousand men ready to attack at his command. Rumors also circulated that the Indians had established secret communications between all the towns and with the nation of Tlaxcala. It was said that an unknown person in Mexico City was implicated in the subversive activity of the Indians in Tepic, and the news was spread that an armed horseman had been seen at meetings with different groups of Indians. The culminating act of this conspiracy was to take place in the capital of the viceroyalty on the day of the Feast of the Virgin of Guadalupe, precisely when the candles were lighted in the chapel. At that moment, the candles, which were to be connected to explosives, were to blow up the shrine to Guadalupe. The confusion that this terrible act would cause would be used by the insurrectionists to attack the palace of the viceroy, which also would have been mined at its corners.

This fantastic conspiracy was accepted as credible by viceregal authorities. As soon as this news spread, the general commander of the Audiencia of Guadalajara, José Abascal, and Captain Francisco de Eliza, commander of the naval department of San Blas, mobilized the troops to suppress the insurrection before it could get under way. Abascal ordered the colonel of the Regiment of Dragoons of New Galicia to advance to the insurrectionary zone with two squadrons, leaving the rest of the force mobilized to go into action at any moment. He also ordered the provincial infantry battalion of Guadalajara to be put on alert and notified the coastal militia. Meanwhile, Captain Francisco de Eliza sent Captain Salvador Fidalgo to Tepic with troops and marines to surprise the Indians when they held their meeting. Apparently, the majority of the population of Tepic knew nothing of Mariano, or they had not paid attention to his communiqués. Others, believing that the Indians were gathering to receive an important person, perhaps the king of Spain himself, as someone said, went to the town to find out about the events. What is certain is that Fidalgo found the Indians gathered and ordered them to surrender. The majority obeyed, throwing their machetes to the ground, saying they had come in peace. Others, however, fearing arrest, attempted to escape. At that moment, a scene of panic and confusion was created: the troops opened fire, killing two Indians, injuring many more, and taking seventy-two prisoners. Fidalgo's troops arrested some two hundred Indians who later were taken to Guadalajara, where many died in prison before their cases were brought before the courts.

When the viceroy received the first news about these events, he saw in them the confirmation that he was facing a real menace to the security of the viceroyalty. This is why he ordered Captain Eliza to be prepared to evacuate San Blas and transfer his detachment to Acapulco. The war with England, the recent skirmishes with English and North American corsairs in the Pacific, and Mariano's insurrection led the viceroy to think of the possibility of a foreign plot. Nor did the viceroy put aside the suspicion that the Indians were preparing a general rebellion by means of secret contacts between each town. News coming from Veracruz seemed to confirm his worst fears. According to the authorities in that region, some Indians from Acayucan had spoken of the crowning of an indigenous king in Tlaxcala whom they proposed to visit and recognize as such. A few days later, an Indian named Juan José García was taken prisoner in Potrero Grande, Nuevo León, for having stolen a mule. Jailed in San Luis Potosí, Juan José García refused to eat for several days and at the end of his hunger strike declared he was Alexander I. His jailers put him in solitary confinement and in irons and chains for several days. Questioned again so that he would tell the truth, García stated that he had been commissioned to visit the viceroy in Mexico City, who was to name him commander-general of the Provincias Internas. As he was unable to get an interview with the viceroy, he transferred to Tlaxcala and then to the port of Veracruz, where he was proclaimed Mariano I. Questioned about this nomination, he said that a royal warrant had granted him this title.

In mid-June 1801, reports of supposed Indian insurrections, fears of foreign plots, and rumors of fantastic coronations were reduced to their true dimension. When Viceroy Marquina received sure information, he learned that Mariano's insurrection in Tepic had been a great hoax thought up by a single person: an Indian named Juan Hilano had been the author of the notices and communiqués attributed to the volatile phantom Mariano. The Indians of Acayucan, who supposedly had gone to subjugate themselves before the recently crowned indigenous king of Tlaxcala, turned out to be beggars who, passing through Tlaxcala, requested meager alms from the indigenous local governor. In turn, Alexander I, or Mariano I, was recognized by the doctors in San Luis

Potosí as a man attacked by a "true melancholy dementia." Finally, the feared attack of the English never took place.[31]

Rumors of uprisings, rebellions, and Indian revolts had been common throughout the tense social history of the viceroyalty. What was new at the end of the eighteenth century and the beginning of the nineteenth century was the insecurity, the growing anxiety of the viceregal authorities before these menacing manifestations of social discontent. The wars with England and other European powers added to the concern for internal security a fear of possible foreign attacks. Thus, in contrast to earlier times, the most fantastic news took on the appearance of reality. This new psychological situation of the viceregal authorities perhaps explains so disproportionate a reply to Mariano's supposed insurrection in Tepic, or the unusual credibility they gave to the rumors of imaginary coronations of indigenous kings. What is certain is that at this time the indigenous myths and signs through which the deepest pulses rose to the surface already moved on their own: they were living phantoms that efficiently transported the accumulated load of indigenous claims; they had a specific weight in both the Indian mentality and that of their dominators.

The King of Spain in the Insurgent Ranks

Just as the religious symbols (the miraculous appearances of the Virgin), the symbols of indigenous resistance (memory of uprisings, insurrections, and crowned indigenous kings), and the indigenous messiahs began to be presences endowed with their own lives that gave messages of different meanings to the indigenous and the Spaniards, so also among the popular classes the figure of the king of Spain became an insurgent symbol and a protective shield of the oppressed social groups' aspirations for liberty. This phenomenon is foreign to developed political societies, where it is clearly absurd and illogical. But it is common in the traditional ones, where mythic and sacred thought is dominant and where there is nothing that could be called modern political thought. In New Spain and in the New Kingdom of Granada (Colombia), this phenomenon is well documented.

Starting in 1801, in the supposed insurrection at Tepic, the presence of the king of Spain is mentioned as supporting the assembly that the Indians had held to plan the insurrection. During that same year, José Bernardo Herrada, the deranged messiah of Durango, bases his rights to the crowning of his indigenous king on a royal warrant granted by the emperor Charles IV. Later, when the French invade Spain, the popular allusions to the messianic figure of the king of Spain appear one after the other. In October 1808, at a ceremony held in Epazoyuca to proclaim the ascension of Ferdinand VII, an Indian named Pablo Hilario, who bore a standard with the image of the Virgin of Guadalupe similar to that carried by the indigenous governor but with the image of Ferdinand VII, yelled: *"Long live Ferdinand VII, and death to all the* gachupines.*"*[32] One year later, the viceregal authorities feared that the diabolical French included in their plans the visit to New Spain of deposed king Charles IV. In preparation for this event, they alerted the population to send him back respectfully if he came alone or to treat him like any enemy if he came accompanied by the French army.[33] That is, at that time, the viceregal authorities themselves were conscious of the charismatic power that the image of the king of Spain had among the indigenous people and the possible use of that image for subversive purposes.

This intuition was fully confirmed during the insurrectionary movement headed by Miguel Hidalgo. According to tradition, the war cry that Hidalgo started in the parish of Dolores was *"Long live Ferdinand VII, long live religion, long live the Virgin of Guadalupe, and death to the* gachupines!*"* Essentially, it is the same cry that had resounded previously in the main plaza in Mexico City and had shaken the viceregal palace in 1624 and 1692. In 1624, the disputes between the viceroy, the archbishop, the Real Audiencia, and the Creoles caused a riot that unleashed the fury of the popular classes in the city. On that occasion, the rioting people shouted: *"Long live the church, long live the faith, long live the king, death to bad government!"*[34] In 1692, a terrible drought and manipulation of grain by the authorities and the landowners caused a popular riot that set fire to the viceregal palace and brought cries for death to the *gachupines.* Among the expressions most repeated by the inflamed multitude were death to the viceroy and the authorities who had commandeered the maize and voices of *"Long live the king, death to the Spaniards and the* gachupines!*"*[35] That is, just as in the popular revolution in the New Kingdom of Granada (1781), in New Spain, the protest of the uprisers separates the acclamation of the figure of the king and condemns bad government: *"Long live the king, death to poor government."*[36]

During the war for independence, the king of Spain is not only the sole Spanish personality proclaimed and respected by the insurgents, but clearly appears as a figure who protects the rebels. In November 1810, a few days after the battle of Monte de las Cruces, some Indians who had participated in it said to their Spanish captors that the king of Spain himself commanded Hidalgo's troops and rewarded the people who joined the rebel armies. According to their version, with the protection of the king of Spain, the rebel army would kill the viceroy and all the *gachupines,* whose properties would be divided up among the poor. The hated tribute, which weighed on the Indians, would be abolished by an edict issued by the king of Spain himself. The deposed king, Ferdinand VII, said other Indians, visited the rural areas of New Spain, and, hidden by a silver mask that covered his face, had been seen traveling with Father Hidalgo.[37]

Here, then, is how the king of Spain, the highest representative of the power that was being fought, appears in the indigenous and popular mentality, invested with the attributes of a messiah. The Spanish monarch takes on, in the popular mind, the rank of the supreme commander of the insurgent army and is seen as a messianic agent whose intercession will bring about the defeat of the royalist forces, the death of all Spaniards, the division of all their property among the poor, and the disappearance of tribute. That is, he embodies the program to liberate the popular classes from the oppression they suffer and, precisely through this transfiguration, preserves the strength, dignity, and prestige of royalty, which in this fashion, with all his power intact, is maintained as an ally and protector of the popular cause. In contrast with political movements, whose end is to unite all their powers to bring down those who have power, the mythic mentality makes the monarch of the oppressor nation sacred: instead of asking for his head, it proclaims him and converts him into a protector power of the insurgent action, into a defender of popular aspirations. In this case, the mythic mentality not only does not distinguish, in the person of the monarch, the representation of the highest political power that oppresses the indigenous people, but sees in him what had traditionally been the monarch in the history of the relationship between the king and the indigenous communities: a paternal power, a patriarchal figure, a source of divine justice, a sacred authority, a mythic entity.[38]

The Battling Virgin

During the war for independence, the Virgin of Guadalupe added new roles to the many that she already had: she consolidated her position as queen and mother of those born in Mexico; she became the protective symbol of the insurgents; she was the charismatic magnet that called the indigenous and popular masses to follow the insurgent armies; and she headed a sort of holy war against the *gachupín* heretics. Early on, the Virgin defined her character as protective symbol of those dissatisfied with Spanish government. In the so-called Conspiracy of the Machetes, put down in 1799, the artisans, laborers, and humble people who participated in it chose her as as propitious symbol to call the people together to kill the *gachupines*, take possession of their wealth, free the prisoners from the jails, and proclaim independence from Spain.[39] Later, her presence is constant in all the phases of the insurgent struggle. Her charismatic name is invoked in the parish of Dolores at the moment at which Hidalgo decides to take up arms against the Spanish government. Afterward, as Hidalgo passes through the parish of Atotonilco, he takes up the image of Guadalupe that was venerated there and converts it into the rebel flag. From that point, the image of Guadalupe travels the battlefields, and with this sacred and patriotic presence, the cry: *"Long live Our Lady of Guadalupe and death to the* gachupines!" the rebel army adds new supporters to its cause from the ranches, haciendas, and towns through which it passes:

> Everywhere soldiers, clergy, hacendados, miners, people large and small, joined up; in some, all citizens with very few exceptions . . . as well as the greatest part of the clergy and other people who know how to read and write and have influence on the multitude, they are Creoles, they not only did not contain the multitude but incited it to disorder and uprising, and all it took was four poor souls in a group of one thousand yelling: *Long live Our Lady of Guadalupe and death to the* gachupines! For the entire [town] to rebel.[40]

Later, these first reactions that spontaneously took up the Virgin of Guadalupe as the symbol of the insurrection were transformed by the rebel leaders into a premeditated strategy. On March 11, 1813, a procla- mation from Morelos obliged the men in his army to wear the national colors (blue and white) on their hats and a "device of ribbon, tape, linen, or paper on which he declared his devotion to the holy image of Guadalupe, soldier and defender of her cult."[41] That same year, in the *Sentimientos de la nación*, Morelos proposed establishing, through a constitutional law, "the celebration of December 12 in all towns dedi- cated to the patron of our liberty, most holy Mary of Guadalupe ." Later, he ordered the official seal of the Chilpancingo Congress to contain the Guadalupan anagram.[42]

In the unleashing of ethnic hatreds, wrongs, resentments, injustices, and vengeance that mark with bloodshed the war against the royalist armies and against Spanish persons and property, the insurgency be- comes a holy war and the soldiers, soldiers of the Virgin, armed defenders of the religion. In his excellent study on independence, Luis Villoro observes that the ignored mass that creates history in the Revolution sees in the war against the Spaniards "something deeper than a claim of their rights. Suspicion in a dark sense that is embarked on in a decisive struggle between the forces of good and those of evil that will end up in the establishment of the kingdom of religion and equality; an eschatological duel in which the faithful defend the religion of Christ from the impious and blasphemous."[43] It is a holy war because the Indians and the popular masses that fought in the insurgency acted as if they were possessed by a religious furor, convinced that they were the "defenders of the religion," threatened by the *gachupín* heretics. It is a religious war because, from one band to the other, insults were traded that qualified the other as a heretic, sacrilegious, or a partisan of Satan. The royalist clergy and the excommunicators of Hidalgo accused him of being the "new Antichrist," "little Mohammed," impious, an atheist, heretic, apostate, schismatic, perjurer, seditious, and an opposer of God, and affirmed that "God is with Ferdinand [VII] and with the Spaniards, because heaven has fought for us." And in turn, the insurgents reply, "All *gachupines* are Jews," and they call them "*gachupín* dogs, heretics!" In the pulpits and confessionals, the "priests of the low clergy incite [the people] to join the insurgent defenders of religion," while the proclamations, the banns, and the edicts of the viceregal authorities denounce the insurgents as atheists, heretics, and Freemasons.[44]

It is a religious war because the very leaders of the insurgent band were religious men, priests who appeared before the people with the bearing of messiahs announcing eternal salvation for those who took up their cause, condemning with terrible anathemas the enemy and handling themselves as warriors illuminated by divine protection. The priests who headed the insurgency embodied the qualities of the traditional charismatic leaders: they were popular leaders, military chiefs, and messiahs concentrated on carrying out a sacred mission—to defend religion and to bring justice to the forsaken. And so were they recognized by the ragged masses who followed them. In the places through which they passed, Father Hidalgo's troops spread this image of their chief: "The priest is a saint; . . . the holy Virgin speaks to him several times a day . . . the *gachupines* are Jews; and . . . those who are killed by them in the war or executed as criminals are martyrs."[45]

Ignacio Allende himself fell into this religious vertigo that seduced the masses, for in September 1810 he stated: "The cause we defend is that of religion and for it we must shed our last drop of blood." Later, he declared to the fighting masses: "Those who die in defense of the just cause will earn a distinguished place among the heroes, in the annals of history, and we will go to heaven as victims of our sacred religion."[46]

It was a religious war, finally, because, for the insurgent masses, the holy religion they defended, the Virgin who protected them, and the warrior priests in whom they placed their earthly life and hopes of salvation in the beyond were forces that were submerged in the mythic, eschatological, and sacred world that nourished their deepest personal experiences and aspirations. As in the holy wars years earlier, taken up by Indians who believed in the Virgin of Cancuc or in the messianic prophecies of Jacinto Canek or Antonio Pérez, in 1810 the followers of the Virgin, of Hidalgo, and of Morelos were masses mobilized by eschatological beliefs, organized by religious men, and directed by traditional goals. They defended the Catholic religion and the holy Virgin of Guadalupe. They wished to establish a new kingdom, but in the religious sense, and they wanted to continue to be Indians, men integrated into the egalitarian traditions and solidarity of their communities.

The Virgin of Guadalupe attracted to the ranks of the insurgency the indigenous masses—thousands of workers and unemployed from the fields and the mines, priests, scholars, military, lawyers, and individuals belonging to the middle and popular sectors in the cities. All of them identified with the insurgency as they were Catholics and adherents of Guadalupe, but the latter did not share the mythic beliefs of the former. They were men educated in the ideals of the Enlightenment and Creole patriotism and they had a modern and secular political plan. Nevertheless, the majority of them, following the tradition of making Guadalupe into a symbol in which the particular aspirations of their devotees fit, also transformed the Virgin of Guadalupe into a battling Virgin. Between 1810 and 1814, a group of lawyers, religious, and individuals of the high and middle groups of the cities founded a secret society baptized with the name "Los Guadalupes." During these crucial years, Los Guadalupes helped develop an insurgent press, trafficked and supplied arms to the army, established an extensive information network that transmitted precious news to the various groups of insurgents, and created forms of protection and safeguards for the families of the combatants.[47]

Sought after by these interests, the Virgin of Guadalupe came to be the principal emblem of the insurgency, the center of a fervent patriotic cult, and the flag of those who fought for independence. In the confusion between traditional religious beliefs and modern political aspirations that is characteristic of this era, the Virgin of Guadalupe was the symbol that gathered both the mythic and the eschatological burden of the indigenous and popular masses as well as the libertarian aspirations of the more developed political groups of the viceroyalty. By gathering these plural claims during the years of the insurgent war and at the moment of political separation from Spain, the Virgin of Guadalupe reached her maximum status as a religious and political symbol of Mexicans. Her old meanings neither decreased nor were lost; to the contrary, during the convulsed years of the war, her ancestral, mythic content was enriched as the pulsations of the various indigenous groups —which transferred into the religious process their myths, their traditional conceptions of the past, their proceedings of cohesion to the community through the announcement of miracles and marvels, and their yearning to see the lost golden age brought about on earth or the egalitarian kingdom of God—were brought into her. For the partisans of the insurgency, the Virgin of Guadalupe proved in these years that the manifestation of the Mother of God in Mexican lands had converted Mexico into a privileged country and its inhabitants into a chosen people.

It is not strange, then, that on September 16, 1823, when the independent nation prepared to celebrate the glorious date when liberty had been declared, the shrine of Guadalupe was the place chosen to honor the remains of the heroes, once again melding religious sentiment with libertarian political symbols. That day, the chronicler of the insurgency, Carlos María de Bustamante, narrates: "the venerable remains of Morelos reached Guadalupe. It must have around 12:30 when they came into the villa and were presented to the collegiate church. Three Indian musicians from different towns accompanied them and, instead of somber chants and music, they played waltzes and cheerful airs."

This mixture of religious fervor and patriotic cult to the heroes was prolonged after the war, particularly on the dates when the freedom cry of Dolores was celebrated. The tone of this religious nationalist cult is described very well by Jacques Lafaye on referring to the honors given to the heroes of independence in the metropolitan cathedral: "The day following that September 16 (1823), since then a national holiday, army formations accompanied the remains of the founding fathers from the convent of Santo Domingo to the cathedral. In a symbolic amalgam of the new national order, the procession in which military and clergy were mixed escorted by a squadron of grenadiers and by the national militia, accompanied the dead heroes to the cathedral. Around the remains of Hidalgo, Morelos, and their early companions, the Mexican national choir . . . sang, perhaps for once in unison."[48] This form of religious nationalism reached its highest symbolic expression in the first president of the republic, who changed his original name (Félix Fernández) to *Guadalupe Victoria*.

The Enlightened Priests

In this war, so contaminated by religiosity, it seems natural that the popular masses would see their leaders as warriors and enlightened prophets, as beings endowed with special powers and protected by sacred forces that led them to perform extraordinary feats. Such is the image of Father Hidalgo that many of his followers spread. The priest, say his people, "is a saint," he has direct contact with the Holy Virgin, to whom "he speaks several times a day." Many partisans of the insurgent cause were convinced that it would end with the establishment of a new kingdom, the setting up of a kind of theocracy, and this is why they declared that their most fervent desire was to "go to Mexico City to put the lord priest on his throne." "Before his own men, Hidalgo appears with a strange seal. The people follow him as a saint or as enlightened, before him priests kneel, a *gard d'corps* preceded him as a sovereign, and his partisans found no better name to give him than that of his most Serene Highness; not your lordship, not excellency, not general, which was his rank, but Highness, a name fitting for those who are glorified above other men."[49]

"Like Hidalgo, Morelos appears closed in a charismatic character, which in the eyes of his troops makes him more of an enlightened prophet than a simple guerrilla chief. They follow him like a father; they call his son Juan 'seer', and one of his Indians, taken prisoner before Cuautla, insists stubbornly that his cadaver be taken inside the besieged plaza so that Morelos can resuscitate him."[50]

The very incandescence of the war, the intense, multiple, unrestrained explosions of frustrations and contained yearnings, the emotional and contaminating force of the mass movements, the cohabitation of individual and collective deliriums, everything favored the manifestation of mythic beliefs and eschatological images in the popular masses, the appearance of new messiahs and enlightened leaders, and the crossing and inventing of the most delirious images. The movement that Hidalgo and Morelos head gathers these manifestations of popular mentality and offers them a conduit through which to express themselves. But in addition, the enlightened leaders of the insurgency owe a great part of their charismatic image to a very conscious sensitivity to the sentiments and demands of their followers. Hidalgo and Morelos are leaders who, in addition to identifying with the popular masses who make up their armies, take on the responsibility of acting on their behalf and representing them. They set themselves up as executors of popular aspirations and demands. If the Revolution at the moment when it is unleashed effectively transfers sovereignty to the people, to the popular armed insurgency that, as of that moment, acts for itself and transforms reality, the decisions that Hidalgo makes in the war are consequences of that new reality. As Luis Villoro says, "Hidalgo's decrees do nothing more than express the effective sovereignty of the people." The majority of his measures have the character of abrogation, manifesting thus the negative character of popular liberty. Starting with his speech of September 16, the abolition of tribute symbolizes the destruction of existing right: "For us—he says—neither the king nor tributes exist any longer. That shameful burden that is only fitting for slaves, we have borne it for three centuries as a sign of tyranny and serfdom; a terrible blotch that we will wash away with our own efforts."[51]

The abrogation of tribute is the sign that announces a deeper modification of reality: the destruction of the old order. This is the sense of the other decisions that Hidalgo makes as representative of the masses that carry out the Revolution. "Invested with the authority that he exercises by acclamation of the nation, Hidalgo abolishes the caste distinctions and slavery, signs of the infamy and oppression that the other classes exercised over the blacks and mestizos."[52]

In Morelos the identification with the aspirations of the popular movement is even more genuine. "Morelos begins his military career as one of many caudillos from the ranks of the low clergy. He is no '*letrado*'; he belongs, to the contrary, to the most humble classes . . . Rising from the people, living always with them, he is the most authentic representative of the popular conscience. His ideas and political positions will be the clear expression of the political movement of liberty. In them the people try to create from its origin a social structure that can replace the old one."[53]

Pressured by the lawyers and literate Creoles that surround him and demand that he define the political plans of the insurgent movement, Morelos states with emotional and simple words the political program centered on popular sovereignty and the disappearance of inequalities that divided the population. He puts into words the ancestral aspiration of the indigenous communities and the oppressed groups to live in equality and converts into a political program the social demands of the most abandoned popular sectors of the viceroyalty:

I want [the nation] to have a government issuing from the people . . . I want us to make a declaration that there is no nobility other than that of virtue, of knowledge, of patriotism, and of charity; that we are all equal, for we come from the same origin; that there be no privileges or lineages; that it is not rational or human or fitting that there be slavery, for the color of the face does not change that of the heart or that of thought; that the children of the peasant and the ditch digger be educated like those of the rich hacendados; that everyone who files a justified complaint has a court to hear it, to help them, and to defend them from the strong and the arbitrary.[54]

In this new era that Morelos preaches, the egalitarian nation governed by virtue, charity, and patriotism will have Catholicism as its sole religion, and it will be a nation by and for those born in it. In his *Sentimientos de la nación*, Morelos establishes that "the Catholic religion will be the only one, without tolerance of others; that the Americans will be those who have jobs; that the laws will moderate opulence and indigence; that [the laws] will include everyone without exception of privileged bodies; and that slavery will be forbidden forever, as will caste distinctions, leaving everyone equal, and the only thing that will distinguish one American from another is vice and virtue."[55]

Thus, by defining this egalitarian project that gathered the social demands of the popular classes and the political aspirations of the marginalized Creoles, Morelos blended the most advanced political and social proposals of the insurgent movement with the deep pulsations of traditional society that formed part of its armies and that he himself represented. This sensitivity that Morelos shows for gathering the hopes and feelings of the popular masses or for declaring the Catholic religion the exclusive faith of the new state or for incorporating it into the official celebrations of the cult to the religious symbol that was most extended and venerated by the population, is manifested also in the effort that he makes to endow the nation with a pantheon of heroes of its own. Morelos is the first rebel chief to elevate the Indian leaders that defended their peoples from Hernán Cortés' troops to the high position of heroes of the country, and he was the first to attempt to blend the cult of heroes of indigenous antiquity with the cult of the heroes of the insurgent movement. In his opening speech at the Chilpancingo Congress (1813), after referring to the country by its old name, Anáhuac, he invokes the "genius of Moctezuma, Cacama, Quautimozin, Xicoténcatl, and Caltzontzin" to celebrate with them the "happy moment in which your illustrious sons have gathered to avenge your outrages and loss of privileges and to free themselves from the claws of Freemasonry's tyranny, which was going to swallow them forever." To this same end, he calls to participation in his congress the "ancestral spirits of the dead, of Las Cruces, Aculco, Guanajuato, and Calderón, Zitácuaro, and Cuautla, united to those of Hidalgo and Allende!" In this way, Morelos associates the indigenous victims of the Spanish Conquest with the leaders and insurgent martyrs killed by the Spaniards and establishes a necessary relation between the ancient conquered nation and the liberating present in which the Mexicans decided to declare their independence from Spain. This is why he says, in the same opening speech to the Chipancingo Congress, that "August 12, 1521, was followed by September 14, 1813. In the former, the chains of our slavery were put on in México-Tenochtitlan, and in the latter, they are broken forever in the fortunate town of Chilpancingo."[56]

The mythic and religious tradition of the indigenous movements, the social demands of the most abandoned groups, and the Creoles' ideals of autonomy, patriotism, and Guadalupan fervor were expressed with all their force in the popular movement that Hidalgo and Morelos headed. This movement, plural and powerful, which for the first time joined the pulsations of the indigenous and popular masses with the political aspirations of the Creole group, found in Hidalgo, and especially in Morelos, its highest expression and its highest capacity for realization. In the subsequent political movements, this intimate relationship between the yearnings and claims of the masses and the actions and programs of the political leaders disappears.

Nevertheless, even when this project did not have continuity in its immediate future, its polyvalent mythic and ideological charge will be present in all later political and social movements. Like the traumatic episode of the Conquest, Hidalgo and Morelos's Revolution will be established in the historical memory as a parting of the waters, an act denying colonial submission, and founding the independent Mexican nation. Beginning then, even when the social and egalitarian programs that replied to the demands of the popular masses are set aside, the presence of myths and symbols of popular rebellion and the mythic images of Hidalgo and Morelos will continue to act in the construction of Mexican nationalism, along with the heroic figures of the other leaders of independence and alongside the inseparable Virgin of Guadalupe. In this strange combination, through which the myth (the Virgin of Guadalupe) becomes historical reality and historical fact is transmuted into myth, the revolution of independence created the myth of the preexisting but enslaved nation (ancient Anáhuac), freed by the cry of Dolores and the declaration of independence. It created also a pantheon of national heroes and, above all, created the project of building a nation based on an ancient history endowed with founding fathers, protected by the divinity, owner of an extensive and rich territory, and destined to live a promising future. The Creoles had already encouraged this project, but Hidalgo and Morelos converted it into a real historical possibility and, above all, gave it the human presence and the emotional charge of the popular masses. They did not imagine a nation for one class or a restricted group; they fought and died for a national project that involved and liberated the majority of Mexicans.

Origin and Founding of a National History

During the viceroyalty, there was no precise idea or conception of the Mexican nation, nor a national history or nationalist historiography, for the simple reason that the country was a viceroyalty, a colony of Spain. This link of political submission impeded the appearance of the idea of nation, that is, a political concept that in most cases manifests itself in situations of autonomy or repulsion of aggression or political subjugation. For almost three centuries in New Spain, the political and ideological conditions to support the idea of an autonomous nation did not exist. On the other hand, as has been seen, the notion of country developed and an exalted patriotic sentiment was manifest, although reduced to the identity with the earth where it had been born, seated on a group of shared religious values (the unity around the Catholic faith and the Virgin of Guadalupe), supported by a progressive recovery of the ancient history of the original inhabitants and directed by the interests and ideological claims of the Creole group. It was, then, a concept of limited homeland that was not shared by the other groups that made up the country and that did not spare the very deep ethnic, social, economic, and cultural divisions that fragmented and opposed the population.

The situation of the viceroyalty changed radically when its political relationship with Spain was modified. Beginning in 1808, the appearance of a political thought centered on the ideas of autonomy and sovereignty of the nation and the formation of a new political reality produced by the insurgent movement created the conditions that allowed the modern idea of nation and the conception of a historical national project to unfold vigorously.

In 1808, Spain was invaded by the armies of Napoleon and Charles IV, and his heir to the throne fell prisoner to the French. Thus, for the first time, the inhabitants of the kingdoms of Spain and the Indies contemplated with alarm the disappearance of the royal tie that united them. In New Spain, while the authorities of the viceroyalty declared that the imprisonment of the monarch did not change in any way "the powers established legitimately and they should continue as they have thus far," the Creoles stated that there was a new political situation and that situation forced raising the problem concerning whom sovereignty resided in and who should assume it in the circumstances of the moment. The Ayuntamiento of Mexico City, which at the time was a redoubt of the Creole group, and Jacobo de Villaurrutia, the only Creole *oidor* of the Real Audiencia, initiated this debate. The Ayuntamiento surprised the highest authorities of the viceroyalty when it argued that the abdications of Charles IV and Ferdinand VII were null, as they were "contrary to the rights of the nation to which no one can give a king if it is not itself by the universal consent of its people."[57]

Thus, for the first time, the political debate held that the king did not exercise sovereignty by divine right, but that it had been granted him by the express will of the nation. It was also stated, then, that there was an original pact between the king and the governed that the monarch could not alter by himself. The Creoles' doctrine of the social pact came from Francisco de Vitoria and Francisco Suárez, two great Spanish writers of political treatises, whose thought had been collected in the eighteenth century by Francisco Martínez Marina and Gaspar Melchor de Jovellanos. These principles of Spanish political thought became mixed with "some ideas of rationalist naturalism [Grocio, Puffendorf, Heinecio] that had quite a bit of influence in all the Hispanic kingdoms during the eighteenth century." Francisco Javier Alegre, an enlightened Jesuit, gathered these two currents in his *Institutorum teologicarum* (1789). In this work he held that "the proximate origin of authority was in the 'consent of the community,' and its foundation in the right of the peoples; the sovereignty of the king—he stated—is only mediate: it is obtained by delegation, by common consent." Citing Puffendorf, he explained a doctrine that coincided also with the Suarist line of thought: "Every empire . . . of whatever type it may be had its origin in a convention or pact between men."[58]

These ideas on sovereignty and the social pact between the king and the governed were the principal sources of inspiration of the first theoreticians of independence. Francisco Primo de Verdad y Ramos, a lawyer who was a trustee of the Mexico City town council, held in 1808 that "authority comes to the king from God, but not in an immediate fashion, rather, through the people." For his part, Juan Francisco Azcárate, also a lawyer and member of the same city council, proposed that this body present the viceroy with a document requesting nonacceptance of the nominations of new authorities in the viceroyalty or of any government decision proceeding from Spain because, in the absence of the king, sovereignty resided in the kingdom of New Spain, in the courts that formed it, and in the bodies that "carry the public's voice," which for Azcárate was, in this case, the town council of Mexico City.

Azcárate explained that there existed a pact between the nation and its sovereign that could not be broken unilaterally; therefore, in the absence of the king, sovereignty returned to its original source, the nation, or to its constituted bodies, that is, principally the town council of Mexico City. Thus, what the Creoles argued was that the basis of this society no longer rested on the king, but on the nation.[59]

Fray Melchor de Talamantes, who was tied to Judge Jacobo de Villaurrutia and to the Creoles who had influence on the town council and in the *Diario de México*, took a further step in this debate: he broadened the concepts on which national representation was based and listed the causes for which a colony exercising its national representation could become independent of its homeland. For Talamantes, national representation was society's right to be considered free and independent of any other nation. This right depended on three principles: nature, strength, and politics. According to Talamantes,

Nature has divided nations by means of oceans, rivers, mountains, diversity of climate, variety of tongues, etc., and under this aspect, the Americas have national representation, as they are naturally separated from other nations, much more so than the kingdoms of Europe are. By strength, nations put themselves in the condition of resisting their enemies ... Considering the Americas in light of this principle, no one can doubt that they have national representation, having resisted, in fact, on many occasions the attacks of foreign powers. The national representation that politics gives rests only on the civil right (direct or indirect suffrage), or what is the same, the quality of citizen that the laws concede to certain individuals of the state.[60]

Talamantes thought that the sovereignty of a nation did not reside in the people, but in the congress that represented them. He held that national representation was inherently the faculty of "organizing one-self," and, based on these considerations, he stated that, as "national representation ... liberty and independence" were "almost identical things"; "as long as colonies can legitimately make themselves independent, separating themselves from their homelands, they will also be capable of taking on national representation." And in what cases can the independence of colonies be legitimate? Talamantes lists twelve reasons:

1. when the colonies are self-sufficient;
2. when they are equal or more powerful than their homelands;
3. when the latter have difficulty governing them;
4. when the government of the homeland is incompatible with the general good of the colony;
5. when the former oppresses the latter;
6. when the homeland has adopted another political institution;
7. when the first provinces that form the principal body of the homeland subject themselves voluntarily to foreign dominance;
8. when the homeland voluntarily submits to foreign domination;
9. when the homeland is subjugated by another nation;
10. when it changes religion;
11. when the homeland threatens to change the religious system; and
12. when separation is demanded by "the general clamor of the inhabitants of the colony."[61]

This search by the Creoles to find the political bases to legitimize their aspirations for autonomy was abbreviated by Servando Teresa de

Mier, who discovered an unobjectionable basis in the very *Carta Magna de Castilla*, written by Alfonso el Sabio. There, argued Mier, it stated explicitly that when there was no king, the nobles and sages of the kingdom and representatives of the towns should gather and constitute a congress to elect a new form of government and its representation. For Mier it was clear that, in the absence of the king of Spain, the American provinces were empowered to call their own meetings or congresses to determine their destiny and to adopt the form of government they elected.

This was the idea that predominated among the members of the Creole party, with two variations. One group (Francisco Primo de Verdad, Juan Francisco Azcárate, and, especially, Fray Melchor de Talamantes) proposed that the gathering or congress be constituted of representatives of the town councils and the "deputies of all the secular and ecclesiastical councils," who should delegate to the congress the exercise of sovereignty. The other current (headed by Jacobo de Villaurrutia) proposed a congress represented by the civil, ecclesiastical, and military corporations and suggested the constitution of a government in which the power of some agencies was counterbalanced by that of the others: a system of division of powers.[62]

The development of this political debate was suddenly interrupted by the coup d'état that in 1808 was headed by merchants and groups most addicted to the traditional state of things. Nevertheless, two years later the ideas and political projects that were then the center of the debates were reborn in Hidalgo's insurrection and took on a new dimension under the influence of popular participation. By means of the transformative action of the Revolution, Hidalgo and Morelos proclaimed the independence of the nation, recognized in the people the original and only source of sovereignty, repudiated the government of the old regime and its laws, and established the basic principles for organizing the freed nation politically and constitutionally. First in the decrees that Hidalgo and Morelos issued during the insurrection, then in the *Acta de independencia* and in the documents before the Chilpancingo Congress (*Manifiesto* of the Congress, *Reglamento y discurso de apertura* of same). Finally, in the *Sentimientos de la nación* and in the *Constitución de Apatzingán*, these constitutional principles of the nation came to form part of the collective memory of the Mexicans.

The principle of the nationalities or of the liberty of people to govern themselves was the insurgents' point of departure for claiming independence: "No people has the right to subjugate another without just cause for aggression." This principle, invoked in similar conditions by other nations, had in Mexico a particular connotation. Mexico proclaimed itself a free and sovereign nation but defined itself as an old nation, prior to the Spanish Conquest, that had been subjugated. It was not, then, a new nation, but a nation that was freeing itself of domination. This is why it said in the *Acta de independencia* that North America had "recovered the exercise of its usurped sovereignty." This is why it was stated in the *Constitución de Apatzingán* that "no nation has the right to prevent another the use of its sovereignty. The title of conquest cannot legitimize acts of force: the people who attempt to do so should be obligated by arms to respect the conventional right of nations."

The principle of popular sovereignty was another great pillar on which the insurgents' political project rested. Gathering the spirit that inspired the popular insurrection in the *Sentimientos de la nación*, Morelos stated that "sovereignty originates immediately from the people"; and in the *Constitución de Apatzingán*, it was asserted that "sovereignty resides originally in the people and its exercise in national representation composed of deputies elected by the citizens." In this last document, it was said that sovereignty by nature is "imprescriptible, inalienable, and indivisible," and its powers were defined: "Three are the powers of sovereignty: the right to make laws, the right to execute them, and the right to apply them to particular cases."

To the founding principles of the insurgent nation were joined others from popular exploits, the enlightened thought of the Creoles, and modern political thought. These affirmed the equality of all Mexicans before the law, ratified the unity of the people around the Catholic religion, and declared that the fundamental objective of the state was the pursuit of a common good and the definition of the new political organization of the nation.[63]

In this manner, the revolution of independence and the political thought that sprang from it affirmed the "subjective characteristics" that, according to theoreticians, explain the formation of a nation: the population's aspiration to constitute an autonomous nation; the loyalty to the nation over any other interest; and the will to maintain the nation united and independent. At the same time, the revolution of independence consolidated and gave a modern political dimension to the "objective characteristics" that define (although they do not explain) the nation: a political organization legitimized by popular consensus; a territorial identity; a shared history; and a common language.[64] For the first time in the history of Mexico, traditional nationalist sentiments (a shared territory, religion, past, and language) were integrated into the modern political project of constituting an independent, autonomous nation dedicated to the pursuit of the common good of its inhabitants. Thus, resting on the armed mobilization of the population and on modern nationalist political thought, the nation elevated itself as free, independent, and in possession of its destiny, and created a future in which to carry out its own historical project, centered on the national state and the autonomous nation. This radical transformation of the present and creation of a horizon open to the future substantially modified the conception of the history of the country, the rescue of its past, and the formation of national historical memory.

Political independence from Spain and the decision to carry out the national political project created a single subject of historical narration: the Mexican nation, the national state. For the first time, instead of an internally fragmented viceroyalty governed by foreign powers, the Mexicans thought of their country, their territory, the different parts that composed it, its population, and its past as a unitary, distinctive entity. From then on, independently of internal visions and contradictions, the nation was thought of as a territorial, social, and political entity that had a common origin, development in time, and a future. The appearance of a political entity that contained in itself all the parts of the nation was the new subject of history that unified the social and cultural diversity of the population in a joint search for national identity.

In turn, the appearance of a conception of historical development centered on the nation gave birth to a history for itself, the development of a writing of history done for the nation and composed by Mexicans. Suddenly, with the dazzling clarity of liberty, the country became aware, at the very point it began to exercise its independence, that the greatest part of its historical memory was created by the conqueror, that it lacked its own interpretation of its historical development, and that the very sources for writing its history were outside its frontiers or had been compiled by its ancient dominators. This discovery explains that the elaboration of a history of their own by Mexicans would inextricably be united with the carrying out of the political project of the national state. Thus, one of the first decisions of the independent governments was to establish archives and museums where the testimony of national history was preserved. With the creation of these institutions, the memory of the past, until then fragmented, expropriated, and alien, began to be a memory recovered and classified by national institutions and under the direction of the historical interests of the nation. Similar to what occurred after the Spanish Conquest, beginning with independence practically the entire past of the country was revised, rethought, and rewritten, but now, under the compulsion of creating an image and a historical memory founded on values recognized as characteristic by the independent nation.

Conclusion

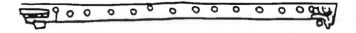

As the title reveals, this book is dedicated to recovering the diverse images of Mexico's past created by the successive generations that have reconstructed, mythicized, hidden, deformed, invented, ideologized, or explained that past. To enumerate these diverse means of recovering the past is equivalent to saying that this is not an orthodox book. It does not propose, as is customary among historians, to explain only the so-called scientific reconstructions of the past, which are, naturally, those elaborated by historians themselves. In addition to studying the images of the past constructed by historians, this book collects the legends, myths, and symbols of the past created by groups that lacked writing and transmitted their traditions in oral form from one generation to the next. It also collects images of the past crystallized in ceremonies, feasts, and popular celebrations that periodically recorded events, foundings, and origins, the memory of which is important for affirming the collective identity.

This book, then, focuses special attention on images of the past created by indigenous and folk groups. It proposes to rescue the collective imagination that, by means of a different temporal dimension from that of the western categories of measuring time and reconstructing the past, composes its own memory of the occurrences, creates a hierarchy of the importance of these events for the collectivity, brings them up to date, and proposes them as social paradigms for living the present and facing the challenges of the future.

It can be said that, since the birth of the profession of historian, the popular representations of the past have been qualified as mythic, legendary, or false, principally because they do not conform to the conceptions that historians accept as scientifically trustworthy. Nevertheless, my decision to consider them as valid testimony in an exercise of reconstruction of historical memory rests on the following argument. Independently of whether they are deformed versions or false interpretations of the past, they were considered true by those who spread them, and were accepted as true by those who heard them and transmitted them to the following generations.

The most powerful argument in favor of myth or the collective image as valid testimony of the representation of the past is that, in spite of the passage of a long period of time since they were first stated, and in spite of the disqualification of these testimonies by those who practiced written history, nowadays these expressions of the collective memory continue to live, and for many people are the most trustworthy instrument for recalling the past and maintaining its identity in the present.

In the case of Mexico, these testimonies are particularly important because, from the most ancient times to date, they have been the principal instrument for preserving, reconstructing, and spreading the memory of past events among the indigenous peoples, the rural population, and urban popular groups. That is, they have been the privileged vehicle for re-creating the historical memory of the majority of the population.

I could add that this book is part of the current of thought initiated by anthropologists and ethnohistorians that makes an effort to open new forms of comprehension for understanding peoples and cultural traditions that are expressed in strange languages, different and sometimes opposed to ours. In this sense, it is a proposal to amplify our comprehension of the multiple forms of reconstructing and spreading the memory of past events.

If today we recognize that, along with the reconstruction of the past carried out under western historiographical methods, there are other equally valid forms of collecting the past, the principal problem in capturing this memory is rooted in the fact that this field does not contain the same richness of already-proven methods that distinguishes traditional historiography. The methods for collecting and explaining the images of the past created by peoples with an oral tradition, or by marginal social groups, are mostly experimental. They arise from the work of anthropologists and ethnohistorians and utilize techniques developed by structuralism, collective psychology, content analysis, history of mentalities, and so on.

Furthermore, with regard to the results that are derived from this investigation, I would mention the following. In the first place, by studying the forms of reconstructing and preserving the memory of the past in ancient Mexico, I discovered that the founding myth of the origins and the cyclical conception of time were the articulating axes of historical memory in antiquity. According to this conception, the cosmos, nature, and human creations had a moment of maximum plenitude. This complete time was the time of original creation, when things were established for the first time and were imbued with the harmony, vigor, and plenitude of primordial creation. Nevertheless, this original creation was later threatened with destruction by temporal happenings, the corrosive passage of time. This is why the actions of the gods and of human beings concentrate on cyclical revitalizing, through ritual, religious ceremony, and collective memory, the full moment of original creation. That is, for the peoples of ancient Mexico, the strongest, most significant historical time was the time past, the time in which for the first time were established the foundations of the cosmos and of human life. Contrary to the western conception of history, the indigenous conception of historical events is turned toward the past, it proposes for the present to preserve and revitalize what was created in the origin, and it insists that the future, instead of being the bearer of disruptive changes, is the bearer of permanence.

By examining the conceptions of history and the past that were manifested in the Conquest and throughout the viceroyalty, I discovered that in this era there was no dominant interpretation of history; rather, multiple interpretations of the past coexisted, produced by diverse sectors of the population, and each one of them was nourished by different concepts of time and the past. There is the imperialist, providential interpretation of history produced by the official chroniclers of the Spanish crown, who present the discovery and conquest of the new lands as a special enterprise expressly indicated by God for the Spanish nation. The fresh and marveled narrations of the soldier-conquerors stand out. These transmit the epic of the Conquest and the encounter with strange civilizations in a direct fashion. Next to these interpretations we find the mystic, Christian conception of history written by the evangelizing friars, who saw in the discovery of indigenous humanity the fulfillment of the prophecies contained in the Book of the Apocalypse and the opportunity to establish in the new lands a celestial city, governed by the ideals of apostolic poverty, love for one's neighbor, and praise of God. Beside these diverse interpretations of history appear the chronicles of the religious orders, which exalt the evangelizing labor of their members, and, much later, the chronicles of the cities of the viceroyalty, which contain a worshipful remembrance of the local and regional environment.

Even when none of these new discourses manage to predominate, what is certain is that as a whole, they propose a new protagonist for history and a new meaning for the writing of history. From that point on, the new protagonist of history is the conquistador, and the purpose of historical narration is to describe the action that this new protagonist unfolds on the American stage. The past and future of indigenous peoples are subordinated to the history that this new agent of historical transformation writes.

Nevertheless, in spite of the destruction of the testimonies of indigenous memory, and in spite of the prohibitions that the Spanish crown dictated concerning the recovery of the past of the vanquished peoples, the indigenous peoples, now without the resource of writing that was lost with the disappearance of their rulers, continued to evoke their past through myth and oral tradition. One of the chapters of this book that is most unusual shows that the conservation and revitalization of ancestral memory was the most powerful resource in the struggle to continue being Indians in a situation of dominance. This was their most effective weapon for resisting the transformation that the conqueror imposed, and the instrument to which they always returned when outside aggression became unbearable and they decided to rebel for the purpose of returning to a lost age in which indigenous values and traditions predominated.

Besides these diverse and internally conflicting memories, there appeared a representation of the past that aspired to fuse these multiple memories into a single one and to represent that as the collective memory of those born in Mexico. This was the memory constructed by the Creoles, by the descendants of Spaniards but born in Mexico. As did the Creoles in other places, those in Mexico experienced an identity crisis between their Spanish ancestry and their loyalty to the land where they had been born. But unlike the continent's other Creoles, those in Mexico resolved this conflict by continually establishing more distance from Spain and creating stronger identification with their native land. According to the interpretation of the Creoles, a religious symbol, the Virgin of Guadalupe, converted Mexican land into sacred land especially privileged by God. Later, a history book, *La historia antigua de México* by Francisco Javier Clavijero, culminated the process that for more than two centuries had troubled Creoles who were trying to find their identity in American roots. Clavijero assumed as proper the until-then foreign and repudiated indigenous past and proposed it as the root for the Creole homeland.

Thus, by integrating indigenous antiquity into the notion of country, the Creoles expropriated the past of the indigenous peoples and made of that past a legitimate and prestigious antecedent of the Creole country. The Creoles' country then had a remote and noble past and a present unified by religious symbols shared by Indians and Creoles.

What is astonishing about this reconstruction is that the idea of a Creole country is founded on two myths: that of the existence of an Indian nation prior to the Spanish Conquest, and that of the miraculous appearance of the mother of God in Mexican territory. Even more astonishing is to observe—during the first decade of the nineteenth century and the ten years of the war for independence, when European political doctrines concerning liberty and the sovereignty of nations and modern forms of organizing the state erupted in the viceroyalty—the presence of multiple folk myths and symbols of the construction of an independent nation.

During these years crucial to the political lives of Mexicans, the populist masses, drawn by the Virgin of Guadalupe, joined the insurgent armies. Like their ancestors, they made a talisman of the image of the Virgin, a weapon that they brandished before the enemy. Father Hidalgo and Morelos, the caudillos of the insurgency, were not simply military leaders to the multitudes that followed them; they were providential men, endowed with supernatural powers, Messiah-like, whose presence alone would produce the triumph of the just cause and the defeat of the perverse Spaniards.

When political independence from Spain was finally achieved in 1821, the feast that celebrated this great event became a populist feast in which were condensed and exploded the collective images of the liberation of the ancient conquered nation, the resentment of the ethnic oppressor, the supremacy of the Virgin of Guadalupe over other cults in the Christian pantheon, and the affirmation of the messianic, providential idea that proclaims a great future for the liberated nation.

In summary, if these reconstructions of Mexican memory are correct, the most important conclusion that can be drawn from this book is the following. During the long period when the ancient cultures of Meso-america developed and during almost all of the viceroyalty, mythical and religious conceptions, of both indigenous and European origin, were dominant in the interpretation of time, of human events, and of historical development.

Notes

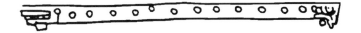

Preface

1. Renan, *Qu'est-ce qu'une nation.*
2. Berlin, *Contra la corriente. Ensayos sobre historia de las ideas,* p. 181. See also idem, *Vico and Herder.*

1. The Nahua Concept of Time and Space

1. See Garibay, *Teogonía e historia de los mexicanos,* p. 27. Garibay includes known texts such as *Historia de los mexicanos por sus pinturas, Histoire du Mechique,* and *Breve relación de los dioses y ritos de la gentilidad* by Ponce de León.

2. The order or succession in which the suns or ages are presented varies greatly from one source to another. Only the *Historia de los mexicanos por sus pinturas* and *La leyenda de los soles* (in the Codex Chimalpopoca) agree on the following order: Earth Sun, Wind Sun, Fire Sun, and Water Sun. This is the order I shall use here. Antonio de León y Gama, the first person to study the Sun Stone, read this same order in the central part of this monument. See León y Gama, *Descripción histórica y cronológica de las dos piedras.* Alfredo Chavero disputed León y Gama's interpretation. He read the following order on the Sun Stone: Wind, Fire, Water, Earth. See Chavero, "La piedra del sol. Estudio arqueológico." Alexander Humboldt was one of the first modern authors to interpret this myth. See Humboldt, *Vistas de las cordilleras y monumentos de los pueblos indígenas de América,* pp. lv–lxx (Labastida's introduction), 221–229. For an explanation of the differences between sources, see Moreno de los Arcos, "Los cinco soles cosmogónicos." See Elzey, "The Nahua Myth of the Suns," pp. 114–135, for an excellent summary of the different interpretations of the order of the suns.

3. *Historia de los mexicanos por sus pinturas* clearly shows this: "And because the counting begins with this first sun and the counting figures go forward continuously, leaving behind six hundred years, at the beginning of which the gods were born." See Garibay, *Teogonía e historia de los mexicanos,* p. 29.

4. Garibay, *Teogonía e historia de los mexicanos,* p. 31.

5. Ibid, p. 23. The version in *Histoire du Mechique* tells that Tezcatlipoca and Quetzalcóatl entered the body of the earth monster Tlaltecuhtli, the former

through his mouth, and the latter through the navel. They joined in the earth's heart. There, with the help of other gods, they created the sky. This same work proposes a third version. Quetzalcóatl and Tezcatlipoca, seeing that the earth goddess, Tlaltecuhtli ("who was filled in every joint by eyes and mouths with which she bit like a savage beast"), walked on the primordial waters, saying: "the land must be made. And saying this they both changed into two large serpents (. . . and) one of them seized the goddess by the left hand and right foot. And they squeezed her so tightly that she split in half and with the half of the back they made the land and the other half they took up to heaven . . . Then, having done that, to compensate the aforesaid goddess for the harm these gods had done to her, all the gods went down to console her and ordered that all the fruit necessary for human life come out of her" (Garibay, *Teogonía e historia de los mexicanos*, pp. 105 and 108).

6. *Historia de los mexicanos por sus pinturas*, in Garibay, *Teogonía e historia de los mexicanos*, p. 33.

7. *Histoire du Mechique* contains a different version of the creation of maize. In this version, the gods descend into the cave where Piltzintecuhtli, son of the first human couple, lives. There they find him lying with his wife, Xochiquétzal. From this union is born Cintéotl, the young god of maize, "who went under the ground and from his hair came cotton, and from one ear a very good seed that they eat with gusto, called *huazontli*." From the other ear another seed springs, and "from his nose another one called *chían*, which is good to drink in the summer; from his fingers came a fruit called *camotli*, which is like turnips, a very good fruit. From his nails a kind of long maize, which is what they eat now, and from the rest of his body came many other fruits that men plant and harvest" (Garibay, *Teogonía e historia de los mexicanos*, p. 110).

8. This version of the cosmogonic myth is derived from the following sources: *Historia de los mexicanos por sus pinturas* and *Histoire du Mechique*, in Garibay, *Teogonía e historia de los mexicanos*; Velázquez, *Códice Chimalpopoca. Anales de Cuauhtitlán y leyenda de los soles*, pp. 119–123; and Sahagún, *Historia general de las cosas de Nueva España*, vol. 2, pp. 258–262. For a comparison of the different versions, see Moreno de los Arcos, "Los cinco soles cosmogónicos." See also Caso's synthesis and interpretation in *El pueblo del sol*; Soustelle, *La pensée cosmologique des anciens mexicains*; and Nicholson, "Religion in Pre-Hispanic Central Mexico."

9. Caso affirms his belief in an evolutionary process because in none of the versions of the cosmogonic account does he find mention of a golden age, of "the good old days." In the *Popol Vuh* of the Quichés, Caso confirms this idea of progress in the cosmogonic creations. That work "tells that the Creator made several tries before He accomplished His perfect work" (*El pueblo del sol*, pp. 27–28). Nevertheless, I believe that this and other "evolutionist" interpretations lack validity. As Elzey says, "The sequence of the world ages is disjunctive. There is nothing inherent in any of the Suns which leads into the next as a higher and more advanced stage" ("The Nahua Myth of the Suns," p. 123).

10. Townsend, *State and Cosmos*, pp. 63–70.

11. Cited by Broda, "Astronomy, Cosmovision and Ideology in Prehispanic Mesoamerica," p. 103.

12. "The surface of the earth was divided into a cross of four segments. The

center, or navel, is depicted as a pierced, precious green stone, uniting the four petals of a gigantic flower, another symbol of the earth's surface.

Each of the four segments of the earth's surface had a different color . . . On the central plateau, the most common distribution gave black to the north, white to the west, blue to the south, and red to the east. Green was the color of the center, the navel of the world. Other symbols, among them the many associated with the four directions of the earthly plane, were a flint stone to the north, a house to the west, a rabbit to the south, and a reed to the east . . . this order establishes a double opposition of death-life (north-south, with the symbols of inert matter and extreme mobility) and female-male (west-east, with the sexual symbols of house and reed)" (López Austin, *The Human Body and Ideology*, vol. 1, p. 58).

13. Ibid., p. 59.

14. See Reyes García, "La visión cosmológica y organización del imperio mexica," pp. 34–40; Broda, "El tributo en trajes guerreros y la estructura del sistema tributario mexica," pp. 130, 132; and idem, "Relaciones políticas ritualizadas: el ritual como expresión de una ideología, " p. 223. Marcus offers an example of this division in the Maya world in *Emblem and State in the Classic Maya Lowlands: An Epigraphic Approach to Territorial Organization.*

15. López Austin, *La constitución real de México-Tenochititlan*, p. 26.

16. See Zantwijk, "The Great Temple of Tenochtitlan: Model of Aztec Cosmovision," and *The Aztec Arrangement*, chaps. 4 and 6.

17. Durán, *Historia de las Indias de la Nueva España*, vol. 1, p. 22.

18. On the repetition of the cosmogonic archetype in human creations and the symbolism of the center as the starting point for all of creation, see Eliade, *El mito del eterno retorno*, pp. 20–28, and idem, *Imágenes y símbolos*, chap. 1.

19. Garibay, *Teogonía e historia de los mexicanos*, p. 29.

20. These and other movements of the sun and the stars were carefully observed and noted in pre-Hispanic astronomical and religious texts. See Aveni, *Archaeoastronomy in Pre-Columbian America*, and idem, *Skywatchers of Ancient Mexico.*

21. "Thus spring is associated with the northeast cuadrant and the north, the point at which the sun reaches its highest point during the summer solstice; summer with the northwest and the west; autumn with the southwest and the south; and winter with the southeast and the east" (Carrasco, "La sociedad mexicana antes de la conquista," pp. 270–271; see also González Torres, *El culto de los astros entre los mexicas*, pp. 140–142).

22. See Carrasco, "La fiesta de los meses mexicanos," p. 52.

23. See the works cited in note 20.

24. See Carrasco, "La sociedad mexicana antes de la conquista," pp. 257–280; and idem, "La fiesta de los meses mexicanos," pp. 55–60. Concerning the fiestas dedicated to the sun cult, see Broda, "Astronomy, Cosmovision and Ideology in Prehispanic Mesoamerica."

25. Thompson, *Grandeza y decadencia de los mayas*, pp. 152–153. See also León-Portilla, *Tiempo y realidad en el pensamiento maya.*

26. See Carrasco, "La sociedad mexicana antes de la conquista," p. 264; Caso, *Los calendarios prehispánicos.*

27. Soustelle, *Daily Life of the Aztecs*, pp. 114–115.

28. On space-time integration in Tenochtitlan, see Zantwijk, "The Great Temple of Tenochtitlan: Model of Aztec Cosmovision"; Broda, "Astronomy, Cosmovision and Ideology in Prehispanic Mesoamerica." See also Umberger, "The Structure of Aztec History," pp. 10–18; idem, "Events Commemorated by Date Plaques at the Templo Mayor," pp. 411–449; and idem, "El trono de Moctezuma," pp. 63–87.

29. These descriptions of the ceremony come from Sahagún, *Historia general de las cosas de Nueva España*, vol. 2, pp. 270–272, and vol. 4, p. 376.

30. Motolinía, *Memoriales*, p. 43.

31. Sahagún, *Historia general de las cosas de Nueva España*, vol. 3, p. 273.

32. See Broda, "La fiesta azteca del fuego nuevo y el culto a las pléyades."

33. See Eliade, *Imágenes y símbolos*; Brandon, *History, Time and Deity*. Brandon offers other examples of this "fear of history." See also Elzey, "The Nahua Myth of the Suns," pp. 131–132.

34. See, for example, Eliade, *Mito y realidad*, pp. 50–51, 55–56, 64–65.

35. Vernant, *Mito y pensamiento de la Grecia antigua*, p. 95.

36. Eliade, *Mito y realidad*, pp. 64–65.

37. See, for example, Bricker, *The Indian Christ, the Indian King: The Historical Substrate of Maya Myth and Ritual*.

38. The reading of this text provoked the following commentary from Bernardino de Sahagún: "This is Plato's thesis, and the Devil taught it here because it is erroneous, completely false, it is against the faith. The statement means: Things will be again as they were in times past; things will live again; and the world, as it is now, will be the same again. This is false and completely heretical" (López Austin, *The Human Body and Ideology*, vol. 1, p. 65).

39. López Austin, *Hombre-Dios. Religión y política en el mundo náhuatl*, p. 97.

40. Barrera Vázquez and Rendón, *El libro de los libros de Chilam Balam*, pp. 62, 49–85.

41. Malinowski, "Myth in Primitive Society," pp. 101–108.

2. Representation and Uses of the Past

1. Coe, *The Maya Scribe*; Tate, *Yaxchilan*, pp. 46–48.

2. Fash, *Scribes, Warriors, and Kings*, pp. 106–110.

3. Ibid., pp. 106–110, 120, 135–136.

4. The best study of historians and the types of historical recordkeeping that the Nahuas practiced is Nicholson, "Pre-Hispanic Central Mexican Historiography."

5. The following is a description of the sage, or *tlamatini*, who appears in the Codex Matritense: "The sage: a light, a torch, a big torch that does not smoke . . . his is the black and the red ink, his are the codices. He himself is writing and knowledge. He is the road, the true guide for others. He guides people and things; he is the guide in human affairs. The true sage is careful and keeps tradition. To him belongs inherited knowledge; it is he who teaches, follows the truth, does not cease to warn. He makes strange faces wise; he gives others a personality; he makes them develop; he opens their ears; he illuminates them. He is the master guide; he shows them the way; on him one depends" (León-Portilla, *La filosofía*

náhuatl estudiada en sus fuentes, pp. 63–72).

6. León-Portilla, *Los antiguos mexicanos a través de sus crónicas y cantares*, pp. 123–135.

7. Eliade, *El chamanismo y las técnicas arcaicas de éxtasis*, pp. 25–44.

8. Chavero, *Obras históricas de don Fernando de Alva Ixtlilxóchitl*, vol. 2, p. 18.

9. During the discovery and conquest of America, the Europeans found peoples who did not know pictographic writing and used only the oral tradition to transmit their knowledge. Thus, Fray Bartolomé de las Casas says: "In some places they did not use this way of writing; rather, news of the old things was passed down from one to the other, from hand to hand.

There was in it an order that kept them from forgetting . . . four or five, perhaps more, were instructed in the antiquities, for which instruction they used the office of historian, referring to them all manner of things that belonged to history, and they took these things into their memories and were made to recite them, and if one could not remember something, the others would amend it and they would remember" (Las Casas, *Apologética historia sumaria*, vol. 2, p. 34).

10. See Dibble, "Writing in Central Mexico."

11. Antonio de Herrera explains this process clearly: "And since their figures were not sufficient, as our writing is, they could not agree exactly on the words, but rather on concepts; but they dared to learn by heart speeches, addresses, and songs. They were very curious so that the young men learned them by memory, and for this purpose they had many schools in which the elders taught the young men things that, traditionally, had always been preserved in their entirety" (Herrera, *Historia general de los hechos de los castellanos en las islas y tierra firme de el Mar Océano*, vol. 3, p. 165).

12. See an analysis of the characteristics of the historical Nahuatl texts and their forms of expression in Calnek, "The Analysis of Prehispanic Central Mexican Historical Texts"; also Nicholson, "Phoneticism in the Central Mexican Writing System"; Robertson, *Mexican Manuscript Proceedings of the Early Colonial Period*, pp. 27–29; and León-Portilla, *Los antiguos mexicanos a través de sus crónicas y cantares*, chap. 2.

13. See Informantes de Sahagún, *Ritos, sacerdotes y atavíos de los dioses*, p. 101. Fray Bartolomé de las Casas claims that the Totonac *tlacuilos* "wrote by means of historical figures, and gave them to the pontiffs or popes, and the popes referred to them in their sermons to the people" (*Apologética historia sumaria*, vol. 2, p. 22).

14. Informantes de Sahagún, *Ritos, sacerdotes y atavíos de los dioses*, p. 93. See also León-Portilla, *Los antiguos mexicanos a través de sus crónicas y cantares*, pp. 68–69.

15. The mestizo historian Ixtlilxóchitl says that "before he died [Huémac] gathered all the stories that the Toltecs had from the beginning of the world and had them painted in a very large book, in which all of their persecutions and troubles were painted, all of their prosperity and good times" (Chavero, *Obras históricas de don Fernando de Alva Ixtlilxóchitl*, vol. 2, p. 18).

16. See León-Portilla, *La filosofía náhuatl estudiada en sus fuentes*, p. 245. Another example: offerings, cult objects, and Teotihuacan antiquities in the Mexica Templo Mayor date to the time of Motecuhzoma Ilhuicaminca (1440–

1469). That is, starting with the Mexica consolidation of political power over neighboring kingdoms, the recovery of the Teotihuacan past began, with the purpose of tying the values of this ancient and prestigious civilization to the new Mexica power (López Luján, *La recuperación mexica del pasado*, pp. 73, 75, 87–89).

17. Fray Francisco de Burgoa says, for example, that "within the barbarity of these nations were found many books in their type, on leaves or fabric made from special tree bark . . . in which all of their stories were written with characters so abbreviated that [on] a single flat leaf were expressed place, location, province, year, month, and day . . . and for this reason the children of the nobles and those who were chosen to be priests taught and were taught from childhood how to form those characters and memorize the stories, and I have had these same instruments in my hands and I have heard them explained by certain elders with some admiration, and they pin or put these papers, or cosmogonic tablets, along the walls of the nobles, for reasons of grandeur and vanity, boasting in their meetings and visits of these materials" (Burgoa, *Palestra historial*, p. 210).

18. Caso, *Reyes y reinos de la mixteca;* see also Smith, *Picture Writing from Ancient Southern Mexico*.

19. See Brundage, *A Rain of Darts: The Mexican Aztecs*, pp. 112–135, 158–173.

20. See chap. 1.

21. "It was believed that the forces manifested themselves as light-heat and that they were diffused over all the earth's surface, bathing and infiltrating all beings . . . Time and transformation—that is, earthly existence itself—were produced by the interplay of heat-light energy spread over the earth and by the past forces still remaining there. Each day a new force, more vigorous than the ones fading from the present, erupted from the sacred trees, interlacing ties between mythical and human time" (López Austin, *The Human Body and Ideology*, vol. 1, p. 205).

22. According to Alfredo López Austin, "On the days named tiger, death, flint, dog, and wind, the forces came from the tree of the north; on deer, rain, monkey, house, and eagle days, they came from the west; on the flower, twisted grass, lizard, ruffed eagle (vulture), and rabbit days, from the south; and on earth monster, reed, serpent, movement, and water days, from the east. The years with the flint sign came from the north; those with the house sign, came from the west; those with the rabbit sign, from the south; and those with the reed sign, from the east" (ibid., p. 66).

23. Ibid., p. 76.

24. See chap. 1 here.

25. Davies, *The Toltecs*, p. 377.

26. Townsend, *State and Cosmos*, p. 71. See also Caso, "El águila y el nopal"; León-Portilla, *Toltecáyotl. Aspectos de la cultura náhuatl*, pp. 159–160; and Umberger, "The Structure of Aztec History," pp. 10–18.

27. Uchamany, "Huitzilopochtli, dios de la historia de los aztecas-mexitzin," p. 213. See also Broda, "Consideraciones sobre la historiografía e ideología mexicas: las crónicas indígenas y el estudio de los ritos y sacrificios"; and the important work by Umberger.

28. Chatelet, *El nacimiento de la historia*, pp. 4–5.

29. See Satterthwaite, "Calendaries of the Maya Lowlands"; and Caso, *Los calendarios prehispánicos.*

30. Berlin, "El glifo 'emblema' en las inscripciones mayas," pp. 111–119.

31. Garibay, *Teogonía e historia de los mexicanos;* Kirchhoff, Güemes, and Reyes García, *Historia tolteca chichimeca;* idem, *Códice Chimalpopoca.*

32. Alfredo López Austin states this interpretation when he says: "other causes originated the recording of the unrepeatable facts: among them, the necessity of a document that would ground the acquired rights in the face of the interests of other peoples; another, the justification for one group in power in the face of a dominated people who perhaps, with some frequency, might ask what title the government gave that group, what their ancestors had done, what relationship they had with the gods, what their family had done for the community." See López Austin, *Hombre-Dios. Religión y política en el mundo náhuatl,* pp. 97–98. Concerning the transition of the mythic and legendary concept of history to a positive and profane history, see Vernant, *Mito y pensamiento de la Grecia antigua,* pp. 334–364; and Chatelet, *El nacimiento de la historia,* pp. 36–56.

33. See Dibble, *Códice Xólotl;* Calnek, "The Historical Validity of the Codex Xolotl," pp. 423–427.

34. See, for example, León-Portilla, *Los antiguos mexicanos a través de sus crónicas y cantares,* chaps. 2 and 4; idem, *Toltecáyotl. Aspectos de la cultura náhuatl,* pp. 15–100; and Garza, *La conciencia histórica de los antiguos mayas.*

35. In this regard, Garibay says that "there is nothing more expressive of the public and community life of Anáhuac than this noisy and solemn expression of melodramatic poems. The public, sometimes in groups of thousands, recited them . . . the repetition of deeds, adorned by poetry, were spectacles the people substituted for reading. They saw their gods personified; they heard about their heroes' deeds and grandeur, and they kept forever the living history of their race and their culture . . . Poetry, music, dance . . . in a grandly solemn scene were the means of making indelible what today is so difficult for us to learn and retain" (*Historia de la literature náhuatl,* vol. 1, p. 356).

36. For these and other examples, see Marcus, "Zapotec Writing," pp. 46–49; and *Mesoamerican Writing Systems,* pp. 391–394.

37. Schele and Freidel, *A Forest of Kings.*

38. See a detailed description of these spectacular hierophanies in Schele, "Palenque: The House of the Dying Sun"; and Tate, *Yaxchilan,* pp. 113–114.

39. The *toltecáyotl* is an example of this veneration of the past and its conversion into revered time. See León-Portilla, *Toltecáyotl. Aspectos de la cultura náhuatl,* pp. 15–35. See also Umberger, "Antiques, Revivals, and References to the Past in Aztec Art," pp. 63–105.

40. See Plumb, *The Death of the Past,* chap. 1.

41. This discovery began with the work of Heinrich Berlin and has been strengthened by the investigations of Tatiana Proskouriakoff, David H. Kelley, Yuri V. Knorosov, and others. See a summary of this story in Garza, *La conciencia histórica de los antiguos mayas.* The best-realized and most innovative study of this subject is Schele and Miller, *The Blood of Kings: Dynasty and*

Ritual in Maya Art. See also Schele and Freidel, *A Forest of Kings.*

42. Cited by León-Portilla, *La filosofía náhuatl estudiada en sus fuentes,* p. 254.

43. Zantwijk, *The Aztec Arrangement,* p. 110; Marcus, *Mesoamerican Written Systems,* p. 265.

44. Zantwijk, *The Aztec Arrangement,* p. 113; Marcus, *Mesoamerican Written Systems,* pp. 265–269.

45. See León-Portilla, *Toltecáyotl. Aspectos de la cultura náhuatl,* pp. 15–100, for an explanation of the various ways the Mexicas incorporated the Toltec tradition into their cultural patrimony. See also Umberger, "Antiques, Revivals, and References to the Past in Aztec Art," pp. 63–105.

46. Zantwijk, *The Aztec Arrangement,* p. 175; Marcus, *Mesoamerican Written Systems,* pp. 264–269.

3. The Conquest: A New Historical Protagonist and a New Historical Discourse

1. See Gerbi, *La naturaleza de las Indias nuevas,* which concentrates on the study of the first people to describe nature in the Americas.

2. See Carbia, *La crónica oficial de las Indias Occidentales,* pp. 76, 91–92.

3. Michel de Certeau refers to a colonization of the American body brought about by western man's discourse of power and conquest writing. See Certeau, *L'Ecriture de l'histoire,* pp. 3–5.

4. See López de Velasco, *Geografía y descripción universal de las Indias.*

5. Acosta, *Historia natural y moral de las Indias.*

6. Momigliano, "Time in Ancient Historiography," pp. 18–19.

7. See a detailed analysis of the Hebrew concept of historical development and time in Brandon, *History, Time and Deity,* pp. 106–140.

8. Ibid., pp. 48–82; Dinkler, "Early Christianity," pp. 171–214.

9. Brandon, *History, Time and Deity,* pp. 184–187.

10. Plumb, *The Death of the Past,* p. 76.

11. Cohn, *The Pursuit of the Millennium,* p. 14.

12. Brandon, *History, Time and Deity,* pp. 95, 104–105.

13. See Cullman, *Cristo e il tempo,* p. 111; Le Goff, "Au Moyen Age: Temps de l'église et temps du Marchand," p. 49.

14. Plumb, *The Death of the Past,* pp. 77–78.

15. Le Goff, "Au Moyen Age: Temps de l'église et temps du Marchand," pp. 48, 51.

16. Brandon, *History, Time and Deity,* p. 196; Munford, *Técnica y civilización,* pp. 30–31.

17. Cohn, *The Pursuit of the Millennium,* discusses these messianic movements in detail.

18. Ibid.

19. Ibid., p. 100.

20. See Baudot, *Utopie et histoire au Mexique,* p. 78.

21. The foregoing summarizes Cohn's discussion of the ideas of Joachim of Fiore in *The Pursuit of the Millennium,* pp. 100–103. See also Lowith, *El sentido de la historia. Implicaciones teológicas de la filosofía de la historia,* pp. 207–228, 299–307. Lowith studies Joachim of Fiore's influence on the philosophy of

modern history. West and Zimdars-Swartz, *Joaquín de Fiore. Una visión espiritual de la historia,* offer a global treatment of his interpretation of history.

22. Casas, *Apologética historia sumaria.* See especially O'Gorman's introduction, pp. lviii–lxxix.

23. See Anglería, *Décadas del Nuevo Mundo;* Fernández de Oviedo, *Sucesos y diálogos de la Nueva España;* López de Gómara, *Hispania Victrix. Primera y segunda parte de la historia general de las Indias,* pp. 156, 168, 194; and Florescano, "Las visiones imperiales de la época colonial."

24. Phelan, *The Millennial Kingdom of the Franciscans in the New World,* p. 18.

25. Ibid., p. 11.

26. Ginés de Sepúlveda, *Tratado sobre las justas causas de la guerra contra los indios,* pp. 133–135.

27. Ibid., p. 101; and also the analysis of these doctrines in Zavala, *La filosofía de la conquista,* pp. 53–54.

28. In the foregoing I have followed the critical studies and interpretations of O'Gorman in Anglería, *Décadas del Nuevo Mundo;* Fernández de Oviedo, *Sucesos y diálogos de la Nueva España;* and O'Gorman, *Cuatro historiadores de Indias.*

29. López de Gómara, *Hispania Victrix. Primera y segunda parte de la historia general de las Indias,* pp. 156, 168, 294.

30. See Phelan, *The Millennial Kingdom of the Franciscans in the New World,* p. 21; also Góngora, "Eschatological Theories in the Writing of Columbus and of the Mendicant Friars"; and Milhou, *Colón y su mentalidad mesiánica en el ambiente franciscanista español.*

31. Phelan, *The Millennial Kingdom of the Franciscans in the New World,* pp. 22–23.

32. On the Franciscans' adoption of eschatological ideas, especially those of Joachim of Fiore, see Cohn, *The Pursuit of the Millenium.* On the influence of these ideas on the first twelve Franciscan evangelizers in New Spain, see Baudot, *Utopie et histoire au Mexique. Les prémiers chroniqueurs de la civilization mexicaine (1520–1569),* pp. 76–90.

33. The best study of the mystic and millenarian ideas of Jerónimo de Mendieta is Phelan, *The Millennial Kingdom of the Franciscans in the New World,* which I follow in this section.

34. Ibid., p. 30.

35. "The advent of the twelve Franciscans is the dawn of the Golden Age of the Indian Church. Furthermore, the friars assume the character of messiahs who have journeyed thousands of miles to deliver the Indians from the bondage of idolatry" (Phelan, *The Millennial Kingdom of the Franciscans in the New World,* p. 35).

36. Ibid., p. 6.

37. Mendieta, *Historia eclesiástica indiana,* vol. 1, p. 18. On Mendieta's ideas concerning the role of kings and the Spanish monarchy in the New World, see Phelan, *The Millennial Kingdom of the Franciscans in the New World,* pp. 5–16, 81–85.

38. Phelan, *The Millennial Kingdom of the Franciscans in the New World,* p. 77.

39. García Icazbalceta, *Códice Mendieta (nueva colección de documentos para la historia de México)*, vol. 2, pp. 5–6; Mendieta, *Historia eclesiástica indiana*, vol. 1, p. 39.

40. Phelan, *The Millennial Kingdom of the Franciscans in the New World*, pp. 66, 98–99. (*Translator's note:* Attempts to find all Phelan quotes in English were only partially successful. The quote from pp. 98–99 here is from the Spanish edition, as well as the Phelan quotes cited in notes 51, 52, 56, and 57.)

41. Ibid., p. 49.

42. Mendieta, *Historia eclesiástica indiana*.

43. Ibid., vol. 3, pp. 184–185; Phelan, *The Millennial Kingdom of the Franciscans in the New World*, p. 100.

44. Phelan, *The Millennial Kingdom of the Franciscans in the New World*, p. 91.

45. García Icazbalceta, *Cartas de religiosos, 1539–1594*, p. 15.

46. Phelan, *The Millennial Kingdom of the Franciscans in the New World*, p. 61.

47. García Icazbalceta, *Cartas de religiosos, 1539–1594*, pp. 5–6; Phelan, *The Millennial Kingdom of the Franciscans in the New World*, p. 67.

48. Mendieta, *Historia eclesiástica indiana*, vol. 3, pp. 222–225.

49. Phelan, *The Millennial Kingdom of the Franciscans in the New World*, p. 106.

50. See Baudot, *Utopie et histoire au Mexique. Les prémiers chroniqueurs de la civilization mexicaine (1520–1569)*, pp. 76, 78.

51. Ibid., pp. 80–90. See also Phelan, *The Millennial Kingdom of the Franciscans in the New World*, pp. 69–72; Castro, *Aspectos del vivir hispánico: espiritualismo, mesianismo y actitud personal en los siglos XIV al XVI*; and Bataillon, *Erasmo y España*, vol. 1, pp. 61–83.

52. Phelan, *The Millennial Kingdom of the Franciscans in the New World*, p. 135.

53. See Le Goff, "Au Moyen Age: Temps de l'église et temps du Marchand," pp. 59–64.

54. The foregoing is based on Zavala, *Recuerdo de Vasco de Quiroga*. On the work and thought of Quiroga, see Aguayo Spencer, *Don Vasco de Quiroga*; Warren, *Vasco de Quiroga and His Pueblo Hospitals of Santa Fe*; Tena Ramírez, *Vasco de Quiroga y sus pueblos de Santa Fe en los siglos XVIII y XIX*; and Miranda Godínez, *Don Vasco de Quiroga y su Colegio de San Nicolás*.

55. Mendieta, *Historia eclesiástica indiana*, vol. 3, pp. 103–104.

56. Phelan, *The Millennial Kingdom of the Franciscans in the New World*, p. 106. For other distinctions between utopian, mystic, and eschatological projects, see Góngora, "Eschatological Theories in the Writing of Columbus and of the Mendicant Friars."

57. Phelan, *The Millennial Kingdom of the Franciscans in the New World*, pp. 69, 84.

58. See Iglesia, *Cronistas e historiadores de la conquista de México*, pp. 17–76.

59. Iglesia, *El hombre Colón y otros ensayos*, p. 111.

60. Ibid., pp. 114–115, 217.

61. For the characteristics of the official chroniclers of the Indies, see Carbia, *La crónica oficial de las Indias Occidentales*; see also Esteve Barba, *Historiografía indiana*, pp. 117–136.

62. Sahagún, *Historia general de las cosas de Nueva España*, vol. 1, pp. 27–28, 31–32, 105.

63. See López Austin, "Estudio acerca del método de investigación de fray Bernardino de Sahagún."

64. Baudot, *Utopie et histoire au Mexique. Les prémiers chroniqueurs de la civilization mexicaine (1520–1569)*, contains a study of the Franciscans' first historical and ethnographic investigations in the New World.

65. Beginning in 1527, foreigners were forbidden to acquire, without special authorization, "paintings or description of the Indies." In 1566 a royal document noted that "every day they make books about the new Indies . . . and they are printed without our permision," for which reason, it ordered "know that books printed . . . without our express permission, that deal with our said Indies, and all that are found will be seized." See Baudot, *Utopie et histoire au Mexique. Les prémiers chroniqueurs de la civilization mexicaine (1520–1569)*, p. 499; Friede, "La censura española del siglo XVI y los libros de historia de América."

66. See Carbia, *La crónica oficial de las Indias Occidentales*. In 1571, when Juan López de Velasco was named chief cosmographer and chronicler of the Indies, he was charged with "making a general history of the Indies," and the viceroy of New Spain was approached: "Your Excellency having named someone to compose the history of the Indies, you are asked to submit whatever facts you can acquire." See Baudot, *Utopie et histoire au Mexique. Les prémiers chroniqueurs de la civilization mexicaine (1520–1569)*, pp. 495–496.

67. This is the case with the obscure chroniclers of the time: Luis Tribaldos de Toledo, Tomás Tamayo de Vargas, Gil González Dávila, Pedro Fernández de Pulgar, Luis de Salazar y Castro, and Miguel Herrero Espeleta. See Esteve Barba, *Historiografía indiana*, pp. 118–132.

68. Phelan, *The Millennial Kingdom of the Franciscans in the New World*, p. 157.

69. See García Icazbalceta, *Bibliografía mexicana del siglo XVI*, pp. 327–376; Ricard, *La conquista espiritual de México*, pp. 102–108; and Edmonson, *Sixteenth-Century Mexico: The Work of Sahagún*.

70. Baudot, *Utopie et histoire au Mexique. Les prémiers chroniqueurs de la civilization mexicaine (1520–1569)*, pp. 475–483.

71. Ibid., pp. 484–485.

72. We must remember that in 1552 the religious orders in Mexico affirmed that the pope had legitimate rights over the country and that, under the influence of their ideas, in 1554 a group of *juristas*, or legal experts, in Mexico solemnly declared that neither idolatry nor the Indians' lifestyle was sufficient justification for the Spaniards' sovereignty over them and that Mendieta came to compare the reign of Philip II to the iron age.

73. See González Dávila, *Teatro eclesiástico de la primitiva iglesia de la Nueva España en las Indias Occidentales*, for an example of the permissions, privileges, approvals, licenses, and censorship official chroniclers of the Indies needed for publication of a chronicle. See Dávila Padilla, *Historia de la fundación*

y discurso de la provincia de Santiago de México, for another example of these requirements.

4. Transformation of Indigenous Memory and Resurgence of Mythic Memory

1. *Chilam Balam de Chumayel* cited by León-Portilla, *El reverso de la conquista*, p. 83.
2. *Chilam Balam* cited by Wachtel, *Los vencidos*, p. 57.
3. León-Portilla, *Visión de los vencidos*, p. 105.
4. "Libro de los coloquios," cited by León-Portilla, *El reverso de la conquista*, p. 21.
5. Méndez Bolio, *El libro de Chilam Balam de Chumayel*, pp. 29–30.
6. Cited by León-Portilla, *El reverso de la conquista*, pp. 78–79.
7. Cited by Wachtel, *Los vencidos*, p. 57.
8. Cited by León-Portilla, *El reverso de la conquista*, p. 81.
9. "La crónica de Chac Xulub Chen," cited by León-Portilla, *El reverso de la conquista*, pp. 89–90. My emphasis.
10. See chap. 1 here and the bibliography on pre-Hispanic calendric systems.
11. See Sahagún, *Historia general de las cosas de Nueva España*, vol. 4, which contains the indigenous versions of the Conquest, and León-Portilla, *Visión de los vencidos* and *El reverso de la conquista*, which add other indigenous testimony.
12. See Barrera Vázquez and Rendón, *El libro de los libros de Chilam Balam*, pp. 12–13.
13. Cited by León-Portilla, *El reverso de la conquista*, pp. 78–79.
14. To distinguish between insurrection and rebellion, I use Henri Favbre's definition: "We understand by rebellion all direct reaction, immediate and spontaneous to specific maltreatment . . . The essential characteristic of rebellion is that it is never premeditated, organized, or subject to direction or control. For this reason, it is as localized in space as it is limited in time, whatever else may be the degree of violence that it attains.

"Insurrection, on the other hand, is a reaction to a state of general crisis the causes and effects of which are much deeper. Insurrection falls within the framework of a restructuring of the colonial situation . . . it constitutes the last phase of a process of reorganization of indigenous society threatened meanwhile by the growing pressure that the ladino society exerts on it" (Favbre, *Cambio y continuidad entre los mayas de México*, p. 287).
15. Aiton, *Antonio de Mendoza, First Viceroy of New Spain*, p. 140.
16. Ricard, *La conquista espiritual de México*, pp. 460–461.
17. Ibid., p. 461. See also Wachtel, *Los vencidos*, pp. 292–295.
18. Chamberlain, *The Conquest and Colonization of Yucatan, 1517–1550*, pp. 238–239.
19. Ibid. See also Barabas, "Profetismo, milenarismo y mesianismo en las insurrecciones mayas de Yucatán," vol. 2, p. 610; Huerta and Palacios, *Rebeliones indígenas de la época colonial*, pp. 46–47.
20. See Huerta and Palacios, *Rebeliones indígenas de la época colonial*, pp. 72–77.
21. Carrasco, "La sociedad mexicana antes de la conquista," pp. 177–179.

22. See Miranda Godínez, *Don Vasco de Quiroga y su Colegio de San Nicolás*, pp. 49–51; Zavala and Miranda, "Instituciones indígenas en la colonia," pp. 56–66.

23. Florescano, *De la colonia al imperio*, pp. 37–38; Moreno Toscano, *Geografía económica de México (siglo XVI)*, pp. 76–78; Gerhard, "Congregaciones de indios en Nueva España antes de 1570," pp. 547–595; idem, "La evolución del pueblo rural mexicano, 1519–1975."

24. Burgoa, *Geográfica descripción*, vol. 1, pp. 340–341. See also Pastor, "Los religiosos, los indios y el estado en la Mixteca, 1524–1810."

25. See Villa Rojas, "Los conceptos de espacio y tiempo entre los grupos mayas contemporáneos," pp. 128–132.

26. Gibson, *The Aztecs under Spanish Rule*, p. 100.

27. Loera y Chávez, *Economía campesina indígena en la colonia. Un caso en el valle de Toluca*, pp. 98–106.

28. Warman, *La danza de moros y cristianos*; Wachtel, *Los vencidos*, pp. 63–92.

29. See Lockhart, "Views of Corporate Self and History in Some Valley of Mexico Towns, Late Seventeenth and Eighteenth Centuries." This is one of the few studies that considers the collective identity of the indigenous peoples as seen in their own statements. It is an excellent analysis.

30. Ibid., p. 42.

31. See the detailed analysis of all of these examples in ibid., pp. 46–54.

32. Ibid., p. 53.

33. Ibid., p. 59.

34. Ibid., p. 62.

35. See Miranda, *Vida colonial y albores de la independencia*, pp. 54–79.

36. Besides Lockhart's excellent analysis of these documents, see Gibson, "A Survey of Middle American Prose Manuscripts in the Native Historical Tradition," pp. 320–321.

37. Chimalpahin, *Relaciones originales de Chalco Amaquemecan*, p. 11.

38. Ibid., p. 20.

39. Ibid., pp. 63–66, 116, 124–127, 166–168.

40. Tezozómoc, *Crónica Mexicáyotl*.

41. See Pomar, "Relación de Texcoco."

42. Muñoz Camargo, *Historia de Tlaxcala*, pp. 50, 55, 59–62, 76–77; idem, *Descripción de la ciudad y provincia de Tlaxcala*.

43. Muñoz Camargo, *Historia de Tlaxcala*, p. 104.

44. With reference to the Tlaxcaltecans, Muñoz Camargo says: "this nation . . . is cowardly, pusillanimous, and cruel when alone; when they are accompanied by the Spaniards, they are devils, daring and bold. Most of them are very simple and very stupid; they are unreasonable and dishonorable to our way of seeing; their code of honor is very different from ours. They do not take offense at getting drunk or eating on the street, although they are learning courtesy and how to reason" (ibid., p. 155).

45. Pomar, "Relación de Texcoco," pp. 23–24.

46. See Alva Ixtlilxóchitl, *Obras históricas*, vol. 2, pp. 25–26, 31.

47. Ibid., vol. 1, pp. 263–265.

48. Ibid., vol. 2, pp. 7–9.

49. Ibid., pp. 8–9.

50. Ibid., p. 271. "These kings were tall and white-bearded like the Spaniards, and for this reason the Indians, when the marquis arrived, thought he was Tupiltzin." See also López Austin, *Hombre-Dios. Religión y política en el mundo náhuatl*, pp. 19–21.

51. Poma de Ayala, *El primer nueva corónica y buen gobierno.*

52. See Wachtel's excellent comparative essay on the historical categories used by Felipe Guaman Poma de Ayala and the Inca Garcilaso de la Vega, "Pensamiento salvaje y aculturación: el espacio y el tiempo en Felipe Guaman Poma de Ayala y el inca Garcilaso."

53. Howe, *Información que el Arzobispo de México D. fray Alonso de Montúfar mandó predicar . . . acerca de la devoción y culto de Nuestra Señora de Guadalupe;* and Maza, *El guadalupanismo mexicano*, pp. 14–17. Torre Villar and Navarro de Anda, *Testimonios históricos y guadalupanos*, pp. 148–149, contains complete information.

54. Sahagún, *Historia general de las cosas de Nueva España*, vol. 3, p. 352.

55. See Maza, *El guadalupanismo mexicano*, pp. 16, 19, 21; Lafaye, *Quetzalcóatl y Guadalupe. La formación de la conciencia nacional de México,* pp. 319–327.

56. Torre Villar and Navarro de Anda, *Testimonios históricos y guadalupanos*, pp. 148–149.

57. Lafaye, *Quetzalcóatl y Guadalupe. La formación de la conciencia nacional de México*, p. 322. O'Gorman, *Destierro de sombras. Luz en el origen de la imagen y culto de Nuestra Señora de Guadalupe del Tepeyac,* is the best study of when and how the image of Guadalupe appeared on Tepeyac and of the miraculous feeling of the apparition.

58. Suárez de Peralta, *Tratado del descubrimiento de las Indias*, p. 161.

59. Sánchez, *Imagen de la virgen María Madre de Dios de Guadalupe milagrosamente aparecida en México, celebrada en su historia, con la profecía del capítulo doce del Apocalipsis . . .* A version of this work that includes only the apparitions of the Virgin is found in Vera, *Tesoro guadalupano. Noticia de los libros, documentos, inscripciones y que tratan, mencionan o aluden a la aparición y devoción de Nuestra Señora de Guadalupe.* Sánchez's complete text and Fr. Mateo de la Cruz's summary are found in Torre Villar and Navarro de Anda, *Testimonios históricos y guadalupanos*, pp. 152–267, 267–281.

60. Torre Villar and Navarro de Anda, *Testimonios históricos y guadalupanos*, p. 164; Maza, *El guadalupanismo mexicano*, pp. 53, 56–57.

61. Maza, *El guadalupanismo mexicano*, pp. 62–73.

62. Torre Villar and Navarro de Anda, *Testimonios históricos y guadalupanos*, p. 257. My emphasis.

63. See the complete version of this work in Spanish in Torre Villar and Navarro de Anda, *Testimonios históricos y guadalupanos*, pp. 282–308.

64. Wasserstrom, *Class and Society in Central Chiapas*, pp. 23, 28–29.

65. Ibid., pp. 32–38. The story of the apparition of the Virgin in Zinacantan is taken from the chronicle of Ximénez, *Historia de la provincia de San Vicente de Chiapas y Guatemala*, vol. 3, pp. 25–343. See a reproduction of this part in Huerta and Palacios, *Rebeliones indígenas de la época colonial*, pp. 143–145.

66. Bricker, *The Indian Christ, the Indian King: The Historical Substrate of Maya Myth and Ritual*, pp. 55–56. This is the best study on the apparitions of the Virgin in this region and the indigenous rebellions associated with those apparitions.

67. See the story of the miracle of Saint Martha in Ximénez, *Historia de la provincia de San Vicente de Chiapas y Guatemala*; Huerta and Palacios, *Rebeliones indígenas de la época colonial*, pp. 146–149; and Bricker, *The Indian Christ, the Indian King: The Historical Substrate of Maya Myth and Ritual*, p. 59.

68. Huerta and Palacios, *Rebeliones indígenas de la época colonial*, p. 145; Bricker, *The Indian Christ, the Indian King: The Historical Substrate of Maya Myth and Ritual*, p. 59.

69. The apparition of the Virgin of Cancuc and the miracles and events related to it are documented in the following works: Huerta and Palacios, *Rebeliones indígenas de la época colonial*, pp. 150–171; Bricker, *The Indian Christ, the Indian King: The Historical Substrate of Maya Myth and Ritual*, pp. 59–69; Klein, "Peasant Communities in Revolt: The Tzeltal Republic of 1712"; Martínez Peláez, *Motines de indios. La violencia colonial en Centroamérica y Chiapas*, pp. 125–167; Wasserstrom, *Class and Society in Central Chiapas*; and Favbre, *Cambio y continuidad entre los mayas de México*

70. See Bricker, *The Indian Christ, the Indian King: The Historical Substrate of Maya Myth and Ritual*, pp. 70–76, for information on and a very complete summary of the principal primary and secondary sources on the Canek insurrection. Huerta and Palacios, *Rebeliones indígenas de la época colonial*, pp. 174–189, includes the stories about this event compiled by Eduardo Enrique Ríos. Quotations in the text come from these sources.

71. All of the quotations and information concerning the movement headed by Antonio Pérez are taken from Gruzinski's excellent study, *Les hommes dieux de Mexique. Pouvoir Indien et société coloniale, XVIe–XVIIe siècles*, pp. 111–179.

72. The little information there is on this important religious movement is found in Taylor, *Drinking, Homicide and Rebellion in Colonial Mexican Villages*, p. 124.

73. Pereira de Queiroz, *Historia y etnología de los movimientos mesiánicos*, p. 144.

74. Ibid.

75. Weber, *Ancient Judaism*; also Pereira de Queiroz, *Historia y etnología de los movimientos mesiánicos*, pp. 40–42.

76. Pereira de Queiroz, *Historia y etnología de los movimientos mesiánicos*, p. 142.

77. Brading, *Prophecy and Myth in Mexican History*, p. 30.

78. Pereira de Queiroz, *Historia y etnología de los movimientos mesiánicos*, p. 336.

79. Ibid., pp. 320–326. For other definitions of the characteristic features of the Messiah, see Weber, *Ancient Judaism*, vol. 1, pp. 93–204, 356–364.

80. Eliade, *Myth and Reality*, pp. 5–6.

81. Ibid., p. 6.

82. Ibid., p. 20.

83. See Gruzinski, "La 'segunda aculturación': el estado ilustrado y la religiosidad indígena en Nueva España (1775–1800)."

5. Creole Patriotism, Independence, and the Appearance of a National History

1. Torquemada, *Monarquía indiana*, vol. 1, p. 226; Brading, *Los orígenes del nacionalismo mexicano*, pp. 21–22. Brading presents one of the best analyses of Creole patriotism, based on the recovery of the indigenous past and on religious myths.

2. Lafaye, *Quetzalcóatl y Guadalupe. La formación de la conciencia nacional de México*, p. 143.

3. Ibid., p. 145.

4. On Boturini, see Miguel León-Portilla's introduction in Boturini, *Idea de una nueva historia general de la América septentrional*; and Matute, *Lorenzo Boturini y el pensamiento histórico de Vico*.

5. The best study of the polemic centered on the enlightened ideas about the physical and social degradation of America is Gerbi, *La disputa del Nuevo Mundo. Historia de una polémica, 1750–1900*.

6. W. Robertson, *The History of America*; see also Keen, *The Aztec Image in Western Thought*, pp. 77–104.

7. See Millares, *Don Juan José de Eguiara y Eguren y su Bibliotheca Mexicana; Fuentes para la historia contemporánea de México*, vol. 1, p. xx.

8. Clavijero, *Historia antigua de México*. On the meaning of Clavijero's work, see Villoro, *Los grandes momentos del indigenismo en México*; Brading, *Los orígenes del nacionalismo mexicano*; Clavijero, *Antología*, introductory study by Aguirre Beltrán; and Pacheco, "La patria perdida (notas sobre Clavijero y la cultura nacional)."

9. Veytia, *Historia antigua de México*.

10. See Bernal, *Historia de la arqueología en México*, pp. 72–74.

11. León y Gama, *Descripción histórica y cronológica de las dos piedras*; Bernal, *Historia de la arqueología en México*, pp. 74–77.

12. Bernal, *Historia de la arqueología en México*, pp. 79–86.

13. Humboldt, *Ensayo político sobre el reino de la Nueva España*.

14. Ibid., p. 6.

15. See Alegre, *Historia de la Provincia de la Compañía de Jesús de Nueva España*; Cavo, *Historia de México*; and Batllori, *La cultura hispano-italiana de los jesuitas expulsos. Españoles, hispanoamericanos, filipinos, 1767–1814*.

16. See Brading, *Mineros y comerciantes en el México borbónico (1763–1810)*, pp. 55–132.

17. Motten, *Mexican Silver and the Enlightenment*.

18. *Historia del arte en México*, vol. 6, pp. 18–100.

19. See Bartolache, *Mercurio Volante (1772–1773)*; Alzate, *Memoria y ensayos*; Wold, *El Diario de México, primer cotidiano de Nueva España*; and Navarro, *Cultura mexicana moderna en el siglo XVIII*.

20. Motten, *Mexican Silver and the Enlightenment*; Howe, *The Mining Guild of New Spain and Its Tribunal General, 1770–1821*; Brading, *Mineros y comerciantes en el México borbónico (1763–1810)*.

21. See Fonseca and Urrutia, *Historia general de la Real Hacienda*; and Florescano and Gil, *Descripciones económicas generales de Nueva España, 1784–1817*, where José María Quirós's *Memoria de estatuto* is published.

22. For a selection of the works of Manuel Abad y Queipo, see Mora, *Obras sueltas*, pp. 178–271.

23. Pérez Marchand, *Dos etapas ideológicas del siglo XVIII en México*.

24. Ibid., pp. 127–132.

25. See González Casanova, *La literatura perseguida en la crisis de la colonia*, pp. 65–82, 83–103.

26. Humboldt, *Ensayo político sobre el reino de la Nueva España*, p. x.

27. Humboldt, *Tablas geográficas, políticas del reino de Nueva España y correspondencia mexicana*.

28. Ibid., pp. xliv–xlv. See also Miranda, *Humboldt y México*.

29. Alamán, *Obras de Lucas Alamán*, vol. 1, p. 10.

30. All of the information about Herrada comes from Van Young's excellent study, "Millennium on the Northern Marches: The Mad Messiah of Durango and Popular Rebellion in Mexico, 1800–1815."

31. The information on Mariano and his alleged insurrection is taken from Archer, *The Army in Bourbon Mexico, 1760–1810*, pp. 98–100.

32. Van Young, "Millennium on the Northern Marches: The Mad Messiah of Durango and Popular Rebellion in Mexico, 1800–1815," p. 406.

33. Archer, *The Army in Bourbon Mexico, 1760–1810*, p. 240.

34. On the grito de Hidalgo, see Hamill, *The Hidalgo Revolt*, p. 123.

35. Feijó, "El tumulto de 1692," p. 661; and Simpson, *Many Mexicos*, p. 143.

36. See Phelan, *El reino milenario de los franciscanos en el Nuevo Mundo*.

37. Van Young, "Millennium on the Northern Marches: The Mad Messiah of Durango and Popular Rebellion in Mexico, 1800–1815," pp. 405–406. See also idem, "'Who Was the Masked Man, Anyway?' Popular Symbols and Ideology in the Mexican Wars of Independence," pp. 18–20.

38. An analysis of these subjects and problems is found in Van Young, "'Who Was the Masked Man, Anyway?' Popular Symbols and Ideology in the Mexican Wars of Independence"; idem, "Millennium on the Northern Marches: The Mad Messiah of Durango and Popular Rebellion in Mexico, 1800–1815"; and Phelan, *El reino milenario de los franciscanos en el Nuevo Mundo*.

39. See Hamill, *The Hidalgo Revolt*, p. 93.

40. Lafaye, *Quetzalcóatl y Guadalupe. La formación de la conciencia nacional de México*, pp. 173–174.

41. Ibid., p. 393.

42. Ibid. See also Villoro, *El proceso ideológico de la revolución de independencia*, p. 103.

43. Villoro, *El proceso ideológico de la revolución de independencia*, p. 84.

44. Pérez Memen, *El episcopado y la independencia de México (1808–36)*, pp. 80–87.

45. Villoro, *El proceso ideológico de la revolución de independencia*, p. 85.

46. Dr. José María Cos, in 1814, characterized the insurgency as a "true religious war." See Pérez Memen, *El episcopado y la independencia de México (1808–36)*, p. 78, and Villoro, *El proceso ideológico de la revolución de independencia*, p. 85.

47. See Timmons, "Los Guadalupes: A Secret Society in the Mexican Revolution for Independence."

48. Lafaye, *Quetzalcóatl y Guadalupe. La formación de la conciencia nacional de México*, pp. 187–188.

49. Villoro, *El proceso ideológico de la revolución de independencia*, pp. 76–77, 85, 86.

50. Ibid., pp. 104–105.

51. Ibid., p. 80.

52. Ibid.

53. Ibid., pp. 98–99.

54. Villoro, *El proceso ideológico de la revolución de independencia*, pp. 100–101.

55. Herrejón, *Morelos, antología documental*, pp. 133–134.

56. Anonymous, "Noticias biográficas del Lic. don Carlos Maria de Bustamante." It is said that Bustamante drew up the speech that Morelos gave at the opening of the Chilpancingo Congress. This does not invalidate the fact that Morelos was the first rebel chieftain to accept these ideas and put them into practice. See Miranda, *Las ideas y las instituciones políticas mexicanas*, p. 318.

57. Villoro, *El proceso ideológico de la revolución de independencia*, pp. 44–45.

58. Ibid., p. 45.

59. Ibid., pp. 45–47.

60. Cited by Miranda, *Las ideas y las instituciones políticas mexicanas*, p. 299. My emphasis.

61. Ibid., pp. 299–300.

62. Villoro, *El proceso ideológico de la revolución de independencia*, pp. 49–52.

63. On the concepts that defined the basic principles of the new nation in political documents and the constitution, see Miranda, *Las ideas y las instituciones políticas mexicanas*, pp. 318–322, 349–364.

64. On the "subjective characteristics" and the "objective characteristics" that explain and define the nation concept, see Rustow, "Nación."

Bibliography

Acosta, José de
    1962   *Historia natural y moral de las Indias.* Edited by Edmundo O'Gorman. Mexico City: Fondo de Cultura Económica.

Aguayo Spencer, Rafael
    1970   *Don Vasco de Quiroga.* Mexico City: Ediciones Oasis.

Aguilar, Héctor, et al.
    1976   *En torno a la cultura nacional.* Mexico City: Instituto Nacional Indigenista.

Aiton, Arthur S.
    1967   *Antonio de Mendoza, First Viceroy of New Spain.* New York: Russell & Russell.

Alamán, Lucas
    1942   *Obras de Lucas Alamán. Disertaciones.* 3 vols. Mexico City: Editorial Jus.

Alegre, Francisco Javier
    1956–1964   *Historia de la Provincia de la Compañía de Jesús de Nueva España.* 4 vols. Edited by Ernest J. Burrus and Félix Zubillaga. Rome: Institutun Historicum S.J.

Alva Ixtlixóchitl, Fernando de
    1975   *Obras históricas.* 2 vols. Edited by Edmundo O'Gorman. Mexico City: Universidad Nacional Autónoma de México.

Alzate, José Antonio
    1985   *Memoria y ensayos.* Edited by Roberto Moreno. Mexico City: Universidad Nacional Autónoma de México.

Anglería, Pedro Mártir de
    1964   *Décadas del Nuevo Mundo.* 2 vols. Edited by Edmundo O'Gorman. Mexico City: Editorial Porrúa.

Archer, Christon I.
    1977   *The Army in Bourbon Mexico, 1760–1810.* Albuquerque: University of New Mexico Press.

Aveni, Anthony F. (ed.)
    1975   *Archaeoastronomy in Pre-Columbian America.* Austin: University of Texas Press.
    1977   *Native American Astronomy.* Austin: University of Texas Press.

1980*a* *Astronomía en la América antigua*. Mexico City: Siglo Veintiuno Editores.

1980*b* *Skywatchers of Ancient Mexico*. Austin: University of Texas Press.

Barabas, Alicia M.
1976 "Profetismo, milenarismo y mesianismo en las insurrecciones mayas de Yucatán." *Actas del XLI Congreso Internacional de Americanistas*. 2 vols. Mexico City: Instituto Nacional de Antropología e Historia.

Barrera Vázquez, Alfredo, and Silvia Rendón (trans.)
1963 *El libro de los libros de Chilam Balam* . . . Mexico City: Fondo de Cultura Económica.

Bartolache, José Ignacio
1979 *Mercurio Volante (1772–1773)*. Mexico City: Universidad Nacional Autónoma de México.

Bataillon, Marcel
1950 *Erasmo y España*. 2 vols. Mexico City: Fondo de Cultura Económica.

Batllori, Miguel
1966 *La cultura hispano-italiana de los jesuitas expulsos. Españoles, hispanoamericanos, filipinos, 1767–1814*. Madrid: Editorial Gredos.

Baudot, Georges
1977 *Utopie et histoire au Mexique. Les prémiers chroniqueurs de la civilization mexicaine (1520–1569)*. Toulouse: Editions Privat.

Berlin, Heinrich
1958 "El glifo 'emblema' en las inscripciones mayas." *Journal de la Société des Américanistes*, n.s. 47:111–119.

Berlin, Isaiah
1976 *Vico and Herder*. London: Hogarth Press.
1983 *Contra la corriente. Ensayos sobre historia de las ideas*. Mexico City: Fondo de Cultura Económica.

Bernal, Ignacio
1979 *Historia de la arqueología en México*. Mexico City: Editorial Porrúa.

Boturini Benaduci, Lorenzo
1974 *Idea de una nueva historia general de la América septentrional*. Mexico City: Editorial Porrúa.

Brading, David A.
1975 *Mineros y comerciantes en el México borbónico (1763–1810)*. Mexico City: Fondo de Cultura Económica.
1980 *Los orígenes del nacionalismo mexicano*. Mexico City: Ediciones Era.
1986 *Prophecy and Myth in Mexican History*. Cambridge Latin American Miniatures. Cambridge: Cambridge University Press.

Brandon, S. G. F.
1965 *History, Time and Deity*. London: Manchester University Press.

Bricker, Victoria Reifler
1981 *The Indian Christ, the Indian King: The Historical Substrate of Maya Myth and Ritual*. Austin: University of Texas Press.

Broda, Johanna
1978 "El tributo en trajes guerreros y la estructura del sistema tributario

mexica." In *Economía, política e ideología en el México prehispánico*, edited by Pedro Carrasco and Johanna Broda, pp. 113–174. Mexico City: Editorial Nueva Imagen.

1978a   "Relaciones políticas ritualizadas: el ritual como expresión de una ideología." In *Economía, política e ideología en el México prehispánico*, edited by Pedro Carrasco and Johanna Broda, pp. 219–255. Mexico City: Editorial Nueva Imagen.

1978b   "Consideraciones sobre la historiografía e ideología mexicas: las crónicas indígenas y el estudio de los ritos y sacrificios." In *Estudios de Cultura Náhuatl*, vol. 13, pp. 97–111. Mexico City: Universidad Nacional Autónoma de México.

1980   "La fiesta azteca del fuego nuevo y el culto a las pléyades." In *La antropología americanista en la actualidad: homenaje a Raphael Girard*, vol. 2, pp. 283–304. Mexico City: Editories Mexicanos Unidos.

1982   "Astronomy, Cosmovision and Ideology in Prehispanic Mesoamerica." In *Ethnoastronomy and Archaeoastronomy in the American Tropics*, edited by Anthony F. Aveni and Gary Urton, pp. 81–109. New York: New York Academy of Sciences.

Brundage, Burr C.
1972   *A Rain of Darts: The Mexican Aztecs*. Austin: University of Texas Press.

Burgoa, Fray Francisco de
1934   *Palestra historial*. Mexico City: Talleres Gráficos de la Nación. *Geográfica descripción*. Mexico City: Talleres Gráficos de la Nación.

Calnek, Edward E.
1973   "The Historical Validity of the Codex Xolotl." *American Antiquity* 38, no. 4: 423–427.
1979   "The Analysis of Prehispanic Central Mexican Historical Texts." *Estudios de Cultura Náhuatl* 13: 239–266.

Carbia, Rómulo D.
1940   *La crónica oficial de las Indias Occidentales*. Buenos Aires: Ediciones Buenos Aires.

Cárdenas, Juan de
1980   *Problemas y secretos maravillosos de las Indias*. Mexico City: Academia Nacional de Medicina.

Carrasco, Pedro
1975   "La transformación de la cultura indígena durante la colonia." *Historia Mexicana* 25, no. 2 (October–December): 175–203.
1977   "La sociedad mexicana antes de la conquista." *Historia General de México*, vol. 1, pp. 165–288. Mexico City: Colegio de México.
1979   "La fiesta de los meses mexicanos." In *Homenaje al doctor Paul Kirchhoff*, edited by Barbro Dahlgren, pp. 51–60. Mexico City: Instituto Nacional de Antropología e Historia.

Casas, Fray Bartolomé de las
1967   *Apologética historia sumaria*. 2 vols. Edited by Edmundo O'Gorman. Mexico City: Universidad Nacional Autónoma de México.

Caso, Alfonso
    1946   "El águila y el nopal." *Memorias de la Academia Mexicana de la
            Historia* 5, no. 2: 93–104.
    1967   *Los calendarios prehispánicos.* Mexico City: Universidad Nacional
            Autónoma de México.
    1975   *El pueblo del sol.* Mexico City: Fondo de Cultura Económica.
    1977   *Reyes y reinos de la mixteca.* Mexico City: Fondo de Cultura
            Económica.
Castro, Américo
    1970   *Aspectos del vivir hispánico: espiritualismo, mesianismo y actitud
            personal en los siglos XIV al XVI.* Madrid: Alianza Editorial.
Cavo, Andrés
    1949   *Historia de México.* Edited by Ernest J. Burros, S.J. Mexico City:
            Editorial Patria.
Certeau, Michel de
    1978   *L'Ecriture de l'histoire.* Paris: Gallimard.
Chamberlain, Robert S.
    1948   *The Conquest and Colonization of Yucatan, 1517–1550.* Washing-
            ton, D.C.: Carnegie Institution of Washington.
Chatelet, François
    1979   *El nacimiento de la historia.* Mexico City: Siglo Veintiuno Editores.
Chavero, Alfredo
    1882   "La piedra del sol. Estudio arqueológico." *Anales del Museo Nacional
            de México* 2: 3–46, 233–267, 291–311, 403–430.
    1952   *Obras históricas de don Fernando de Alva Ixtlilxóchitl.* 2 vols.
            Mexico City: Editora Nacional.
Chimalpahin, Francisco de
    1965   *Relaciones originales de Chalco Amaquemecan.* Translated by
            Silvia Rendón. Mexico City: Fondo de Cultura Económica.
Clavigero, Francisco Saverio
    1958–1959 *Historia antigua de México.* 4 vols. Edited by Mariano Cuevas,
            S.J. Mexico City: Editorial Porrúa.
    1976   *Antología.* Edited by Gonzalo Aguirre Beltrán. Mexico City: Sep-
            Setentas.
    1979   *The History of Mexico.* 2 vols. New York: Garland.
Cline, Howard
    1972   "The 'Relaciones Geográficas' of the Spanish Indies, 1577–1586." In
            Handbook of Middle American Indians, vol. 12, pp. 185–242.
            Austin: University of Texas Press.
Coe, Michael D.
    1973   *The Maya Scribe and His World.* New York: The Grolier Club.
    1980   *The Maya.* London: Penguin.
Cohn, Norman
    1957   *The Pursuit of the Millennium.* Fairlawn, N.J.: Essential Books.
Cullmann, Oscar
    1962   *Christ and Time.* London: SCM Press.
    1964   *Cristo e il tempo.* Bologna.

Davies, Nigel
1977   *The Toltecs.* Norman: University of Oklahoma Press.
Dávila Padilla, Agustín
1955   *Historia de la fundación y discurso de la provincia de Santiago de México.* Mexico City: Editorial Academia Mexicana.
Dibble, Charles E.
1971   "Writing in Central Mexico." In *Handbook of Middle American Indians,* vol. 10, pp. 322–332. Austin: University of Texas Press.
1980   *Códice Xólotl.* 2 vols. Mexico City: Universidad Nacional Autónoma de México.
Dinkler, Enrich
1955   "Early Christianity." In *The Idea of History in the Ancient Near East,* edited by Robert C. Denton. New Haven, Conn.: Yale University Press.
Durán, Diego
1951   *Historia de las Indias de Nueva España y islas de Tierra Firme.* Mexico City: Editora Nacional.
1964   *The Aztecs: The History of the Indies of New Spain.* Translated by Doris Heyden and Fernando Horcasitas. New York: Orion Press.
Edmonson, Munro S. (ed.)
1974   *Sixteenth-Century Mexico: The Work of Sahagún.* Albuquerque: University of New Mexico Press.
Eliade, Mircea
1954   *The Myth of the Eternal Return.* New York: Pantheon Books.
1963   *Myth and Reality.* New York: Harper & Row.
1964   *Shamanism Archaic Techniques of Ecstasy.* New York: Pantheon Books.
1965   *Imágenes y símbolos.* Madrid: Editorial Taurus.
Elzey, Wayne
1976   "The Nahua Myth of the Suns: History and Cosmology in Pre-Hispanic Mexican Religions." *Numen* 23, pp. 114–135.
Esteve Barba, Francisco
1964   *Historiografía indiana.* Madrid: Editorial Gredos.
Fash, William L.
1991   *Scribes, Warriors and Kings.* London: Thames and Hudson.
Favbre, Henri
1972   *Cambio y continuidad entre los mayas de México.* Mexico City: Siglo Veintiuno Editores.
Feijó, Rosa
1965   "El tumulto de 1692." *Historia Mexicana* 14, no. 4: 656–679.
Fernández de Oviedo, Gonzalo
1972   *Sucesos y diálogos de la Nueva España.* Edited by Edmundo O'Gorman. Mexico City: Sep-Setentas.
Florescano, Enrique
1977   "Las visiones imperiales de la época colonial." *Historia Mexicana* 27 (October–December): 195–230.
1980   *De la colonia al imperio.* Mexico City: Siglo Veintiuno Editores.

.escano, Enrique, and Isabel Gil (eds.)
1973   *Descripciones económicas generales de Nueva España, 1784–1817.* Mexico City: SEP-INAH.

Fonseca, Fabián, and Carlos de Urrutia
1945   *Historia general de la Real Hacienda.* 6 vols. Mexico City: Vicente G. Torres.

Friede, Juan
1959   "La censura española del siglo XVI y los libros de historia de América." *Revista Historia de América,* no. 47: 45–94.

Fuentes para la historia contemporánea de México
1961–1962   3 vols. Mexico City: Colegio de México.

García Icazbalceta, Joaquín (ed.)
1886–1892   *Códice Mendieta (nueva colección de documentos para la historia de México).* Mexico City: Imprenta de Francisco Díaz de León.

1941   *Cartas de religiosos, 1539–1594.* Mexico City: Editorial Salvador Chávez Hayhoe.

1981   *Bibliografía mexicana del siglo XVI.* Edited by Agustín Millares Carlo. Mexico City: Fondo de Cultura Económica.

Garibay, Angel María
1953   *Historia de la literature náhuatl.* 2 vols. Mexico City: Editorial Porrúa.

1965   *Teogonía e historia de los mexicanos.* Mexico City: Editorial Porrúa.

Garza, Mercedes de la
1975   *La conciencia histórica de los antiguos mayas.* Mexico City: Universidad Nacional Autónoma de México.

Gerbi, Antonello
1960   *La disputa del Nuevo Mundo. Historia de una polémica, 1750–1900.* Translated by Antonio Alatorre. Mexico City: Fondo de Cultura Económica.

1978   *La naturaleza de las Indias nuevas.* Translated by Antonio Alatorre. Mexico City: Fondo de Cultura Económica.

Gerhard, Peter
1975   "La evolución del pueblo rural mexicano, 1519–1975." *Historia Mexicana* 24 (April–June): 566–678.

1977   "Congregaciones de indios en Nueva España antes de 1570." *Historia Mexicana* 26 (January–March): 347–395.

Gibson, Charles
1964   *The Aztecs under Spanish Rule.* Stanford, Calif.: Stanford University Press.

1975   "A Survey of Middle American Prose Manuscripts in the Native Historical Tradition." In *Handbook of Middle American Indians,* vol. 15, pp. 311–321. Austin: University of Texas Press.

Ginés de Sepúlveda, Juan
1979   *Tratado sobre las justas causas de la guerra contra los indios.* Mexico City: Fondo de Cultura Económica.

Góngora, Mario
1975   "Eschatological Theories in the Writing of Columbus and of the Mendicant Friars." In *Studies in the Colonial History of Spanish*

America, pp. 206–216. London: Cambridge University Press.

González Casanova, Pablo

1958 *La literatura perseguida en la crisis de la colonia.* Mexico City: Colegio de México.

González Dávila, Gil

1959 *Teatro eclesiástico de la primitiva iglesia de la Nueva España en las Indias Occidentales.* Madrid: José Porrúa Turanzas.

González Torres, Yólotl

1975 *El culto de los astros entre los mexicas.* Mexico City: Sep-Setentas.

Gruzinski, Serge

1985a *Les hommes dieux de Mexique. Pouvoir Indien et société coloniale, XVIe–XVIIe siècles.* Paris: Editions des Archives Contemporaines.

1985b "La 'segunda aculturación': el estado ilustrado y la religiosidad indígena en Nueva España (1775–1800)." *Estudios de Historia Novohispana* 8: 175–201.

Hamill, Hugh M.

1966 *The Hidalgo Revolt.* Gainesville: University of Florida Press.

Herrejón, Carlos

1985 *Morelos, antología documental.* Mexico City: SEP (100 de México).

Herrera, Antonio

1945 *Historia general de los hechos de los castellanos en las islas y tierra firme de el Mar Océano.* 5 vols. Buenos Aires: Guarania.

Historia del arte en México

1982 12 vols. Mexico City: SEP-INBA-SALVAT.

Howe, Walter

1948 *Imagen de la virgen María de Dios de Guadalupe milagrosamente aparecida en México, celebrada en su historia, con la profecía del capítulo doce del apocalipsis . . .* Mexico City: Imprenta de la Viuda de Bernardo Calderón.

1964 *Información que el Arzobispo de México D. fray Alonso de Montúfar mandó predicar . . . acerca de la devoción y culto de Nuestra Señora de Guadalupe.* Mexico City (1556).

1968 *The Mining Guild of New Spain and Its Tribunal General, 1770–1821.* New York: Greenwood Press.

Huerta, María Teresa, and Patricia Palacios

1976 *Rebeliones indígenas de la época colonial.* Mexico City: Instituto Nacional de Antropología e Historia.

Humboldt, Alexander

1966 *Ensayo político sobre el reino de la Nueva España.* Edited by Juan A. Ortega y Medina. Mexico City: Editorial Porrúa.

1970 *Tablas geográficas, políticas del reino de Nueva España y correspondencia mexicana.* Mexico City: Dirección General de Estadística.

1974 *Vistas de las cordilleras y monumentos de los pueblos indígenas de América.* Translated by Jaime Labastida. Mexico City: Secretaría de Hacienda y Crédito Público.

Iglesia, Ramón

1944 *El hombre Colón y otros ensayos.* Mexico City: Colegio de México.

1980 *Cronistas e historiadores de la conquista de México.* Mexico City:

Colegio de México.

Informantes de Sahagún
1958   *Ritos, sacerdotes y atavíos de los dioses.* Mexico City: Universidad Nacional Autónoma de México.

Israel, J. I.
1975   *Race, Class and Politics in Colonial Mexico, 1610–1670.* Oxford: Oxford University Press.

Keen, Benjamin
1971   *The Aztec Image   in Western Thought.* New Brunswick, N.J.: Rutgers University Press.

Khon, Hans
1975   "Nacionalismo." In *Enciclopedia Internacional de las Ciencias Sociales,* edited by David L. Sills, vol. 7, pp. 306–311. Madrid: Editorial Aguilar.

Kirchhoff, Paul; Linda Odena Güemes; and Luis Reyes García
1976   *Historia tolteca chichimeca.* Mexico City: INAH-CISINAH-SEP.

Klein, Herbert S.
1966   "Peasant Communities in Revolt: The Tzeltal Republic of 1712." *Pacific Historical Review,* no. 35: 247–263.

Lafaye, Jacques
1977   *Quetzalcóatl y Guadalupe. La formación de la conciencia nacional de México.* Mexico City: Fondo de Cultura Económica.

Le Goff, Jacques
1979   "Au Moyen Age: Temps de l'église et temps du Marchand." In *Pour un autre Moyen Age. Temps, travail et culture en Occident,* pp. 46–65. Paris: Gallimard.

León-Portilla, Miguel
1959   *La filosofía náhuatl estudiada en sus fuentes.* Mexico City: Universidad Nacional Autónoma de México.
1961a   *Los antiguos mexicanos a través de sus crónicas y cantares.* Mexico City: Fondo de Cultura Económica.
1961b   *Visión de los vencidos.* Mexico City: Universidad Nacional Autónoma de México.
1964   *El reverso de la conquista.* Mexico City: Editorial Joaquín Mortiz.
1968   *Tiempo y realidad en el pensamiento maya.* Mexico City: Universidad Nacional Autónoma de México.
1981   *Toltecáyotl. Aspectos de la cultura náhuatl.* Mexico City: Fondo de Cultura Económica.

León y Gama, Antonio de
1978   *Descripción histórica y cronológica de las dos piedras.* Mexico City: Miguel Angel Porrúa.

Lipschutz, Alejandro
1971   *Los muros pintados de Bonampak.* Santiago de Chile: Editorial Universitaria.

Lockhart, James
1991   "Views of Corporate Self and History in Some Valley of Mexico Towns, Late Seventeenth and Eighteenth Centuries."*Nahuas and Spaniards: Postconquest Central Mexican History and Philology.*

UCLA Latin American Studies, vol. 76. Los Angeles: UCLA Latin American Center Publications, Stanford University Press.

Loera y Chávez, Margarita
1981   *Economía campesina indígena en la colonia. Un caso en el valle de Toluca.* Mexico: Instituto Nacional Indigenista.

López Austin, Alfredo
1961   *La constitución real de México-Tenochtitlan.* Mexico: Universidad Nacional Autónoma de México.
1973   *Hombre-Dios. Religión y política en el mundo náhuatl.* Mexico City: Universidad Nacional Autónoma de México.
1976   "Estudio acerca del método de investigación de fray Bernardino de Sahagún." In *La investigación social de campo en México,* edited by Jorge Martínez Ríos, pp. 9–56. Mexico City: Universidad Nacional Autónoma de México.
1980   *Cuerpo humano e ideología.* 2 vols. Mexico City: Universidad Nacional Autónoma de México.
1988   *The Human Body and Ideology: Concepts of the Ancient Nahuas.* Translated by Thelma Ortiz de Montellano and Bernard Ortiz de Montellano. Salt Lake City: University of Utah Press.

López de Gómara, Francisco
1946   *Hispania Victrix. Primera y segunda parte de la historia general de las Indias.* Madrid: Biblioteca de Autores Españoles.

López de Velasco, Juan
1971   *Geografía y descripción universal de las Indias.* Edited by M. Jiménez de la Espada. Madrid: Biblioteca de Autores Españoles.

López Luján, Leonardo
1989   *La recuperación mexica del pasado teotihuacano.* Mexico City: Instituto Nacional de Antropología e Historia.

Lowith, Karl
1958   *El sentido de la historia. Implicaciones teológicas de la filosofía de la historia.* Madrid: Editorial Aguilar.

Malinowski, Bronislaw
1955   "Myth in Primitive Society." In *Magic, Science and Religion,* pp. 101–108. New York: Doubleday.

Marcus, Joyce
1976   *Emblem and State in the Classic Maya Lowlands: An Epigraphic Approach to Territorial Organization.* Special Publications. Washington, D.C.: Dumbarton Oaks.
1980   "Zapotec Writing." *Scientific American* 242, no. 2 (February): 46–49.
1992   *Mesoamerican Written Systems. Propaganda, Myth and History in Four Ancient Civilizations.* Princeton, N.J.: Princeton University Press.

Martínez Peláez, Severo
      Motines de indios. La violencia colonial en Centroamérica y Chiapas. Puebla: Cuadernos de la Casa Presno.

Matute, Alvaro
1976   *Lorenzo Boturini y el pensamiento histórico de Vico.* Mexico City: Universidad Nacional Autónoma de México.

Maza, Francisco de la
1984   *El guadalupanismo mexicano.* Mexico City: Fondo de Cultura Económica–Secretaría de Educación Pública.
Méndez Bolio, Antonio
1930   *El libro de Chilam Balam de Chumayel.* San José, Costa Rica.
Mendieta, Gerónimo de
1945   *Historia eclesiástica indiana.* 4 vols. Mexico City: Editorial Salvador Cháves Hayhoe.
Meyerson, J. I.
1956   "Le temps, la memoire et l'histoire." *Journal de Psychologie,* pp. 333–357.
Milhou, Alain
1983   *Colón y su mentalidad mesiánica en el ambiente franciscanista español.* Valladolid: Casa Museo de Colón.
Millares Carlo, Agustín
1957   *Don Juan José de Eguiara y Eguren y su bibliotheca mexicana.* Mexico City: Universidad Nacional Autónoma de México.
Miranda, José
1962   *Humboldt y México.* Mexico City: Universidad Nacional Autónoma de México.
1972   *Vida colonial y albores de la independencia.* Mexico City: Sep-Setentas.
1978   *Las ideas y las instituciones políticas mexicanas.* Mexico City: Universidad Nacional Autónoma de México.
Miranda Godínez, Francisco
1972   *Don Vasco de Quiroga y su Colegio de San Nicolás.* Morelia: Fimex.
Momigliano, Arnaldo
1966   "Time in Ancient Historiography." *History and Theory* 6: 1–23.
Mora, José María
1963   *Obras sueltas.* Mexico City: Editorial Porrúa.
Moreno de los Arcos, Roberto
1967   "Los cinco soles cosmogónicos." *Estudios de Cultura Náhuatl* 7: 183–210.
Moreno Toscano, Alejandra
1968   *Geografía económica de México (siglo XVI).* Mexico City: Colegio de México.
Motolinía, Toribio de
1903   *Memoriales de . . .* Mexico City: Edición de Luis García Pimentel.
Motten, Clement G.
1972   *Mexican Silver and the Enlightenment.* New York: Octagon Books.
Munford, Lewis
1977   *Técnica y civilización.* Madrid: Alianza Editorial.
Muñoz Camargo, Diego
1947   *Historia de Tlaxcala.* Mexico City: Publicaciones del Ateneo Nacional de Ciencias y Artes de México.
1981   *Descripción de la ciudad y provincia de Tlaxcala.* Edited by René Acuña. Mexico City: Universidad Nacional Autónoma de México.

Navarro B., Bernabé
1964 *Cultura mexicana moderna en el siglo XVIII.* Mexico City: Universidad Nacional Autónoma de México.

Nicholson, Henry B.
1971 "Religion in Pre-Hispanic Central Mexico." In *Handbook of Middle American Indians*, vol. 10, pp. 395–445. Austin: University of Texas Press.
1971 "Pre-Hispanic Central Mexican Historiography." In *Investigaciones contemporánea sobre historia de México*, pp. 38–81. Mexico City: Universidad Nacional Autónoma de México–University of Texas at Austin.
1973 "Phoneticism in the Central Mexican Writing System." In *Mesoamerican Writing Systems*, edited by E. P. Benson, pp. 1–46. Washington, D.C.: Dumbarton Oaks.

O'Gorman, Edmundo
1972 *Cuatro historiadores de Indias.* Mexico City: Sep-Setentas.
1986 *Destierro de sombras. Luz en el origen de la imagen y culto de Nuestra Señora de Guadalupe del Tepeyac.* Mexico City: Universidad Nacional Autónoma de México.

Pacheco, José Emilio
1976 "La patria perdida (notas sobre Clavijero y la cultura nacional)." In *En torno a la cultura nacional*, edited by Aguilar et al. Mexico City: Instituto Nacional Indigenista.

Pastor, Rodolfo
1981 "Los religiosos, los indios y el estado en la Mixteca, 1524–1810." Paper presented at IV Meeting of Mexican and North American Historians, Chicago, 8–12 September.

Pereira de Queiroz, Isaura
1969 *Historia y etnología de los movimientos mesiánicos.* Mexico: Siglo Veintiuno Editores.

Pérez Marchand, Monelisa
1945 *Dos etapas ideológicas del siglo XVIII en México.* Mexico City: Colegio de México.

Pérez Memen, Fernando
1977 *El episcopado y la independencia de México (1808–36).* Mexico City: Editorial Jus.

Phelan, John L.
1970 *The Millennial Kingdom of the Franciscans in the New World.* Berkeley and Los Angeles: University of California Press.
1972 *El reino milenario de los franciscanos en el Nuevo Mundo.* Translated by Josefina Vázquez de Knauth. Mexico City: UNAM, Instituto de Investigaciones Históricas.
1980 *El pueblo y el rey. La revolución comunera en Colombia, 1781.* Bogotá: Carlos Valencia Editores.

Plumb, J. H.
1971 *The Death of the Past.* Boston: Houghton Mifflin.
1974 *La muerte del pasado.* Barcelona: Barral Editores.

Poma de Ayala, Felipe Guaman
1980 *El primer nueva coronica y buen gobierno*. 3 vols. Edited by John V. Murra and Rolena Adorno. Translated by Jorge L. Urioste. Mexico City: Siglo Veintiuno Editores.
Pomar, Juan Bautista
1941 "Relación de Texcoco." In *Relaciones de Texcoco y de la Nueva España*. Mexico City: Editorial Salvador Chávez Hayhoe.
Renan, Ernest
1882 *Qu'est-ce qu'une nation*. Paris: Ed. Levy.
Reyes García, Luis
1979 "La visión cosmológica y organización del imperio mexica." In *Mesoamérica. Homenaje al doctor Paul Kirchhoff*, edited by Barbro Dahlgren, pp. 34–40. Mexico City: Instituto Nacional de Antropología e Historia.
Ricard, Robert
1947 *La conquista espiritual de México*. Mexico City: Editorial Juspolis.
Robertson, Donald
1959 *Mexican Manuscript Painting of the Early Colonial Period*. New Haven, Conn.: Yale University Press.
Robertson, William
1777 *The History of America*. London.
Robicsek, Francis, and Donald M. Hales
1981 *The Maya Book of the Dead. The Ceramic Codex*. Charlottesville: University of Virginia Art Museum.
Rustow, Dankwart A.
1975 "Nación." In *Enciclopedia Internacional de Ciencias Sociales*, edited by Dario L. Sills, vol. 7, pp. 301–306. Madrid: Aguilar.
Sahagún, Bernardino de
1956 *Historia general de las cosas de Nueva España*. 4 vols. Mexico City: Editorial Porrúa.
Sánchez, Miguel
1982 *Imagen de la virgen María Madre de Dios de Guadalupe milagrosamente aparecida en México, celebrada en su historia, con la profecía del capítulo doce del Apocalipsis . . .* In *Testimonios históricos Guadalupanos*, edited by Ernesto de la Torre Villar y Ramiro Navarro de Anda, pp. 152–281. Mexico City: Fondo de Cultura Económica.
Satterthwaite, Linton
1965 "Calendaries of the Maya Lowlands." In *Handbook of Middle American Indians*, vol. 3, pp. 603–631. Austin: University of Texas Press.
Schele, Linda
1977 "Palenque: The House of the Dying Sun, " in *Native American Astronomy*, edited by A. F. Aveni, pp. 42–56. Austin: University of Texas Press.
Schele, Linda, and David Freidel
1990 *A Forest of Kings: The Untold Story of the Ancient Maya*. New York: Morrow.

Schele, Linda, and Mary Ellen Miller
1986   *The Blood of Kings: Dynasty and Ritual in Maya Art.* New York: George Braziller.
Sepúlveda, Juan Ginés de
1979   *Tratado sobre las justas causas de la guerra contra los indios.* Mexico City: Fondo de Cultura Económica.
Simpson, Lesley Byrd
1961   *Many Mexicos.* Berkeley and Los Angeles: University of California Press.
Smith, May Elizabeth
1973   *Picture Writing from Ancient Southern Mexico.* Norman: University of Oklahoma Press.
Soustelle, Jacques
1940   *La pensée cosmologique des anciens mexicains.* Paris: Hermann et Cie Editeurs.
1974   *La vida cotidiana de los aztecas.* Mexico City: Fondo de Cultura Económica.
Suárez de Peralta, Juan
1949   *Tratado del descubrimiento de las Indias.* Mexico City: Secretaría de Educación Pública.
Tate, Carolyn E.
1992   *Yaxchilan. The Design of a Maya Ceremonial City.* Austin: University of Texas Press.
Taylor, William B.
1979   *Drinking, Homicide and Rebellion in Colonial Mexican Villages.* Stanford, Calif.: Stanford University Press.
Tena Ramírez, Felipe
1977   *Vasco de Quiroga y sus pueblos de Santa Fe en los siglos XVIII y XIX.* Mexico City: Editorial Porrúa.
Tezozómoc, Fernando de Alvarado
1949   *Crónica de Mexicáyotl.* Translated by Adrián León. Mexico City: Universidad Nacional Autónoma de México.
Thompson, J. Eric S.
1959   *Grandeza y decadencia de los mayas.* Mexico City: Fondo de Cultura Económica.
Timmons, Wilbert H.
1950   "Los Guadalupes: A Secret Society in the Mexican Revolution for Independence." *Hispanic American Historical Review* 30: 453–479.
Torquemada, Juan
1943–1944   *Monarquía indiana.* Facsimile edition. 3 vols. Mexico City: Editorial Salvador Chávez Hayhoe.
Torre Villar, Ernesto de la
1966   *Los "Guadalupes" y la independencia.* Mexico City: Editorial Jus.
Torre Villar, Ernesto de la, and Ramiro Navarro de Anda
1982   *Testimonios históricos y guadalupanos.* Mexico City: Fondo de Cultura Económica.
Townsend, Richard F.
1979   *State and Cosmos in the Art of Tenochtitlan. Studies in Pre-*

Columbian Art and Archaeology, no. 20. Washington, D.C.: Dumbarton Oaks.

Uchamany, Eva Alexandra
1978   "Huitzilopochtli, dios de la historia de los aztecas-mexitzin." *Estudios de Cultura Náhuatl* 13: 211–237.

Umberger, Emily
1981   "The Structure of Aztec History." *Archaeoastronomy* 4, no. 4: 10–18.
1984   "El trono de Moctezuma." *Estudios de Cultura Nahuatl* 17: 63–87.
1987   "Events Commemorated by Date Plaques at the Templo Mayor." In *Aztec Templo Mayor*, edited by Elizabeth Hill Boone, pp. 411–449. Washington, D.C.: Dumbarton Oaks Research Library and Collection.
1987   "Antiques, Revivals, and References to the Past in Aztec Art." *Res* 13, Spring, pp. 63–105.

Van Young, Eric
1984   "'Who Was the Masked Man, Anyway?' Popular Symbols and Ideology in the Mexican Wars of Independence." *Proceedings* of the Rocky Mountain Conference on Latin American Studies Annual Meeting, vol. 1, pp. 18–35.
1986   "Millennium on the Northern Marches: The Mad Messiah of Durango and Popular Rebellion in Mexico, 1800–1815." *Comparative Studies in Society and History* 28, no. 3: 385–413.

Velázquez, Primo Feliciano (ed. and trans.)
1945   *Códice Chimalpopoca. Anales de Cuauhtitlán y leyenda de los soles*. Mexico City: Imprenta Universitaria.

Vera, Fortino Hipólito
1887–1889   *Tesoro guadalupano. Noticia de los libros, documentos, inscripciones y que tratan, mencionan o aluden a la aparición y devoción de Nuestra Señora de Guadalupe*. 2 vols. Amecameca de Juárez: Impresión del Colegio Católico.

Vernant, Jean Pierre
1973   *Mito y pensamiento de la Grecia antigua*. Barcelona: Editorial Ariel.

Veytia, Mariano
1944   *Historia antigua de México*. 2 vols. Mexico City: Editorial Leyenda.

Villa Rojas, Alfonso
1968   "Los conceptos de espacio y tiempo entre los grupos mayas contemporáneos." In *Tiempo y realidad en el pensamiento maya*, edited by Miguel León-Portilla, pp. 119–162. Mexico City: Universidad Nacional Autónoma de México.

Villaseñor y Sánchez, Joseph Antonio de
1932   *Teatro americano*. 2 vols. Mexico City: Editora Nacional.

Villoro, Luis
1950   *Los grandes momentos del indigenismo en México*. Mexico City: Colegio de México.
1986   *El proceso ideológico de la revolución de independencia*. Mexico City: Secretaría de Educación Pública.

Wachtel, Nathan
1973   "Pensamiento salvaje y aculturación: el espacio y el tiempo en Felipe

Guaman Poma de Ayala y el inca Garcilaso." In *Sociedad e ideología. Ensayos de historia y antropología andinas*, pp. 162–228. Lima: Instituto de Estudios Peruanos.

1976　*Los vencidos*. Madrid: Alianza Editorial.

Warman, Arturo
1972　*La danza de moros y cristianos*. Mexico City: Sep-Setentas.

Warren, Fintan B.
1963　*Vasco de Quiroga and His Pueblo Hospitals of Santa Fe*. Washington, D.C.: Academy of American Franciscan History.

Wasserstrom, Robert
1983　*Class and Society in Central Chiapas*. Berkeley and Los Angeles: University of California Press.

Weber, Max
1952　*Ancient Judaism*. Glencoe, Ill.: Free Press.
1969　*Economía y sociedad*. Mexico City: Fondo de Cultura Económica.

West, Delno C., and Sandra Zimdars-Swartz
1986　*Joaquín de Fiore. Una visión espiritual de la historia*. Mexico City: Fondo de Cultura Económica.

Wold, Ruth
1970　*El Diario de México, primer cotidiano de Nueva España*. Madrid: Editorial Gredos.

Ximénez, Fray Francisco
1929　*Historia de la provincia de San Vicente de Chiapas y Guatemala*. Guatemala City: Tipografía Nacional.

Zantwijk, Rudolf van
1962　"La paz azteca. La ordenación del mundo por los mexicas." In *Estudios de Cultura Náhuatl*, vol. 3, pp. 101–135. Mexico City: Universidad Nacional Autónoma de México.
1963　"Principios organizadores de los mexica, una introducción al estudio del sistema interno del régimen azteca." In *Estudios de Cultura Náhuatl*, vol. 4, pp. 187–222. Mexico City: Universidad Nacional Autónoma de México.
1976　"La organización social de México-Tenochtitlan naciente." In *Actas del XLI Congreso Internacional de Americanistas*, vol. 2, pp. 188–208. Mexico City.
1981　"The Great Temple of Tenochtitlan: Model of Aztec Cosmovision." In *Conference on Mesoamerican Sites and World-Views*, pp. 71–86. Washington, D.C.: Dumbarton Oaks.
1985　*The Aztec Arrangement. The Social History of Pre-Hispanic Mexico*. Norman: University of Oklahoma Press.

Zavala, Silvio
1965　*Recuerdo de Vasco de Quiroga*. Mexico City: Editorial Porrúa.
1972　*La filosofía de la conquista*. Mexico City: Fondo de Cultura Económica.

Zavala, Silvio, and José Miranda
1973　"Instituciones indígenas en la colonia." In *La política indigenista en México*, edited by Alfonso Caso et al., vol. 1, pp. 43–206. Mexico City: Instituto Nacional Indigenista.

Index